Dadabhai Naoroji

Dadabhai Naoroji

Series Editor
Dr. M.H. Syed

Editor
M.A. Khan **N.P. Sharma**

Himalaya Books Pvt. Ltd.
'Ramdoot', Dr. Bhalerao Marg, Girgaon, Mumbai - 400 004
Tel : (022) 23863863. Fax : (022) 23877178
Email : himpub@vsnl.com

First Edition : 2011

Published by : **H.B.P.L.**
"Pooja Apartments", 4-B, Murari Lal Street, Ansari Road,
Darya Ganj, New Delhi-110 002
Phones : 23270392, 23278631 Reliance : 30180392 to 396
Fax : 011-23256286 Email : hphdel@vsnl.com

Sole Distributers : HIMALAYA PUBLISHING HOUSE PVT. LTD.

Branch Offices

Mumbai : "Ramdoot", Dr. Bhalerao Marg, Girgaon, Mumbai-400 004.
Phones : 23860170/23863863 Fax : 022-23877178
Email : himpub@vsnl.com
Website : www.himpub.com

Nagpur : Kundanlal Chandak Industrial Estate, Ghat Road, **Nagpur 440-018.**
Phone: 2738731, 3296733 Telefax : 0712-2721215

Bengaluru : No. 16/1 (Old 12/1), 1st Floor, Next to Hotel Highlands,
Madhava Nagar, Race Course Road, **Bengaluru - 560 001.**
Phone : 22281541, 22385461, Telefax: 080-22286611

Hyderabad : No. 3-4-184, Lingampally, Besides Raghavendra Swamy Matham,
Kachiguda, **Hyderabad - 500 027.** Phone: 040-27560041,
27550139, Mobile:- 09848130433 Telefax: 040-27560041

Chennai : No. 85/50, Bazullah Road, T. Nagar, **Chennai - 600 017.**
Phone: 044-28344020, 32463737, 42124860

Pune : No. 527, "Laksha" Apartment, First Floor, Mehunpura,
Shaniwarpeth, (Near Prabhat Theatre), **Pune - 411 030.**
Phone: 020-24496323/24496333/32326733

Lucknow : Jai Baba Bhawan, Near Dr. Sanjiv Awasthi, Church Road,
Kurshi Road, Aliganj, **Lucknow - 226 024.**
Phone: 9305302158, 9415349385

Ahmedabad : No. 114, "SHAIL", 1st Floor, Opp. Madhu Sudan House, C.G.Road,
Navrang Pura, **Ahmedabad – 380 009.**
Phone: 079-26560126, Mobiles: 09327324149,09314679413

Ernakulam : No. 39/104 A, Lakshmi Apartment, Karikkamuri Cross Rd.,
Ernakulam, **Cochin – 682011**, Kerala.
Phone: 0484-2378012, 2378016, Mob.: 09344199799

Bhubaneswar : 5 Station Square, **Bhubaneswar (Orissa) - 751 001.**
Mobile: 9861046007, E-mail:-orissa@himpub.com

Indore : Kesardeep Avenue Extension, 73, Narayan Bagh, Flat No. 302,
IIIrd Floor, Near Humpty Dumpty School, Narayan Bagh,
Indore (M.P.) 452 007 Mobile: 09301386468

Kolkata : 108/4, Beliaghata, Main Road, Near ID Hospital, Opp. SBI Bank
Kolkata - 700 010. Mobile: 09910440956

Printed at : Shri Krishna offset Press Delhi-93

Preface

Biography, is now a form of literature, very much in vogue. In fact, biography is a description or account of someone's life and the times, which is usually published in the form of a book. A biography is more than a mention of personal facts (life, education, work, relationships and death), it also portrays the subject's experience of events. Technically speaking, a work is biographical, if it covers, all of a person's life. Biography writing has a long history. A biography is real. Ancient Greeks developed the biographical tradition, which we have inherited, although until the 5th century AD, when the word 'biographia' first appeared, in Damascius' "Life of Isodorus," biographical pieces were called simply "lives". It is quite likely that the Greeks were drawing on a pre-existing eastern tradition. Certainly Herodotus' "Histories" contains more detailed biographical information on Persian kings and subjects. The earliest surviving pieces, which we would identify as biographical are Isocrates' "Life of Evagoras" and Xenophon's "Life of Agesilaos," both from the fifth century BC. "Parallel Lives" by Plutarch, a Greek writing under the Roman empire, is a series of short biographies of eminent men.

The Golden Age of English biography emerged in late eighteenth century, the century in which the terms "biography" and "autobiography" entered English lexicon. The classic works of the period were Samuel Johnson's "Critical Lives of the Poets" and James Boswell's "Massive Life of Johnson". Generally American biography followed English model. By World War I, cheap hardcover reprints had become popular. The decade of the 1920s witnessed a biographical 'boom'. Later, biographical writings developed a lot and today biographies are written and compiled in the finest form of the genre. In India too, biography, as a form of literature has been evolved, cultivated and polished over the years. Here is an effort to promote this tradition further.

This series of biographies of great men, great women and celebrities in all walks of life is an adventurous academic endeavour, in its own right. A team of researchers and compilers has worked for a good period of time to accomplish the project. For this purpose, hundreds of books by eminent authors and editors have been consulted and referred to. We have benefited from various works, liberally, in order to illustrate and enrich this effort of ours. Present book is devoted to the great personality of Dadabhai Naoroji.

The "Grand Old Man of India", Dadabhai Naoroji was a great nationalist. He established the "East India Association" in England to serve as a forum for the ventilation of grievances, against the exploitation by British Government. He, in his book, *"Poverty and Un-British Rule in India"*, exposed that poverty and economic backwardness of India were not inherent in local conditions, but were caused by colonial rule, which was draining India of its wealth and capital. Dadabhai Naoroji, a great leader of Indian national movement, was the first Indian to become a Member of the House of the Commons, on the Liberal party's ticket, where he fervently pleaded the cause of his country. He was elected president of the Indian National Congress, thrice. He also founded Bombay Association. He established the 'London Indian Society', for a closer relationship, between the Indians and the Englishmen. Naoroji dedicated his entire life and wealth to the National Movement. He kept in touch with youths, all through his life and continuously developed his thought and acts in a radical direction.

This is a compact and comprehensive account of the above mentioned great life, which is bound to attract the attention of scholars, researchers, students and the general readers alike. Let's hope this humble effort would receive a warm welcome and due applause.

— ***Editors***

Contents

1

An Illustrious Life

The great leader of the first generation of Indian politicians. Dadabhai Naoroji was born in a middle class Parsi family on 4 September 1825 when the East India Company held its sway in our country. His father, Naoroji Palanji Dordi was a Parsi priest with moderate economic means and lived in a small house in Khadak in Bombay. The system of education in the Bombay presidency or elsewhere in our subcontinent was not in proper stage of development. The lead, however, was given by Mountstuart Elphinstone, who founded a society known as the Native Education Society in Bombay. It was conducted under the patronage of the government. Young Dadabhai joined it and this was the foundation of his career. It was entirely free education.

The life during school days has been recorded by Dadabhai thus: 'The awakening of the soul came to me when I was about fifteen. I remember as if it were only yesterday, how at a certain spot on a certain road I made a vow never to use low language. From that time forward, as my education advanced, other resolutions to do this, and not to do that followed, and I think I may say that I faithfully adhered to them.' He also confessed very frankly another weakness. 'As a boy I was accustomed to have my little drink before dinner. One day, there was no liquor in the house, and I was sent to have my drink at a shop opposite. Never did I forget the shame and humiliation I felt at being there. It was enough. The drink shop never saw my face again.

In the nineteenth century, child marriage both of male and female was very much in vogue in our country. In spite of the efforts of our reformers the social evil remained in our society. The Parsi families too could not escape the effect of this social system. Dadabhai's mother was keen that his son should get married at an early age and in order to avoid social criticism he was to married to Gulbai daughter of Sorabji Shroff. He was hardly eleven and his wife was seven years old.

After a few years the Native Education Society developed into the Elphinstone Institute which was accorded the status of a college. Indeed young Dadabhai was a brilliant students who by dint of his hardwork, sincerity and obedience pleased his teachers who, on their part, considered him as 'The Promise of India'.

After his college education, proposal were made for this brilliant young man. The Chief Justice Sir Erskine Perry recommended his name for the law course in England. But fearful of the proselytising activities of several missionaries at that time, the proposal was not agreeable to the family as well as to the Parsi community. He was also offered a job in the Bombay Secretariat but he did not accept it as his own teachers advised him not to do so ultimately he was appointed Assistant Professor of Mathematics and after a short span of two years he was elevated to the chair of Professor of Mathematics and Natural Philosophy. He discharged his academic function with a sense of responsibility marked with highest degree of distinction. He also became an active member of the Bombay Branch of the Royal Asiatic Society. He participated in several social gatherings and suggested solution for the elimination of social evils of our society.

After a few years, Dadabhai changed his profession from a teacher to a businessman. In 1855, the commercial firm of the Camas decided to open a business firm in London with a branch at Liverpool. They sent an invitation to Dadabhai to join them as a partner. He readily agreed to join the firm although he had no experience worth its name. This indeed was a turning point in his career When the teachers and the students came to know of his decision, they expressed unhappiness to lose an able and popular teacher like him. But Dadabhai was adamant and ultimately he was accorded a touching farewell by the members of the staff and the students who greatly eulogised the services of a very patriotic and knowledgeable teacher.

Having been relieved from the college, he left for England on 27 June 1855. He was accompanied by Muncherji Hor-musji Cama and Khurshedji Rustomji Cama to establish a new firm in England. On arrival there they established a firm which dealt with opium, mine and spirits. Dadabhai remained in the firm for a short while, but he was not happy with the commodities which the firm sold. His conscience pricked him. He soon made up his mind to give it up and having made a firm decision, he came back to India in order to give a better thought to the line of action for his future career.

It was the era of Gladstone, John Bright, and Cobden. Whereas young Dadabhai was impressed by the political ideology of these leaders, he was much influenced by John Mill, Carlyle and Herbert Spencer. He thus made up his mind to carve out his career without and kind of hurdles being imposed by his partners. Rather he began to show the sense of independent thinking keeping in view the poverty of the people of India.

He came back to England in 1859 when he was only thirty four and established his own business firm under the name of Dadabhai Naoroji and Co. In a few years he flourished in his business. He also began to show in socio-political life in the areas in which he lived. He was an active member of the Liverpool Literary and Philosophic Society, the Royal Institute of London, the Royal Society of Great Britain and Ireland and several other cultural societies. He got himself interested in the cotton trade and studied several aspects of this trade in Liverpool.

At this point of time Naoroji began he show much interest for opportunities of young educated Indians in the Indian Civil Service. He opened forcefully that Indians were equally competent to compete for this examination and could be absorbed adequately in the Civil Service. In this regard, he sought the help several British members of the House of Commons. The Raj was this made aware of the growing genuine demands of the educated Indians who were keen to compete for this examination.

During all these years, Dadabhai was a true helper and guide to several Indian students who had gone to England for higher studies. He used to meet them at regular intervals and discussed with them their problems which they faced abroad. He never hesitated in sending memorials to the highest authority of the Raj in this regard and sought solution of their numerous problems.

He was constantly in touch with D.E. Wacha, a prominent Congress leader of the time. He always apprised Dadabhai of numerous socio-economic and political developments in the Indian subcontinent. He also made him acquainted with the doings of the Bombay Presidency Governor as well as the Viceroy of India." This correspondence made him full aware of the happenings in India which Dadabhai could discuss with the British members of Parliament.

14 June 1895

[The monopoly of the growth, manufacture, and sale of opium had, since the time of Warren Hastings, been a source of revenue to the Government of India. The opium was exported to China, where its consumption was generally admitted to have had harmful effects on large numbers of the population. Christian missionaries in China had been agitating in England for the suppression of the opium trade, and about 1888 a Society was formed there for the suppression of that trade under the Presidentship of Sir Joseph Pease (1828-1903). Pease was a scion of an old Quaker family which had large business connections. Joseph entered Parliament in 1865, and remained M. P. till his death. He was a Strong Gladstonian Liberal. He was created a baronet in 1882. A resolution condemning the opium trade was introduced by Pease in the House of Commons in April 1891 and passed. Suppression of the trade was, however, bound to create financial difficulties for India, and so in June 1893 Alfred Webb had proposed the appointment of a Royal Commission to enquire into Indian finances and to suggest what subsidy would have to be paid to India by the British Treasury if the opium trade was suppressed. Gladstone, however, proposed instead that a Royal Commission should be appointed to enquire whether the growth, manufacture and sale of opium should be prohibited in India except for medicinal purposes. This was carried, and a Commission was accordingly appointed with Lord Brassey as President. The commission visited India in the cold weather of 1894-95 to take evidence there, and submitted its report in May 1895. The answer of the majority of the Commission to the main term of reference—whether the growth, etc. of opium should be prohibited—was in the negative. But H. J. Wilson, one of the members, disagreed, and he appended a Memorandum to the report in which he pointed out how the Government of India had prevented any evidence, not favourable to itself, from being submitted to the Commission.

Even before the observations of the Government of India on the Commission's report had been received, Pease moved, on 14th May 1895, that the Government of India should be urged so stop the cultivation of the poppy, etc. The motion was defeated by a large majority: 59 voting for, and 176 against.]

My dear Dadabhai

I have yours of the 24th ultimo. I am sorry to say I was not able to write to you last week.

Of course, it was a foregone conclusion that the debate on Opium should end in a majority against Sir J. Pease's amendment. I have carefully gone through the report and must sorrowfully admit that Mr. Wilson's charges against the tampering of witnesses are well-founded. It was notorious that the Government of India and the subordinate administrations had been gerrymandering witnesses for weeks before the appointment of the Commission.

It is at the same time a great pity that the Anti-Opiumists indulged in exaggerations and married their own cause. However, the battle should be continued. I am glad to learn from your letter that you tackled your own amendment as a rider to Sir John's motion. It was necessary. We should boldly say it out how the bugbear of the deficit from diminished opium revenue could be laid low. The emissaries of Government and the apologists in the press here and on your side have been deliberately misleading the ignorant British public and frightening the tax-payers of by holding out the threat of fresh taxation. I have been already singly combating this humbug here. Even our own newspaper writers seem to understand next to nothing of the significance of the real issues involved. They are simply carried away by the superficial cant of these interested and partisan writers. All this shows, how much more have our own educated people to learn of the very a b c of [a] revenue problem like that of opium.

I am not forgetting the Simultaneous Examination question. In fact, you must have noticed from my closing speech at the Belgaum Conference, copy of which was posted to you, that I most vigorously exhorted all the delegates to attend to the despatch of the petitions through me. As the summer vacation is over now and people are resuming their avocations I am soon going to issue a whip in the matter to our mofussil friends.

What about the scope of the Royal Commission? And what about its visits to India? Kindly enlighten us on these two points.

I was concerned at the news of your indisposition. I hope you are now thoroughly recovered and are strong as ever, specially for the coming affray. Let us all pray for your complete success at Finsbury at the General Election. You deserve to be returned with a thumping majority.

Yours sincerely
D. E. Wacha
21 June 1895

My dear Dadabhai

I have yours of 31st May. Touching your enquiry as to the writer from whose leaflet I quoted that extract about mistrusting Anglo-Indian opinion in the columns of the Kziser-e-Hind of 5th May last, I may mention that it was our valued friend Mr. Worsworth. You know those dozen leaflect we issued in 1885 at the time of the General Election. Some were written by Sir William Wedderburn, one by Crawley Bowey, two by Mr. Telang, two by me, one by Mr. Javerilal and so on.

I am glad Sir William Wedderburn has prepared a second note on Westland's Budget. He kindly forwarded me and Mr. Mehta an advanced copy which both of us have read with keen interest. We must congratulate the Committee on having so ably and lucidly criticised the statements of Sir James Westland. The note must carry conviction home in the mind of every unbiasse member of the House. Mr. Browne wrote to say a copy has been forwarded to Sir James. This is as it should be. If there be any errors, let him point them out. We can correct them and then stand firmer on our legs. But I doubt if our heaven-born Finance Minister will condescend to say we are right or wrong. At the best he will acknowledge the copy.

In this connection we wish you would enlarge a bit on that absurd table of net revenue and expenditure converted into sterling. Show up its absurdity mercilessly for the table deserves that fate. Not only that let us demonstrate to Parliament how the Finance Minister attempts to mislead it by such futile statistics and how far reliance can be placed on his figures.

I think it is also needful in showing the enhanced charges on account of Military expenditure to include the total capital outlay on military railway on the frontier. I think they come up to about 17 crores. Moreover, these have been losing railways. So that adds to the original outlay.

I am really sorry that Sir J. Pease precipitated the debate on the Opium Commission Report It was ill-considered tactics. Possibly he wishes to forestall the report of the Government of India, knowing well that it would further strengthen the Commissioner. So that a division forced prior to the receipt of such report might be a good thing. Sir John must have been sanguine that he would carry the House with him; and thus by a majority on his side render any report from the Government of India nugatory. If such be the reasons which impelled him to force on the debate, he has acted most unwisely. This premature discussion has done great harm to our cause in more ways than one and I am sorry for it. But all is not lost yet. If the evidence is carefully sifted the Society may find abundant evidence to damage the officials and the Commission and wipe away the present nasty defeat. Mr. Fowler of course had an easy victory. What more could be expected when not even two persons in the House had completely gone over the report? Of course he was plausible all through and besides he got the opportunity he wanted to dish the antiopiumists. I fully believe Mr. Wilson is in the right.

But it is a pity that our own right cause should have been marred by precipitate debate. All along they have tried by noisome and other means to silence Truth and hold up its opposite as if that were the Truth! I am sure the Government here will now go in more extensively for cultivation of the poppy.

They are so much at their wits' end that they would do anything now to raise more revenue from opium, for it is the only thing left to them after adding 7 Crores and more to taxation. I have written 2 article in the Kaiser supporting the view of our anti-opium friends; and I have written a third for next Sunday. I dare say you will have read all these.

Lord Sandhurst is doing very well. His reply to the address of the Poona Sarvajanik Sabha was well conceived and courteous in tone. A little friendly advice to the Sabha not to exaggerate facts and to keep a little more confidence in the officials has been construed by the Anglo-Indian press into a kind of mild rebuke. It is nothing of the kind. We say it was right and proper. His Lordship is moving diplomatically and with great tact and judgement. He observed in his speech that he read with interest my address at the Belgaum Provincial Conference. Mr. Malabari wrote to me a few days ago from Mahableshwar to say his Lordship would like to have a talk with me. I think of seeing him by appointment.

Yours sincerely
D.E. Wacha

P.S.—There is an article in the June number of the Fortnightly Review on "Hong Kong and the Straits Settlements" by Mr. E.S. Gundrey. You will find in it how much of financial injustice is done to the Straits and how the non-official members of the Legislative Council of that Settlement resented such arbitrary blackmail on account of military expenditure and resigned their seats in a body. Not a single non-official gentleman has since cared to accept office though offered. There is a good deal in the article which reminds us of the iniquities of the War Office in connection with our own country.

D.E.W.
28 June 1893

My dear Dadabhai

I have yours of the 6th Inst. The week on your side, judging from the telegrams, has been of a most eventful character. The Ministry has been obliged to resign. And Lord Salisbury steps back again into power and place. The Bannerman incident appears to be the last straw that broke the back of the camel of the Liberal Cabinet. But the end one way or the other was inevitable. We have not yet heard who is to be our next autocrat at Westminster. Two names have been telegraphed as candidates for the Secretaryship of India—Lord Hamilton and Curzon. I do not think Lord Salisbury would be so injudicious as to set up that pompous puppy, who has been posing as a sort of civil authority on frontier affairs, under the inspiration of Lord Roberts and other fireeaters, as our Secretary of State. For that matter he may as well give the reins to the ambitious whilom Governor of Bombay who yearns after the Indian Viceroyalty. Anyhow he has better experience. I should prefer Sir J. Fergusson as an eminently safe and fair-minded person. But it is of no [use] speculating as the telegraph will announce in a few hours more who is to be the arbiter of our destinies till the new Parliament comes into existence. Perhaps, to avoid all bickerings Viscount Cross may as well fill the post again, though one cannot say what further mischief this cress-grained minister may do. Between him and Lord Lansdowne must be shared the greater portion of the mischief created by their repressive and retrograde policy.

I received a telegram from London requesting me to sec that all India sends to Finsbury its thanks and that it expresses a strong vote of confidence in you. The telegram did not say from whom it came! But I presume it must be from our good friend Sir W. Wedderburn. Well, I may say I have promptly compiled with the message as you will see from the copy of the circular I have addressed to the fifty Congress Centres. I am also privately writing to our leading friends in Madras and Calcutta to keep their constituencies in their respective Presidencies alert on the subject. Too rapid elections are rather hard on poor members. And in your case the hardship is doubly enhanced by your being an Indian who has to court on Anglo-Indian friends as your adversaries. Of course, the Salisburians will try their utmost to storm Finsbury and defeat you. But we all suppose Finsbury is strong and radical to the core. If so none but you will carry the day. Has your rival, Mr. Mainwaring, any chances of success ? And what is the attitude of Mr. Penton? I read somewhere that he is friendly towards you.

We know nothing of the real situation of Bhownuggree. Of course, he advertises himself and sends long extracts to prove to the world of India what a mighty whole he is and how anxious are the Conservatives to rally round him and carry him successfully through the election. We know how much of this should be discounted. But after all the elections are a mixture of party politics and party passion. Simply for the sake of spiting you the Tories might do their best to support the candidature of Bhownuggree at Bethnal Green. The India Office influence, I am sure, will be exerted to the utmost. Still it is a question of strength and how far Mr. Howell would be able to stand against him. He is an old Liberal who has served that constituency for many a year. But let the fate of Bhownuggree be what it may India will be anxiously interested in yours. But we have all are confident (sic) of hope that you will win and that you have wonderfully improved your chances at Finsbury.

As to the Royal Commission, I fear, it will make little progress during the next four months—at any rate we do not think member will find time to sit with the elections impending on them. Everybody will try to look more after his constituency than anything else. But the non-parliamentarians of the Commission, who are mostly officials, will have a fine time of it. I should not be surprised that they rush through while you may be engaged elsewhere, and so too Sir W. Wedderburn and Mr. Caine. At any rate they will have fine time to concoct and lay the faggots against India whilst you are all busy elsewhere.

Moreover, we shalln't know anything about their doings as it is reported that the Commission is to sit in camera! Wonderful Commission! Parliament sits with open doors and yet such are the mighty secrets touching the Indian administration that *the* Commission must sit with closed doors! There is little hope from a Commission of this character. We give up ail hopes of even a modicum of reform. It would be an agreeable surprise were our forecasts to be belied. Let us see.

I note all you say about the Opium Commission. I and you are at one in the matter. I formed the same opinion about Lord Brassey that you did. You seem to have forgotten that we both called on him together at Government House and we both compared notes after our interview that he was only a waxen figure in the hands of the bureaucracy here and no good can ever be expected from him.

But I must be brief. You will be nearer and nearer your election preparations when this reaches you. The cry "to arms" has already been raised. Let the victory so far as you are concerned be yours. We shall hail with redoubled joy the day when you are again returned.

Yours sincerely
D. E. Wacha
5 July 1895

My dear Dadabhai

I have two letters of yours to acknowledge—one of the 13th and the other of the 20th ultimo—the latter owing to early arrival of the Caledonia.

18 January 1896

My dear Dadabhai

I have your two letters of the 27th December and 2nd Inst.

The number of India to hand gives the summary of the proceedings of the first two days of the Congress as telegraphed by Reuter. Mr. Hewart speaks of them as "meagre". I thought they were sufficiently full. It was I [who] telegraphed them. Of course, it was done late at night, but I took sufficient care to see that due prominence was given to the most important topics which would interest and instruct people on your side. I therefore omitted to wire all humdrum and oft-repeated resolutions and confined myself to the most burning ones. The first day's telegram, moreover, had been seen by Dr. Banerji and approved of by him. However you will have are this received the full proceedings. So I [need] not say more on this topic. Perhaps you will feel disappointed that no special resolution by the Congress itself was passed about your getting back into Parliament. In reference to this I may mention that I had urged it on Mr. Surendranath who thought that his having referred to the matter in his speech was ample. Sometimes in the hurry of the moment our friends take such superficial views that one feels discouraged. This time the Subjects Committee actually did a great deal of its work against time and therefore hurried on with many resolutions, some of which were of an inconsequential character. Due regard is not paid to the pressing and the weighty.

As to your private matters I am always open to Mr. Muncherji for advice and support. It gives me pleasure to do anything which has a personal reference to yourself. I religiously follow my view that in your matter I have a stern filial duty to discharge. I reverence you as I reverence my parents. I am glad you think of called (sic) Manekbai on your side. Nothing could be better.

Lord Sandhurst was good enough to give me a second interview which was as satisfactory as the first I had some months ago. He is really anxious to elicit the opinion of the genuine leaders of public opinion. He put me many questions to which I replied—all about Legislature, Municipality, Education, Congress, Conference and so forth. Also about Mr. Ranade, Mr. Tilak, Mr. Wadia, Mr. Dharamsi, Mr. Sayani and so on. His Lordship is certainly winning more and more popularity which is indeed an excellent sign under our present discouraging Tory regime. An occasional letter from you and Sir William will be very good. Of course, when you have to compliment him on something specially good. It will keep him in touch with ourselves and encourage him. He fully reciprocates all the good wishes and sympathy we show to him. Last Thursday be attended our Corporation Meeting and sat out during the whole proceedings, carrying a good impression of our debating ability. We were discussing the budget and he must have been fully impressed with our critical way of discussing it. It must have made it clear to him how far we are capable of intelligently discussing provincial and imperial budgets. Altogether his present way of governing is the only redeeming feature in the dismal gloom of rank repression and reaction all round.

India has done well in castigating Lord Elgin. Let Mr. Hewart now and then give an honest good word for Lord Sandhurst. I may mention that he has become a regular subscriber to India through a local bookseller. But I am going to present him with a copy of the issues of India for the last 3 years; also with the reports of our own Association.

Yours sincerely
D.E. Wacha
25 January 1896

My dear Dadabhai

I have no letter of yours to acknowledge as the Mail is not in.

Meanwhile the Government of India has inflicted another severe financial injustice on poor India. It has again scarified her interests to those of Manchester. As there will be a surplus of 50 lakhs owing to improved exchange and increase in railway and other items of revenue, Manchester is to be made a present of nearly 40 lakhs out of it, by the reduction of the import duties on cotton from 5 to 3} per cent. We have nothing to say so far. If Manchester cried against protection and complained that she was handicapped against Indian mills to the extent of 1 per cent she has now got all she wanted and cannot now complain of even the shadow of protection. But the Government seems to have gone out of its way, while doing this, to increase the burden on poor India and at the same time create another kind of protection and that among Indians themselves. The burden is this. All mills in India hitherto paid excise on yarns only above 20, a duty amounting to 7 lakhs per annum. This excise is abandoned. All yarns above and under 20° are made free. At the same time all cloths manufactured by Indian mills are taxed 3½ %—above 20° and under. That is to say coarse cloths under 20°, which never entered into competition and which Government admitted so, are now for the first time taxed! This is grievous injustice, specially after giving Manchester what she wanted. Now this duty is estimated to realise 12 lakhs. So that, as the Millowners have pointed out, while Manchester's burden is diminished by 30 per cent (the total duty of 1,25,00,000 Rs. will now yield at the reduced rate of 3 1/2 per cent Rs. 88,00.000) the burden of Indian mills has been increased by 12 lakhs—or say an increase of 5 lakhs which is equal to 70 per cent. In the one case there is an increase of 70 and in the other a diminution of 30! Look at the anomaly! Have you ever heard that when Government has a surplus and is prepared to remit taxes that one favoured class, because omnipotent and voiceful, should get off a greater portion of its burden, while another poor and least able to bear it should be taxed higher! This is political economy and practical finance with a vengeance. The coarser cloths are consumed by the meases.

They are the ultimate consumers. So the increased duty will be paid by them, when they are already ground down by the enhanced salt duty and the petroleum tax apart from paying their land revenue in an artificially enhanced Rupee. It is impossible to characterise in fitting terms the political and financial injustice of this odious measure. The Government has actually gone out of its way uncalled for and gratuitously laid the burden on the shoulders of poor India. And look at this precious principle of protection.

They have allayed it for Manchester but given rise to it in India. The handloom weaver is now protected to the extent of 3½ per cent as he will now weave all his coarser cloth from duty-free yarn. He will undersell the millowner. And he will also be protected against Manchester because he can now weave even his finer cloth from duty-free yarn while Manchester will have still to pay 3i on his finer goods. You will thus perceive that while they have failed to kill the bugbear of protection and remove the so-called inequality they have introduced new inequalities which did not exist and actually handicapped our rising industry for no earthly reason whatever. There is a strong feeling of indignation among all classes of the people, European and Native, which will find expression in a public meeting on the 28th Inst called by the Sheriff You see how we are treated. What hope is there for India under the Conservatives? Please read summaries of both the dailies which contain sensible articles. I cannot write more today. Please read this letter to Sir W.W. as I have no time to write to him.

Yours
D. E. Wacha
1 February 1896

My dear Dadabhai

I have yours of the 9th January.

There is widespread indignation on the Cotton Duties Bill. The agitation is deriving greater force but there is no chance of the Government being bent into changing its course. It is really very despairing this latest phase. And I need not particularise the political features of the situation. You can as much realise them as I do. I have written a long letter to Sir William Wedderburn to interpellate the Secretary. Much good cannot come of it. But still a debate might have a good moral effect, unless the Conservatives and Unionists vote in solid phalanx and throw India overboard altogether. Really Englishmen ought to be ashamed of themselves.

We are moving in the matter of the Portrait fund. Moos's people are behaving shabbily according to Mr. Muncherji. This is most deplorable.

Yours sincerely
D. E. WACHA
Bombay 8 February 1896

My dear Dadabhai

I have yours of the 16th January; also the evidence of the Royal Commission which, you may rest assured, will remain, with me as a confidential paper till it is made public. It is arduous work to wade through it, specially as it has no index and the different topics have not yet been classified as is usually done in such cases. All the same I am going though, it. Meanwhile I have read out your last letter to Mr. Mehta. He has taken time to consider the matter. Of course, everyone is agreed that at this juncture nothing could be better for India than that its best and most influential men should go before the Commission. As lawyers, Messrs Mehta, Banerji and Ghose could very well stand the severest cross-examination and greatly strengthen the non-official views submitted by you and others. As to Mr. Banerji I presume he will not hesitate to be a witness, specially as he is an annual visitor to London. Even Mr. Ghose may sacrifice his large practice to do the same. But I am not quite confident about Pherozeshah. He hesitates and hesitates. His health has been greatly impaired and

I and other friends have been urging on him the desirability of seeking a change to England. But he has not yet made up his mind. I shall strongly urge on him now to go so that he may benefit himself and the country. You are quite right in saying that we may not have another such opportunity for another generation and that we shall have to blame ourselves if we fail in our duty at the present moment. It is this inherent weakness of our countrymen which emboldens our far from sympathetic rulers now steeped in intense selfishness, and forgetful of all righteous principles, to forge stronger and stronger chains to keep us "slaves" as you rightly observe.

Yours sincerely
D. E. WACHA
15 February 1896

My dear Dadabhai

I have yours of the 23rd ultimo.

The Duty affair is still engaging the public mind and everywhere the feeling of indignation is slowly finding vent. Several towns have passed resolutions boycotting Lancashire stuffs. But I fear these are mere academic resolutions. The Government cares not a fig for these. The only effectual boycotting is to cancel orders for a couple of months. But our merchants are disunited. We suffer every way on account of want of unity among ourselves— politically, socially and commercially.

Yours sincerely
D. E. WACHA

Early Years

Naoroji was the son of Maneckbai and Naoroji Palanji Dordi, born into a poor family of Parsi-Zoroastrian priests in Navsari in Southern Gujarat. His father died when he was four, leaving his illiterate mother to raise him. Naoroji was educated at Elphinstone College, Bombay. At the early age of 25, he was appointed leading Professor at the Elphinstone Institution in 1850, becoming the first Indian to hold such an academic position. Being an Athornan (ordained priest), Naoroji founded the Rahnumae Mazdayasne Sabha (Guides on the Mazdayasne Path) on 1 August 1851 to restore the Zoroastrian religion to its original purity and simplicity. In 1854, he also founded a fortnightly publication, the *Rast Goftar* (or The Truth Teller), to clarify Zoroastrian concepts. By 1855 he was Professor of Mathematics and Natural philosophy in Bombay. He travelled to London in 1855 to become a partner in Cama and Co, opening a Liverpool location for the first Indian company to be established in Britain. Within three years, he had resigned on ethical grounds. In 1859 he established his own cotton trading company, Naoroji and Co. Later he became professor of Gujarati at University College London.

In 1867 Naoroji helped establish the East India Association, one of the predecessor organisations of the Indian National Congress. In 1874 he became Prime Minister of Baroda and was a member of the Legislative Council of Bombay (1885-88). He was also a member of the Indian National Association founded by Sir Surendranath Banerjee from Calcutta a few years before the founding of the Indian National Congress in Bombay, with the same objectives and practices. The two groups later merged into the INC, and Naoroji was elected President of the Congress in 1886. Naoroji published *Poverty and Un-British Rule in India* in 1891.

Naoroji moved to Britain once again and continued his political involvement. Elected for the Liberal Party in Finsbury Central at the 1892 general election, he was the first British Indian MP. He refused to take the oath on the Bible as he was not a Christian, but was allowed to take the oath of office in the name of God on his copy of *Khordeh Avesta*. In Parliament he spoke on Irish Home Rule and the condition of the Indian people. In his political campaign and duties as an MP, he was assisted by Muhammad Ali Jinnah, the future Muslim nationalist and founder of Pakistan. In 1906, Naoroji was again elected president of the Indian National Congress. Naoroji was a staunch moderate within the Congress, during the phase when opinion in the party was split between the moderates and extremists.

Naoroji was a mentor to both Gopal Krishna Gokhale and Mohandas Karamchand Gandhi. Naoroji was the paternal uncle of famous industrialist J. R. D. Tata. He was married to Gulbai from the age of eleven. He died in Bombay on 30 June 1917, at age 92.

Birth and Childhood

Dadabhai Naoroji was born in Bombay on 4th September 1825, the son of Maneckbai and Naoroji Palanji Dordi, a poor Athornan (priestly) Parsi family. At the age of 4, Dadabhai's father died and his mother was left the difficult task of bringing up the family, and she managed admirably. According to prevailing customs, she arranged the marriage of Dadabhai to Gulbai at the early age of 11. For the rest of her life, Maneckbai remained a close companion and mentor to Dadabhai. "She made me what I am" noted Dadabhai in 1901 when he gave an account of his early life in "The Days of my Youth."

Dadabhai became a scholar at the Elphinstone Institution (now Elphinstone College, Bombay) and had a brilliant academic career. In 1850 at the early age of 25, he was appointed Assistant Professor, and 4 years later, Professor of Mathematics and Natural Philosophy at the Elphinstone Institution. Professor Orlebar of the college called him "The Promise of India". Dadabhai, being an Athornan (ordained priest), founded the Rahnumae Mazdayasne Sabha (Guides on the Mazdayasne Path) on 1st August 1851. The ethos of the Rahnumae at its inception was to restore the Zoroastrian religion to its original purity and simplicity. The society is still in operation in Bombay.

Visit to England: On 27th June 1855, Dadabhai sailed for England to join the first Indian business firm of the mercantile Cama family. In 1859, Dadabhai established his own business firm under the name of Dadabhai Naoroji and Co.

The London Anjuman: On 31st October 1861, an association was founded in the name of "THE LONDON ANJUMAN" and Dr. Dadabhai Naoroji was its Patron, Founder and First President.

Other Activities: During his time in England, Dadabhai endeavoured to educate the British people about their responsibilities as rulers of India. He delivered speeches and published articles to support his opposition to the unjust and oppressive regime of the British Raj. In 1867 he helped to establish the East India Association of which he became the Honorary Secretary. The purpose of the Association was to keep Britain well informed of India's plight and needs and to secure fair treatment for India's people. This was his first political move and his colleagues were not slow in realising his aspirations, echoing Professor Orlebar's sentiment as "The Promise of India".

Dadabhai presented to the British people the "Drain Theory", which put before them the facts and figures illustrating systematic bleeding of the wealth and resources of India. His ideas were put into a volume called "Poverty and unBritish rule in India". This was a charge against the British Empire, and he asked for immediate appointment of a Royal Commission to look into the charges. Dadabhai was one of the members of the Royal Commission.

Dadabhai went back to India in 1869 but soon returned to England to give evidence before the Parliamentary Commission on Indian Finance. Dadabhai returned to India in 1874, having been appointed Dewan of Baroda State. He came back to England in 1886 with the idea of getting into the British Parliament to enable him to fight from within the system, and further the cause of his native country India.

Election to Parliament: Dadabhai was elected to Parliament on the 5th of July 1892 and entered the House of Commons as a Liberal, representing the Central Finsbury constituency. He delivered his maiden speech in the House of Commons in August 1892. This was indeed a historic occasion as Dadabhai Naoroji became the first ever Indian/Asian Member of the British Parliament. Dadabhai immediately championed various causes in the House of Commons. He made many speeches both in England and in India on political reforms, fair play and justice for India, which spearheaded the beginning of the freedom struggle. He was renowned as the founding father of Indian Nationalism.

Other Members of Parliament: Dadabhai's success on being elected to the Parliament was followed by two other Indian Parsi Zoroastrians; Sir Muncherji Merwanji Bhownagree and Sir Sorabji Saklatvala. Dadabhai's reputation and his help facilitated the political careers of both these gentlemen.

Indian National Congress: Dadabhai was one of the moving spirits and founder of the Indian National Congress. He took part in the inauguration of the Indian National Congress that was held in Bombay in 1865, before his departure to England. Dadabhai was thrice elected President of the Congress.

Dadabhai Naoroji had attempted to keep the Freedom movement on a moderate path during the formative years of the Congress. He had put his faith in the British. He believed that if they were informed of India's problems, they would reform their method of rule. However, his experience of the British political system and years of dealing with British officialdom led to increasing disillusionment. Dadabhai began to despair when even moderate claims were not considered. In 1904 Dadabhai demanded "SWARAJ" Self Government for India. Dadabhai said "Indians were British citizens with a birthright to be free" and that they had "every right to claim an honourable fulfilment of our British pledged rights". "It is futile to tell me that we must wait till all the people are ready. The British people did not -wait for their Parliament". "Self-government is the only and chief remedy. In self-government is our hope, strength and greatness". "I am a Hindu, a Muslim, a Parsi, but above all an Indian First".

Enter Mahatma Gandhi: On 1st September 1888, Gandhi sailed from Bombay with a letter of introduction to Dadabhai. Mahatma Gandhi wrote "...you will, therefore oblige me greatly if you will kindly direct and guide me and make necessary suggestions which shall be received as from a father to his child". Gandhi further wrote: "The story of a life so noble and yet so simple needs no introduction from me or anybody else. May it be an inspiration to the readers even as Dadabhai living was to me". "And so Dadabhai became real DADA to me".

The Grand Old Man: The Grand Old Man of India once asked "Is it vanity that I should take great pleasure in being hailed as the Grand Old Man of India? No, that title, which speaks volumes for the warm, grateful and generous hearts of my countrymen, is to me, whether I deserve it or not, the highest reward of my life".

A great life nobly lived, spanning nearly a whole century, great, indeed in the greatness of its simplicity, purity and benignity and lofty in its concept of man's mission on earth, came to an end on 30th June 1917. Dadabhai passed away at the ripe old age of 93.

Tributes: Sir Narayen Chandravarkar at the "Memorial Meeting" paid a warm affectionate tribute to the life and character of the dear departed sage of India.

"If we take stock of his life and his example, may I not say with perfect justice and truth that in his career, in all he did, in all he suffered and in all he taught, he was the prophet Zoroaster's religion personified because he was the man more than anybody else of pure thought, of pure speech and pure deeds".

Sir Dinshaw Wacha in a speech full of feeling said: "There is no doubt.. Dadabhai served his country with a sacrifice and singleness of purpose which it may be rightly said, without exaggeration, was rare. A devout follower of Zoroaster, he faithfully followed the ethics of that Great Prophet - pure in thought, word and deed".

Kusoom Vadgama, a prominent writer in London in her recent book "India in Britain" writes: "One whose contributions to Britain by any standards remain memorable and who represented culture, intelligence and public spirit was Dadabhai Naoroji, the first Indian Member of Parliament".

The Backdrop

Not many years ago, there lay seven desolate islets where the city of Bombay has now sprung up, forming the main gateway between the East and the West. Here, scattered along the coastline, were several fishing villages of the early settlers.

One of these, known as Mandvi, after the old mandovim or custom house, has since been transformed into a busy emporium. Bhatrias, Banias, Khojas, Bohras, and Memons, pillars of Indian commerce, muster strong in this labyrinth of storehouses and slums, but the otherwise ubiquitous Parsi is rarely to be found. It was not so a hundred years ago, when several Parsi families had their homes in this locality.

One of those inhabitants was a poor priest, Naoroji Palanji Dordi, who lived with his wife, Manekbai, in a lowly house in Khadak. Great was the joy of this couple when, on September 4, 1825, a son was born to them, their first and only child. They named him Dadabhai. What made them select this Hindu name?

Was it a mere accident, or was it because the fairy godmother, who visits the homes of Indian children on the Chhathi, or the sixth night after their birth, I whispered to the fond mother that her son was destined to fill a large space in contemporary history and to become the Grand Old Man—the Dada—of Hindustan?

Be that as it may, Dadabhai carried his lofty destiny in Ms. name. To love and serve Mother India, as none of her sons had done before him, to get grey in that service and still to knock at England's door for the redress of India's wrongs, to teach his countrymen to be free, and then in the twilight of old age to see them placed on the path of self-government—this was the mission of his life; and he gloried in it as much as he rejoiced in the tide "Dada" with which his countrymen loved to honour him.

Is it vanity (he once asked) that I should take a great pleasure in being hailed as the Grand Old Man of India ? No, that title, which speaks volumes for the warm, grateful, and generous hearts of my countrymen, is to me, whether I deserve it or not, the highest reward of my life.

Dadabhai's ancestors came from Navsari, a small town in the territory of the Gaikwad of Baroda, originally known as Nagmandal, or snake-land. It is related that finding its climate as salubrious as that of the ancient city Sari, in Iran, the early Parsi settlers of the place called it Nao Sari, or "New Sari." "What Bombay owes to the enterprise of the Parses in British India, Navsari owes to the achievements of their co-religionists in the Gaikwad's dominions. It is the pride of this stronghold of Parsi priesthood and the religious centre of the Parses of Western India that it has produced some of the most famous dasturs (prelates) and desais (headmen), who owned extensive territories, enjoyed great prerogatives, and rendered eminent services to society under successive rulers, and that it has been the birthplace of men like the first Sir Jamshedjee Jejeebhoy and Jamshedjee Tata, who have shed lustre on the Indian people.

Many a resident of Navsari claims that the town is the birthplace of Dadabhai also, but there is no warrant for it. His ancestors were, no doubt, domiciled in Navsari. The branch of the Dordi family, in which Dadabhai was born, owned an estate in the Dharampore State, about twenty miles from Navsari. Here his grandfather, and his father, too, before he settled in Bombay, carried on agricultural pursuits. The family record, however, shows a long unbroken chain of priests tracing their descent from Zarthost Mobed, the oldest known ancestor, who was the first Parsi priest to arrive in Navsari. In those days a Parsi priest considered it a religious duty to have his son admitted to the priesthood. Had Dadabhai's father lived until he attained the age of initiation, he would probably have insisted on Dadabhai becoming a Mobed and ministering to the spiritual needs of his community. It is interesting to speculate how in that event he might have devoted himself to the religious interests of the Parsi community with the zest of a reformer even more fervid than the spirit of patriotism which marked his advocacy of the secular interests of his motherland. How vehemently would he have denounced religious tyrannies instead of the economic disabilities and political injustice under which he found his country groaning for redress! A word from such a priest might have silenced the din of many bitter controversies; the priesthood might probably have been restored to its ancient dignity; and the religious and social progress of the community greatly accelerated.

This, however, was not to be, unfortunately for the Parsi priesthood, but fortunately for all the people of India, including the Parses. The regeneration of the country was of far greater moment than the reformation of a particular creed. It was, therefore, ordained that Dadabhai should make the first gap in the family record of uninterrupted sacerdotal service, and become the high priest of Indian Nationalism. Dadabhai, however, did go through the Navar ceremony, qualifying him for priesthood, when he was fourteen years of age.

Gujarat is the "Garden of India" and Navsari is the "Garden of Gujarat" famous for its fragrant flowers and perfumes, "the like of which," says Abul Fazal, the historian, "is nowhere to be found." Tradition relates that one of the ancestors of Dadabhai, Chandji Kamdin, made the best perfumes of the day. His fame travelled from Navsari to Delhi and reached the ears of Nur Jahan Begam. She desired to know the recipe and induced her husband, the Emperor Jahangir, to send for Chandji with his perfumes. On receipt of the royal invitation Chandji left for Delhi with jars of four select varieties of attar, which he laid at the feet of the Emperor. In return, he was entertained in Delhi as a royal guest and was granted a hundred bighas of land with the tide of Mulla Jamasp.

"How far this account is correct," wrote Dadabhai in reply to certain questions put to him by a journalist, in the year 1881, "I am unable to say till I see all the documents connected with the matter.

This laconic reply was typical of the man. Never to accept a statement without verification, never to make a statement without being convinced of the truth of it, was the rule of his life; and if he did say anything which was not borne out by facts, even his bitterest critic refrained from questioning his credentials.

It was left to Dr. Jivanji Modi to examine the documents and sift all the evidence. His erudite research has thrown much light on the historic background on which the tradition rested. In a paper read before the Bombay Branch of the Royal Asiatic Society, on March 22, 1920, he points out that the royal order, issued in the name of "Victorious Nur-ud-din Muhammad Jahangir Badshah Gazi," announced the grant of land measuring approximately a hundred bighas in the town of Navsari, exempt from all taxes, "in aid of the livelihood of Mulla Jamasp and his nephew Mulla Hoshang, two members of the Dordi family."

The firman, which is now in the possession of the Dordi family, dated August 24, 1618, records the facts that Mulla Jamasp and Mulla Hoshang waited on the Emperor and presented to him "four goblets of oil fulel (prepared from jasmin)." "Chandji" was one of the Hindu names then current among the Parsi community. While granting the firman, Jahangir substituted for that name the Iranian name Jamasp.

According to the traditional account, the perfume was taken to Delhi in response to the wishes of Nur Jahan, but it appears from Jahangir's autobiography that on the date of the royal decree the Emperor was in Ahmedabad. There is no doubt, however, that Mulla Jamasp did on one occasion visit the Mughal Court, for his name is mentioned in the list, given in the Bombay Gazetteer, of the author is indebted for further particulars concerning the history of the Dordi family to Dr. Jahangir Behramji Dordi, F.R.C.S., who is now maintaining the traditions of his illustrious house for social service and civic usefulness, the Parses who visited the Court of Akbar. Whether he went to Ahmedabad with the offering, in response to an invitation, or simply took the opportunity of paying homage to the sovereign, whose father's Court he had visited and whose hospitality he had enjoyed, is a matter of surmise. In all other respects the family tradition and history go together.

Mulla Jamasp was a direct descendant of Zarthost Mobed, who settled in Navsari about the year 1201, and Dadabhai was the ninth in descent from Mulla Jamasp. His parents lived in comparative poverty, but his ancestors appear to have seen better days.

The names of some of the Dordis figure with those of the elders of the Parsi community in communal records, which show that Dadabhai's impulse for patriotic service had its roots in his ancestry. Mehernosji Dordi rose to the position of an Akbar, or leader, not only of the Parsi fraternity of Navsari, but also of the whole population of the place. Mehernosji's eldest son, Bachaji, was one of a mission of five famous Parses of the time, who visited the Gaikwad's headquarters at Songadh in 1740, as a result of which the fire-temple of the Parses was removed to Udwada, where it remains to this day.

Mehernosji's second son, Behramji, was at one time the richest man in Navsari. He was, however, robbed during one of the raids of the Pindaris, which were common in those days, of all the bars of gold he had concealed in the basement of his residence. He died broken-hearted the same day. Another ancestor of the family, Sorabji Burjorji, was well known in Navsari as Hafiz, the title conferred on men versed in scriptural lore. This shows that the family was renowned for learning also, while its connection with the celebrated Desai family of Navsari bespeaks its high social status.

A curious origin has been suggested of the family name Dordi. One day some Parsi priests of Navsari went to a dinner. An ancestor of Dadabhai's family, Behramji Mehernosji, turned up rather late and tried to conceal himself, or, according to another account, perambulated the place in search of a seat company thereupon ejaculated,

Mulla Jamasp's Line of Descent

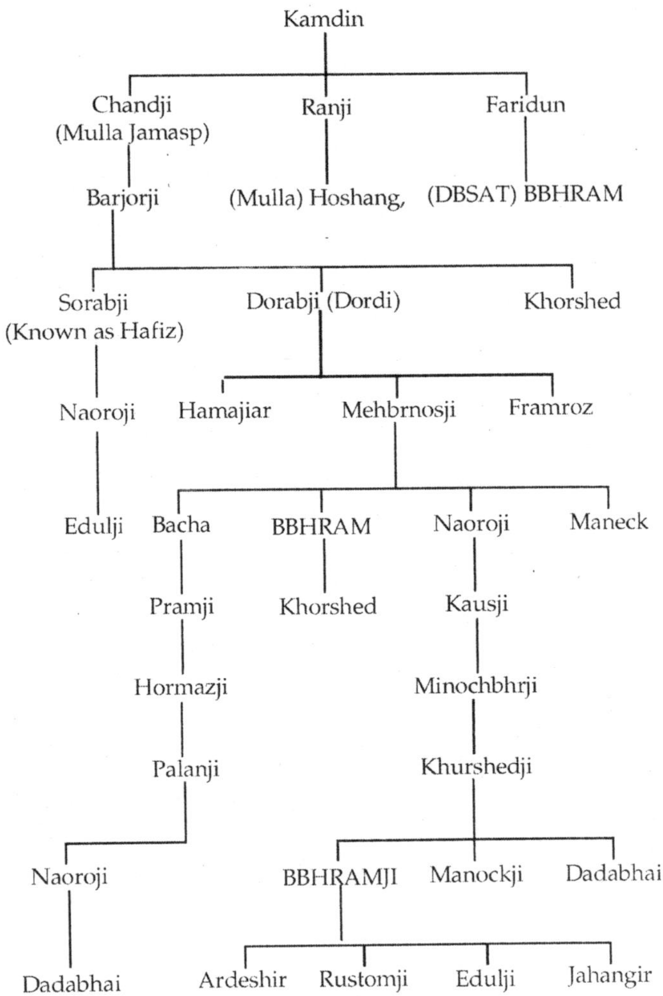

"Why are you twisting and turning like a dordi (rope made of coir) ?" Thereafter the name stuck to the man and his descendants. According to the local account, this nickname was given to Behramji in the year 1764, but the family records show that he had been gathered to his forefathers long before that date. There is a confusion of names and dates in the traditional account. Perhaps the name was given to some other headstrong member of the family for his inflexibility of decision and tenacity of purpose, qualities which the hero of our story inherited and displayed in an eminent degree.

"Maharaj," said Dadabhai once to Mulharrao Gaikwad when pressed to do what he, as his Prime Minister, thought would cause more harm than good, "my name is 'Dordi.' You know, Your Highness, that you may burn a dordi, but can never take the twist out of it. So is it with me. When once I form a decision, nothing will dislodge me from it."

A striking illustration of such courage of conviction and determination was his stupendous struggle to enter the House of Commons. It was the most romantic dream of his life; the chances for its fruition seemed extremely slender, but Dadabhai carried on his election campaign for seven years, undeterred by the coldness or antagonism of friend or foe and undismayed by repeated reverses. After his first failure to win the suffrages of the electors of the Holborn division of Finsbury, in the year 1886, he nursed the Central Finsbury constituency for five years in spite of the opposition of the executive of his own Liberal Party. When he appeared to be leading a forlorn hope, W. A. Chambers, one of the British friends most keenly interested in Dadabhai's success, called on him. This liberal-minded Englishman, who was a member of a leading firm of civil engineers and architects in Bombay and was well known for his active sympathy with India in her struggle for freedom, was also a voter in Central Finsbury. In the course of their conversation concerning the attitude of the officials of the Liberal Party, Dadabhai warmed up and said: "They think they can keep down the mild Hindu, but I will teach them a lesson. I will stick to this constituency." He did, indeed, stick to it and conquered.

There are no nursery annals to entertain us with the details of Dadabhai's childhood. Whether he was an infant prodigy maturing into brilliant boyhood, we have no evidence to show.

All that we know is that little Dady had the misfortune to lose his father when he was only four years old. "One of the first fancies which took possession of my mind as a little child," he tells us, "was that, as my father was dead, the moon, like other friends, was in sympathy with me. And whether I went to the front or back of the house, the moon always seemed to go with me. I liked sympathy then, and like it now."

His gifted mother, however, supplied to a large extent the want of a father's care and protection. It was in India an age of ignorance and submerged womanhood, but her natural intelligence was remarkable. She was, as he used to recall in later days, his constant companion, nurse, teacher, guardian-angel, all in one, and continued to be the good genius of his life for over fifty years. The shadow of adversity hung over the little household; nevertheless she sent him to school and toiled for his maintenance. Thanks to her diligence and care, he escaped unscathed from the contaminating influences of his environment.

In a brief account of his early life, which he contributed to "The Days of My Youth" column of T. P. O'Connor's journal M.A.P., in the year 1904, he observed:

There is one who, if she comes last in this narrative, has ever been first of all, my mother. "Widowed when I, her only child, was an infant, she voluntarily remained a widow, wrapped up in me, her everything in the world. She worked for her child, helped by a brother. Although illiterate, and although all love for me, she was a wise mother. She kept a firm hand upon me.

She was the wise counsellor of the neighbourhood. She helped me with all her heart in my work for female education and other social reforms against prejudices of the day. She made me what I am.

In the same account he gives us a few more glimpses of his childhood. That being the only chapter of autobiography left by him, it seems best to draw on it freely to complete this narrative of those early days.

How things, little in themselves, lead to important results!

In the early twenties of the last century there was formed at Bombay a society called the "Native Education Society," which established a school in two branches, English and vernacular.

The Mehtaji (master) of my indigenous school did not know very much about the experiment of the Native Education Society.

But it was enough for him that it was conducted under Government auspices. So he sent his son to the school and persuaded my mother to send me also, and this was the foundation of my whole life's career. The education was then entirely free. Had there been levied the fees of the present day, my mother would not have been able to pay them. This incident made me an ardent advocate of free education and of the principle that every child should have the opportunity of receiving all the education it is capable of assimilating, whether it is born poor or with a silver spoon in its mouth.

Being quick at multiplication tables and at mental arithmetic, and being also little of size and fair of colour, I was a regular "exhibition boy" at my indigenous or native school. On special occasions all the boys of the school used to be lined up in the open by the side of the road, and there, surrounded by crowds of people, I, along with other little boys, was smartly exercised in mental gymnastics amid the loud wawas (cries of bravo) of the admiring audience.

Owing to the fairness of my complexion, and, I think I may say, the prettiness of my little limbs, I was also always an object of show at weddings, processions, etc. generally appearing as an English general or admiral or in some gorgeous Indian Royal or Court dress brocade. Fond parents and friends of the child thus exhibited used to say of him: "Oh, he is my dear Jonglo (Englishman)!" Little did I dream then that I should spend much of my manhood and older life in the country of the Jonglos arid don their dress in reality. I was particularly reminded of these days of processions and my childish joy in the different dresses I wore, especially the English Court dress, when, in Court dress, I formed one of the deputation from the committee of the Imperial Institute, who received the late Queen Victoria on die occasion of the opening of that building. I well remember how the thought passed through my mind: "Here I am, a real courtier now!"

When I entered the school, there were two European masters— one for the literary, the other for the arithmetic, department.

Some difference of opinion having arisen between them, they divided the school into two parts, each taking die whole education of his own division. One of the two was a strict disciplinarian, the other anything but that. My lot fell with the latter. Practically we were allowed to do as we liked, but I was not disposed to be idle. I must be active in some way or the other. There was no enforcement of lessons, so I looked about for an occupation.

I had a retentive memory and could repeat any story I heard both in spirit and in letter, and I was full of stories. So most of my school hours were passed in "spinning yams" to an admiring circle of schoolfellows. So lax was discipline that often we would coolly march out of school and spend the whole day in games.

In this way something like a year of regular study was lost tome.

Yet I cannot say that even that truant year did not do me some good. My storytelling powers and skill at games made me a leader among the boys, and I acquired the self-confidence and reliance which comes with such a position.

As a boy I took a great interest in, and was considered pretty smart at, Indian cricket (gilli-danda). In the pursuit of that active and absorbing game we boys did not in the least seem to mind the hot sun, and during the half-hour for lunch at midday we used to play regularly on the Esplanade.

In the streets of great cities one's ears are not infrequently assailed by foul language. Dadabhai's soul shrank with horror from it.

Another incident of my childhood I give upon my mother's authority and not from personal recollection. According to my mother, whenever any boy used bad language to me, I used to reply, "Your bad words will remain in your mouth."

The awakening of the soul came to me when I was about fifteen. I remember, as if it were only yesterday, how at a certain spot on a certain road I made a vow never to use low language.

From that time forward, as my education advanced, other resolutions to do this and not to do that followed, and I think I may say that I faithfully adhered to them.

Happy the man who can thus lay his hand on his heart and claim fidelity to his better self! The following startling story gives an idea of the unwholesomeness of the general surroundings.

As a boy I was accustomed to have my little drink before dinner. One day, there was no liquor in the house, and I was sent to have my drink at a shop opposite. Never did I forget the shame and humiliation I felt at being there. It was enough. The drink shop never saw my face again.

In another reminiscence he tells us how at a school exhibition he deprived a jackdaw of his borrowed feathers.

I remember at one of the school examinations a fellow-pupil, having learned the "ready-reckoner" by heart, carried off the prize I had expected. But at the distribution of prizes, when questions outside the book were asked, he faltered and broke down. I seized the opportunity, rushed out of the ranks, and answered. There and then an English gentleman among the company gave me a prize, and Mrs. Postans, the lady traveller, who was also present, has made a special note of the incident in her book Western India.

In this book Mrs. Postans described Dadabhai as a little Parsi lad "with an overhanging forehead and small sparkling eyes," which "peculiarly attracted attention." "The moment a question was proposed to the class," she writes, "he quickly took a step before the rest, contracted his brows in deep and anxious thought and with parted lips and fingers eagerly uplifted towards the master, rapidly worked his problem and blurted out the solution with a startling haste. The little fellow seemed wholly animated with a desire of excelling, and his mental capabilities promised him a rich reward."

One wonders if "the little fellow" would have risen or fallen in the estimation of this lady if she had been told that on his tiny shoulders he was carrying the burden of a married man! Infant marriages were then a rule among Parses. The earlier the age at which a mother succeeded in securing a husband for her girl, the greater was her exultation. Marriages were even arranged, in rare cases, in anticipation of the birth of a bride or bridegroom, and Dadabhai would have been a good-for-nothing fellow had his mother failed to secure a wife for him before he was in his teens. So we find him married during his eleventh year to Gulbai, daughter of Sorabji Shroff, aged seven.

The Promise of India

It was a critical hour for the advanced students of Dadabhai's school when Assistant Professor Bal Gangadhar Shastree visited it to select half a dozen boys for a new college class.

Young Dady felt his fate trembling in the balance. Although he was the brightest boy of the class, he was put very near the bottom. The teacher of the class had a partiality for the sons of rich people, a common failing of schoolmasters of that type, Poor as he was, Dady could not stand it. It was not in his nature to conceal resentment; he often rebelled against such injustice, but it made matters worse for him. Bal Gangadhar, however, picked him out with unerring judgement and pronounced him fit for the higher form. Thereafter he toiled on, winning academic laurels which culminated in his appointment as Professor of Mathematics.

Among the educational institutions which revolutionised the life and thought of the people of the Bombay Presidency during the nineteenth century none was more conspicuous than the Elphinstone Institution, popularly known as the Sisoti (Society's) School, and among the distinguished Sisoti boys who powerfully stimulated the activities of the people of India and transformed their ideals of national life none was more prominent than Dadabhai. The genesis of this institution throws some light on the conditions under which Dadabhai received his early education.

In the beginning of the nineteenth century India was steeped in ignorance. Only in a few nooks and corners the lamp of knowledge was dimly lit. The rulers of the country were so engrossed in the work of consolidating the conquered territories that they had no time to think of the immediate intellectual wants of the people or of the danger inherent in the ignorance of the multitude.

It is astonishing how backward, until recently, was British educational policy. There was no public grant-in-aid for education in England until 1834; no educational enactment of any real importance until the year 1870. Even then England would probably have remained inactive, had not the Prussian victories in the Franco-German War demonstrated to the world the immense advantage of an educated rank and file.

Such innate conservatism may account for the indifference of the early authorities; but another factor also appears to have encouraged the policy of inaction pursued during the regime of the East India Company. This was the conflict between self-interest and duty, the conflict of interests of the people with those of their alien rulers, which was to be the theme of hundreds of Dadabhai's orations and appeals to British statesmen. Should the torch of knowledge and liberty be kindled in those regions, would there not be a growing demand for more light and more freedom until the subject people were acknowledged to be fit for self-government and allowed to throw off the yoke of an alien ascendency ? The Directors of the East India Company, therefore, looked upon the educational efforts of Christian missionaries with grave misgivings and warned their satrap, the Marquis of Hastings, that such activities would give rise to political aspirations which might jeopardise the rule of the Company. Lord Hastings, however, manfully replied that it would be a betrayal of national morality to perpetuate ignorance for the sake of sordid political considerations.

Very little, however, was done by the State for the furtherance of that object. Consequently, during the days of Dadabhai's infancy, education in Bombay was a haphazard affair. There was not a single Government school in the City. The benevolent missionary bodies and the Bombay Education Society conducted a few schools on Western lines, and their work was supplemented by indigenous schools owned and run by penurious Mehtaji, who held their classes on the verandahs of houses. Chairs and tables were unknown; slates and pencils were novelties; the student carried with him a portable patti, or a piece of wood, on which he traced die letters of the alphabet and numerals with a reed pen dipped in a chalky fluid. Sweeping the school premises in the morning and doing household work for the teacher formed part of the curriculum—and striking recognition of the place of manual training in the scheme of elementary education!

The origin of school sports in Bombay is generally traced to the game of gilli-danda, the game which Dadabhai used to describe in England as "Indian cricket." Perhaps we may also trace the early beginning of school gymnastics to the indigenous modes of enforcing discipline, which prevailed in the schools until the closing years of the last century. To be on the rack from morning to evening, or to kneel on pebbles for hours together with their fingers touching the toes and with a heavy stone balanced on the back, as a punishment for some trivial offence, was the lot of almost all the students. Nor was it an uncommon incident to see some of the more refractory boys swung across the beams in the classroom with a rope round their bodies. Just underneath a large quantity of grass was spread and ignited; and in that position the young pupils of the stern martinets of the day had to manoeuvre as best they could to protect their bodies from being scorched.

While Dadabhai was yet an infant, a great educational movement was set on foot in Bombay. Mountstuart Elphinstone, who was then Governor of Bombay, was an ardent advocate of education. Although the prevailing official view was against Western education, and Macaulay had not yet raised his powerful voice in favour of teaching European sciences to Indians through the medium of English, this distinguished administrator sympathised with the aspirations of a few Indians for promoting higher education among the people. The Native Education Society was established under his patronage and received his constant support.

When he retired in 1827, the Princes and the people of India raised a large sum for perpetuating his memory by the foundation of "professorships for teaching the youths of the country the languages, literature, sciences, and moral philosophy of Europe."

The college classes were subsequently amalgamated with the school classes conducted by the Native Education Society, and the combined school and college, named the Elphinstone Institution, was placed under the control of a Board, This was the college where Dadabhai was taught by Professors Bell, Harkness, Henderson, Orlebar, and Reid. Of life at the institution there is, however, no record. Neither Dadabhai nor any of his contemporaries has told us what subjects were then taught, what methods were in vogue, whether politics were forbidden ground, whether the professors mixed freely with the boys, what their idiosyncrasies were, what impressions were made by them on the plastic minds of the first batch of students who joined the college classes, what traces of each one's personality were left in the hearts of their pupils. We gather, however, from the reports of the Institution that Professor Bell taught Mathematics and Natural Science, Professor Henderson History, and Professor Harkness English Literature and Philosophy. In his reminiscences of old Bombay, Sir Dinsha Wacha says that he had heard that those early professors were "most excellent in their own branches of knowledge". Harkness was "an Aberdeen man, Scotch to the backbone and Scotch in his broad accents, besides a man of stem discipline. He was hot-tempered and often used to fly into a rage, But age had mellowed him, specially in his later days before he retired in 1862." On his retirement, the grateful Elphinstonians of the day voted him a marble bust, which now adorns the Framji Cowasji Institute Hall in Bombay.

Here, then, Dadabhai learnt to commune with the best minds in the realm of literature. Here all that was noble in him was illumined by the study of the life and labours of the heroes of the world. Here dawned on him, while he was yet in his teens, the consciousness of the debt he owed to society. Among the books he read we find the pride of place given to the great Persian epic, Firdausi's Shahnama. Another favourite book, a constant companion, was a Gujarati treatise, The Duties of Zoroastrians, the burden of which was pure thought, pure speech, pure deed.

But (says he) the literature I had most to do with and most enjoyed was, of course, English. Watt's Improvement of the Mini settled my style and mode of thought—never two words when one was enough, clearness of thought and diction. So I bade farewell to the fine and flowery.

This made him an orator and an author always comprehensible to the simplest minds.

As education advanced (he adds) thought gradually developed itself in different directions. I realised that I had been educated at the expense of the poor, to whom I myself belonged, so much so that some of my school books came from a well-to-do classmate, a Cama, one of the family with whom I was destined subsequently to have so much to do in public and private life.

The thought developed itself in my mind that, as my education and all the benefits arising therefrom came from the people, I must return to them the best I had in me. I must devote myself to the service of the people....

In the year 1840 Dadabhai received the Clare Scholarship; two years later he was admitted to the newly opened class of Normal Scholars. There was another Parsi scholar, Kavasji Edulji Masani, who shared with him the honour of being the earliest to be admitted to that class, the highest rung of the academic ladder in those days. Both were close comrades until their paths fell apart; both were great at mathematics, but in his mastery of natural philosophy and political economy Dadabhai stood unrivalled.

Among his other fellow-students was Bomonji Pestonji Master, who worked for some time with Dadabhai and Kavasji Masani as a teacher in the Elphinstone School and afterwards distinguished himself as a member of the Municipal Corporation of Bombay, reputed for his wit and humour. Another companion was Kavasji Edulji Khambatta, known for the felicity of diction which marked his contributions to the English columns of the Rast Goftar, the progressive journal started by Dadabhai.

During those happy college days Dadabhai was the shining light of die Elphinstone Institution, the pride of his professors and fellow-students. In appearance he was handsome, with singularly.

Dadabhai as Professor

Tucky the lad whose academic career could dazzle not only as professors but also the Chief Justice of the day. Dadabhai had that good fortune. His work as a brilliant student came constantly to the notice of Sir Erskine Perry, Chief Justice of the Supreme Court of Bombay, who happened to be the President of the Board of Education. He suggested that Dadabhai should be sent to England to qualify himself as a barrister. It needed, however, quite a fortune to carry out the project, whereas Dadabhai and his mother did not seem to possess between them a hundred rupee note. His good uncle, Rustamji Desai, maintained them, but neither he nor any other relative could give or lend him the money required for the purpose. Hearing this, the large-hearted judge offered to contribute half the expenses himself, provided the other half was borne by the elders of the Parsi community.

Gifted with quick intelligence and the aptitude of a terse debater, fluent and forceful in speech and patient and persevering in action, Dadabhai would have been an ornament to the Bar and the Bench, had his lot been cast that way. He himself eagerly looked forward to such a career but was doomed to disappointment. The proposal of the Chief Justice was at first welcomed by some of the leaders of the community, particularly by the liberal-minded Camas, who were the pioneers of social reform and patrons of education in Bombay, but it fell through because the orthodox among them scented disaster in that generous offer.

Conversion of the heathen appears to take a secondary place among the beneficent activities of the saintly souls who now preach the Word of God in the East. Their predecessors, however, were particularly keen on proselytism as the primary object of their mission. To break through the citadel of Hinduism was not a very difficult task for them, but the staunch followers of Zoroaster, who had abandoned their homes and sought refuge in India, for the preservation of their faith, could not think of any calamity more appalling than the renunciation of the ancient creed by even a single soul. They, therefore, took special care to guard Parsi youths from the snares of the missionary. No Christian evangelist could hope to enter their sanctuary. Nevertheless, a few of the more ardent missionaries, of whom Dr. John Wilson was the most prominent, ventured to cast covetous eyes on some of the schoolboys. The method of these zealous followers of the Cross was simple—for one hour given to Christianity a gift of four hours' English, History, Geography, and Mathematics. At last, in the year 1839, they succeeded in inducing two lads, Dhanjibhoy Naoroji and Hormusji Pestonji, to embrace Christianity. Nothing ever convulsed the Parses more, or caused them greater chagrin and humiliation, than these two solitary cases of conversion. The whole community was up in arms. The missionaries were anathematised as "devils in human shape"; and brochures denouncing Christianity were written as tracts for the times.

So bitterly were the feelings of the community outraged that a disturbance of the peace was apprehended. It was alleged that the Parsi leaders were inciting their followers to violence and scheming to get forcible possession of the two lads, "with the ulterior object of sending them to Navsari and there terminating their existence." Thereupon they sent a representation to Government affirming their earnest desire to prevent any disturbance.

They had appealed to the tribunal of justice and as law-abiding people they were willing to bow to its decision. The law, however, could not give them relief, inasmuch as the boys had come of age. This kept die embers of controversy smouldering for years, and it made the creed-bound Zoroastrian fight shy of anything savouring of Christianity.

In course of time, however, the Parses were reconciled to the work of the missionaries, and they marked their appreciation of it by liberal donations to the missions. They even looked upon the two converts with respect when they had taken Holy Orders and had become Christian priests. The Rev. Dhanjibhoy died in England in the year 1905. When the cables announced the death of "D. Naoroji," people thought the Grand Old Man of India had passed away.

When Sir Erskine Perry proposed to send Dadabhai to England, six years had elapsed since the conversion of the Parsi youths, but the passions roused by that incident had not yet spent their force. Orthodox Parses would have nothing to do with anything English. It was, therefore, impossible for the leaders of the community to accept the proposal. On his retirement, Sir Erskine was appointed a member of the India Council.

Dadabhai was then in England, engrossed in the study of problems of far greater importance than Law and unconsciously qualifying himself as an advocate to plead the cause of India before the bar of the British public. "It is as well my proposal was not accepted," said the ex-judge to him one day at the India Office, "as I am sure that your life has been of more public service than if you had become a lawyer."

For the time being, however, it seemed as if Dadabhai had lost a golden opportunity. The humble chair of "Head Native Assistant-Master" of the Elphinstone School was all that could be offered to him on the completion of his academic career. By that time, however, he had come perilously near the portals of the

Government Secretariat. The Secretary to the Board of Education had secured for him an appointment in the Bombay Secretariat.

Dadabhai was on the point of accepting it, but, fortunately, sage advice of some of the professors saved him from a post where he would have been bound down to the narrow outlook of a subordinate official.

The Assistant Master's place was a stepping-stone to the Assistant Professorship of Mathematics. Referring to the appointment in their report for the year 1850-51, the Board of Education spoke of him as "one of the most experienced as well as able men ever educated within the walls of the Institution."

They expressed the hope that he would continue his career with the same single-minded straightforwardness of purpose which had hitherto characterised him. "Go on in the same, steady, straightforward course, and with the same single-minded views," wrote Dr. Stovell, Secretary to the Board of Education, "and you may prove in time a great blessing to your countrymen."

Two years later, Dadabhai was appointed Professor of Mathematics and Natural Philosophy. It was the first professorship ever held by an Indian in any prominent college in the country.

The appointment, therefore, attracted more attention in those days than that of a Minister does at the present time. It was regarded as a fitting recognition of the Indian intellect, and it made Dadabhai's countrymen feel some inches taller. The Board of Education made a special reference to it in their report for the year 1854-55. "We feel sure," they observed, "that the distinction he has thus won by a long and laborious devotion to mathematical studies and by a able discharge of his duties in the Institution will stimulate him to still greater exertions."

The enthusiasm with which the public hailed the appointment was shared by Government. They congratulated the Board of Education on having seen in the honourable distinction conferred on Dadabhai a fulfilment of the hope expressed by the founders of the Professorships, nearly thirty years ago. Dadabhai considered it the greatest event in his career. Down to the end of his life he felt proud of that distinction. "Several honours came to me during my lifetime," said he on one occasion, "but no other title created in me that sense of pride which I felt in being known as a Professor." On another occasion, when, as a member of the House of Commons, he was at the zenith of his fame, he wrote,

> "To me it is the dearest tide and honour. It is my delight, and many a schoolfellow and pupil call me 'Dadabhai Professor' to this day."

To be a professor, to mould the mind of youth and age alike, to be the preceptor not only of his pupils but of all the two hundred and fifty million people of India and, in a sense, of those in authority over them, was the destiny for which "The Promise of India" had been marked out. On that account, perhaps, he was turned aside from the byways to which he was lured by well-meaning friends, who could not then have dreamt of die position he was to occupy amongst the nation-builders of the world.

Subsequently, the forces of destiny conspired to terminate his career as a professor and to take him to another country, 6,000 miles away, where the great work of his life for the freedom of his motherland was to be accomplished.

Before, however, we cross the seas with him, let us have a glance at the record of his work as Professor in the Elphinstone Institute. How many students are befogged in their school and college days by the mysteries of mathematics! As this subject was also the stumbling-block of a large majority of Dadabhai's pupils, he did his best to make it as interesting to them as possible and to infuse in them his own love and enthusiasm for the science. Those who were specially weak in the subject were asked to sit with him after college hours, and he took keen delight in solving their difficulties. This, however, was not all. Accustomed to do everything thoroughly, he saw how necessary it was that the foundations of instruction in that abstruse subject should be laid in the lower classes on scientific lines. He, therefore, set about improving the teaching of the subject in the lower classes and undertook the work of supervision of the mathematical classes of the school division, in addition to his own duties. He also conducted periodical examinations of the classes and issued reports bringing to light the merits or demerits of individual teachers. So systematically did he carry out this work that Principal Harkness specially eulogised his efforts in his report on the work of the Institution for the year 1853-54. "In Mr. Dadabhai's report and tables of results," he observed, "will be shown the work of the year in Mathematics and Natural Philosophy in the hands of an intelligent and zealous Native Professor, who has for many years devoted himself to this department."

To what extent the Professor's love for mathematics moulded his life and character and influenced his code of ethics it is difficult to say. It will, however, be seen, as the story of his life is unfolded, that mathematical precision was the keynote not only of his private conduct and judgement but also of his political conduct and of the public agitation he led. Nothing less than a demonstrative proof could make him accept a statement; nothing short of what was just and fair could give him satisfaction.

Similarly, all his complaints against the rulers resolved themselves into the indictment that they were not governing India on principles precisely British. All his demands on behalf of India were simply appeals for a precise and just interpretation of and adherence to declarations solemnly made by the Crown and British statesmen. Many of Dadabhai's pupils, who subsequently held high positions in life, spoke admiringly of his efficiency as a teacher and his solicitude for his pupils. None who came under his spell could forget his winning simplicity, charm of manner, and unfailing courtesy. None could forget the debt of gratitude he owed to so gifted and kind-hearted a teacher for his advice and guidance. His most distinguished pupil, Ramakrishna Bhandarkar, who subsequently made a name for himself as the greatest Orientalist in India, often used to say that it was impossible to forget Dadabhai's "masterly teaching and kindness to students." Simple in manners and habits himself, he impressed upon his pupils the dignity of simplicity and weaned a good many of them, by his own example, from their weakness for ostentation.

The spirit of the reformer was, however, still more conspicuous in his work, during those early years, as a pioneer of social reform and a leader of thought in Bombay City and presidency.

The End

The quietest year of Dadabhai's life was 1916; even so, it is memorable for a unique event. Rather late in the day, the Bombay

University decided to confer on Dadabhai and Pherozeshah Mehta the Honorary Degree of Doctor of Laws.

That University could not have been accused of lavishness in the distribution of the highest distinction within its gift. During the thirty years that had elapsed since the institution of the degree, it had been conferred only four times. Pherozeshah Mehta died before the day fixed for the special Convocation for conferring the degree (January 18). Dadabhai was mercifully spared. In point of time he belonged to pre-University days, but he was a product of the renaissance which had given birth to the University and had from the beginning a share in the new intellectual life. Dadabhai summed up in his life, said the erudite Vice-Chancellor, the Rev. Dr. D. Mackichan, in his address on the occasion, the history of that great intellectual revival. Into the serene academic atmosphere of the University the heated air of politics should not enter. Nevertheless, a reference to Dadabhai's political career could scarcely have been avoided.

This only I should like to be permitted to say (said the Vice-chancellor) regarding a career which has been so largely concerned with the problems of the government of India that the honour and success of that career were due in large measure to the high qualities of personal life and character which were so conspicuous in every part of it. Men of all shades of political opinion were quick to discern the transparent honesty, the simplicity of purpose, the unselfish patriotism of the man who sought to interpret to Great Britain the needs and aspirations of his countrymen.

British political life is peculiarly sensitive to character. India's Grand Old Man owes as much to the influence of a blameless character as did his great prototype in Britain to the conviction which had wrought itself into the British mind regarding the loftiness of his motives and the purity of his life. While in this University we do not concern ourselves with politics, we are deeply concerned with character, and today we pay the tribute of our admiration to Mr. Dadabhai Naoroji's patience under adversities and disappointments, to his unwearied perseverance in the maintenance of his convictions and to the unselfish love of his country and nation which inspired him throughout his many conflicts.

There was a grave risk in the exertion which Dadabhai had undertaken in appearing in person at the Convocation. Dadabhai braved it, and the Fellows of the University and the general public were rejoiced to find that the venerable recipient of the academic distinction was none the worse for it. After the Convocation he took a drive in the City. A procession was formed outside the precincts of the University. Dadabhai took his seat in a motor car with his daughter Manekbai and her husband Dadina. The car was followed by those of many leading citizens.

The streets were thronged with admiring crowds, and the scenes of enthusiasm throughout the journey to Pedder Road reminded one of the pageants of the earlier days. They marked the most fitting recognition of his worth and work. All honours paled before such a testimony of popular affection and esteem.

The time for the realisation of Dadabhai's dream of self-government was drawing near. Negotiations were going on between the Viceroy and the Secretary of State. Congress workers in the East and in the West and their British friends were busy preparing proposals for constitutional reforms which would satisfy the aspirations of the rising generation of India. An essential principle of self-government had already been indicated by Lord Hardinge, namely, provincial autonomy, with a gradual transfer of authority from officials to the representatives of the people. It was believed that the representations of a United India on so vital a problem would receive a fair hearing from the British people and the Imperial Parliament.

Dadabhai's earnest wish and prayer was that he might live to witness the inauguration of the reforms which would place India securely on the road to self-government. He was, however, taken suddenly ill two months before the declaration of August 20, 1917, was made, guaranteeing increased association of Indians in every branch of the Administration and the gradual development of self-governing institutions with a view to the progressive realisation of responsible government in India as an integral part of the British Empire, guaranteeing, that is to say, practically all that Dadabhai was demanding.

It was a case of general debility, but it caused grave concern. Dadabhai was removed from his house in Versova to Palitana

House, Cumballa Hill, Bombay, the residence of Mr. Maneck Captain. Here, on June 30, the greatest of great Indians of the day passed away peacefully, surrounded by all the members of his family, except his two daughters who were in Kashmere.

After his body was consigned to the Tower of Silence, according to Parsi rites, Sir Narayenrao Chandavarkar paid a glowing tribute to his memory:

If we take stock of his life and his example, may I not say with perfect justice and truth that in his career, in all he did, in all he suffered, and in all he taught, he was the Prophet Zoroaster's religion personified, because he was the man more than anybody else of pure thought, of pure speech and of pure deeds.... The sun that rose, just ninety-three years ago, over India is set, but, I say, it is set to rise again in the form of regenerated India, for Dadabhai lived and worked for us with a devotion which must remain for all of us an inspiring example.

Many a tribute poured in from the four corners of the Globe, many a public meeting was held, many a monument was raised and is still being raised to his memory, but what monument could be greater than the rejuvenated India he left behind?

2

An Eventful Career

Early Activities

By its charter of 1833, the East India Company had secured a twenty years lease of life. To renew or not to renew its charter, to mend or end its rule, was the burning question of the day throughout the year 1852. It supplied the necessary impetus to Young Bombay to plunge into politics.

After 1833 the Company had ceased to be a trading corporation and had become a ruling body. The machinery set up for the traders, who had become soldiers of necessity, and administrators by accident, was cumbrous indeed. There were three separate governments: the Governor-General in Calcutta, the Madras Government and the Bombay Government. The two local Governments of Bombay and Madras had to refer every important question to the highly centralised Government at Calcutta, which in its turn had to send home particulars of everything it said or did. Ostensibly, the supreme authority lay with the Directorate in Leadenhall Street; but it was in fact a mere ministry of patronage without any authority beyond that of suggestion, criticism, and obstruction. All its powers were subject to the Board of Control, which was endowed with absolute authority, but was void of any responsibility. The Board's government was carried on in secret.

Only when called upon, it presented to Parliament statements which were often outrageously curtailed and garbled. In theory, the triumvirate in India was expected to exercise coordinate jurisdiction, but in practice the different authorities were found to thwart and retard the operations of one another. The education of the people was neglected and improvements for the internal development of the country ignored. The defects of such a system of government, unsuited to the rapidly changing conditions of the country, could no longer pass unchallenged.

With the spread of Western education, the Indian people began to feel that they had a right to demand that the country should no longer be governed in the spirit of a commercial concern. Even at that early date, when there was not a single university in the land and no army of discontented graduates, the greatest grievance of the people was the exclusion of Indians from the service of the State. When the Company's charter had been renewed, a clause was specially introduced in the Act of 1833 to the effect that no native of India, or natural-born subject therein, should be disqualified from office by reason only of religion, place of birth, descent, or colour. Although this clause conferred absolute eligibility on Indians, it was rendered nugatory by the maintenance of a distinction between the covenanted and uncovenanted services. Young men educated at Haileybury College were sent over from England to superintend the collection of revenues and to administer justice.

A good opportunity to ventilate these grievances was presented by the application of the Company for an extension of its political existence. It looked as if the leaders of the different parties in England, the Ministers, the President of the Board of Control, and the Members of the Court of Directors had agreed among themselves that the Company's Charter should be renewed for a further term of twenty years. An Association had been formed in Manchester, which had its own axe to grind, to bring the defects of the Constitution to light and to ask for a change in the administration. The British public, however, took little interest in the matter. Even the House of Commons did not attach any importance to it. The people of India, however, who dreaded the continuance of the same antiquated regime, could not afford to look on.

The Bengalis took the lead and formed an association' for sending representations to the British Government. Young Bombay followed suit. In this matter the elders were not against the youthful reformers, but with them. British friends also sympathised with the movement. On August 26, 1852, a meeting of the "native inhabitants" was held in the rooms of the Elphinstone Institution, and on the same evening was inaugurated the first political association in the Bombay Presidency, named the Bombay Association.

Among those present was Dadabhai. He was a Government servant, but that did not prevent him from taking part in the proceedings and delivering a neat little speech. It was his maiden speech on politics and would appear to be a very tame affair in these days of political fervour. It has, however, to be read in the light of the circumstances prevailing in mid-Victorian days. Public life in India was then at a very low ebb. The tide of national consciousness had not yet set in. People had only a hazy notion of their rights and wrongs. At such a stage, advocates of reform could merely appeal to the sense of fair play and justice among the authorities. The hour for self-assertion had not yet struck. Dadabhai himself has told us how modest the aspirations of the early reformers were. In a Congress manifesto, which he penned fifty-three years later, he says: "How limited our political ideas and aspirations of that time were! The extent and causes of the increasing poverty in India we had hardly any conception of, nor had we fully realised our rights and duties as free British citizens."

The maiden speech is, however, of peculiar interest to us, inasmuch as in it is foreshadowed the political creed which sustained Dadabhai in later life despite terrible disappointments.

The word grievance (said he) has nowadays become very common. It is in the mouth of everybody. But I apprehend few have any idea of the real importance of the term. Under the British Government we do not suffer any great zoolum (oppression). We are comparatively happier under the kind Government than we are likely to be under any other. Whatever evil we have to complain of originates from one cause, viz., the ignorance of European, officers coming fresh from home. With regard to many of the habits, customs, and usages prevailing in this country, these officers may pass laws or regulations injurious to the nation and yet fancy they have done their duty conscientiously. The authorities think them to be right, while the natives think otherwise. But if an Association like this be in existence, we can suggest improvements. These suggestions coming from such an Assembly must be listened to and perhaps adopted. The real grievances that I am aware of are those relative to the state of the Kunbis (peasants) in the interior and the judicial and revenue systems.

But we want facts regarding all these, and the present meeting is one step in the enquiry.

If we analyse this speech, we find the root principles of his political philosophy. India's wrongs should not blind her to the benefits of British rule. The permanence of that rule was the starting-point and foundation of all hopes. India's destiny had been linked up with it, and she had no desire to change the yoke for any other. The authorities erred, but, it might be, with the best of motives. They might consider to be right what Indians might regard as wrong, and might follow a policy harmful to the interests of India. The remedy lay in agitation. People should combine to give expression to their convictions, and their voice must be heard. Herein lay the principal justification and hope for all the agitation Dadabhai conducted—a nation's united voice is bound to be heard.

Heretofore the critics of the British administrators were their own countrymen. Now, however, commenced the investigation by Indians themselves of their country's wrongs. With every further step in that enquiry, the list of grievances increased.

With every effort to bring them home to the authorities, the hopes of obtaining a sympathetic hearing received a rude shock.

But, however discouraging the outlook, the keynote of Dadabhai's policy remained the same. It induced a general belief among the Indian politicians of the day that the English people in their own country were different from their kinsmen out in India. The officials on the spot might turn a deaf ear to the representations of the people, but the liberty-loving people of England would, they hoped, willingly listen and, with their traditional love for justice and freedom, extend a helping hand to their Indian fellow subjects.

These hopes were not so readily fulfilled. That, however, did not shake in the least the confidence of Dadabhai. In his opinion it merely served to warn the people of India that they had not made adequate effort to rouse the conscience of the British public.

After a lapse of fifty years, speaking before an English audience on the condition of India, he reiterated the same sentiments:

"The Congress has for its object to make you understand your deficiencies in government, the redress of which would make India a blessing to you and make England a blessing to us, which it is not unfortunately at present".

During the closing years of the nineteenth century there was rising a new generation, whose estimate of British rule and British character was founded only on experience of evasion of promises and repression. A growing section of the people was deriding the idea of dependence on the British public for the redress of India's woes. Salvation seemed to lie not in supplication but in self-assertion, not in submission but in counteraction.

The advanced party was preaching the gospel of violence. The patience of even the moderates among the Indian National Congress was sorely tried. A good many of its members felt that faith in British justice was a sorry crutch to lean on. Yet their weather-beaten general did not falter for a moment and went all the way from London to Calcutta, in the year 1906, to reaffirm the basic principles of his creed, Our faith and our future (said he) are in our own hands. If we are true to ourselves and to our country and make all the necessary sacrifices for our elevation and amelioration, I for one have not the shadow of a doubt that in dealing with such justice-loving, fair-minded people as the British, we may rest fully assured that we shall not work in vain. It is this conviction which has supported me against all difficulties. I have never faltered in my faith in the British character and have always believed that the time will come when the sentiments of the British nation and our gracious Sovereign proclaimed to us in our great charter of the Proclamation of 1858 will be realised, viz. "in their prosperity will be our strength; in their contentment our best reward."

When, at last, he doffed his armour and was living in retirement, Dadabhai continued to preach the same gospel of faith in British justice. He told his friends once that he had met a Bengali anarchist in London who argued that, while fifty years of preaching and supplication had proved of no avail, half an ounce of lead had worked wonders and would still work wonders. "I felt staggered," said Dadabhai, "and could not very well repudiate the claims that were put forward to the credit of the bomb, but the idea was wholly repugnant to my feelings and convictions.

I still believe that India's real salvation lies in the hands of the British public." Faith in the conscience of the British public was, indeed, part of his fibre. The messages that he sent forth to his countrymen year after year from his retirement breathed the same spirit of confidence in the British people's love of liberty and free institutions.

Did the interests of India and England conflict so violently as to render separation inevitable? No; he believed, with his British colleagues, A. O. Hume and William Wedderburn, that the interests of the Indian people and the British people were essentially the same and that the continuance of the British connection could be made to conform to the best interests of India. It is necessary to hold these root principles of Dadabhai's political creed steadfastly before our eyes, if we would appreciate correctly the spirit of his agitation throughout his whole life—an agitation so desperate at times that, despite his genuine love for the British public and his unswerving loyalty to the Crown, among the Anglo-Indian public during the past century his name spelt sedition!

The Bombay Association drew up a petition, for submission to the Imperial Parliament, asking for an enlightened system of government for the millions of British Indian subjects. It is a far cry from 1852 to 1938; the document has not the same significance today. Nevertheless, it reads as if it were directed against some of the grievances of modern times. The question that loomed large in the petition was that of admission of Indians into the Civil Service. As a means to that end, the establishment in each Presidency of a university for training public servants was recommended. It was also suggested that the Councils of local Government should be opened for educated Indians. The Government grant of .£12,500 for the education of millions was altogether inadequate. The petitioners asked for an increase, and urged that a larger share of the land revenue might be spent on public works in the district from which it was levied.

This indictment of the Company's government caused a rift in the Association. Soon after the text of the petition was published, the English journals that had at first blessed the movement began to fall foul of it. Several Indians also seceded from the movement; notable among them were Sir Jamshedjee Jejeebhoy Ramlal Thakoreseedas, Manockji Cursetji, and Mahomed Ameen Rogay. Manockji Cursetji also issued a pamphlet entitled A Few Passing Ideas for the Benefit of India and Indians the burden of which was, "first creep, then walk, then run/' The most indignant of the Anglo-Indian newspapers was the Telegraph and Courier. That English institutions could be established in India, or that the country could be governed by the people and for the people, was a notion to which, in the opinion of that oracle, no honest politician could ever lend the slightest countenance.

Might we not as well attempt, asked the writer, to assimilate the natural productions of the two hemispheres as strive to naturalise in the East the growth of Anglo-Saxon civilization?.

Even were the soil fitted for its reception, would the tree of Liberty flourish after its transplanting? Should it not be raised from the seed and not the graft.

There was, however, at least one journalist who could look beyond his nose.

It would be a lamentable mistake (he observed in the Spectator) to suppose that a movement like this can be disposed of by being "put down" or "put off," nor would it be a less mistake to suppose that to grant the claims of this petition in substance would be a concession to the Natives at the expense of the British.

On the contrary, it would commence, in a more thorough style than we have yet attempted, the work of identifying the Natives, their affections and progress with English institutions, thus recruiting the alien civil force, by which we hold the country, with a far more numerous militia of attached volunteers.

Little, however, could the writer of these words of political prescience have dreamt at the time that, within four years, the need for enlisting a numerous militia of attached volunteers would be tragically brought home to the British public by the Mutiny of 1857, 'which sent a thrill of horror from one end of the United Kingdom to the other.

The Bombay Association's petition created a stir in England. Several friends of India, including Sir Edward Ryan, Sir Erskine Perry, Lord Monteagle, John Bright, and Joseph Hume, raised their powerful voices in favour of the petitioners, while the cynical Cobden was one of the few who could not see any advantage either to the Indians or to their foreign masters in this vast possession. "Hindustan," he said in a subsequent letter, "must be ruled by those who live on that side of the globe. Its people will prefer to be ruled badly—according to our notions—by its own kith and kin than to submit to the humiliation of being better governed by a succession of transient intruders from the antipodes." His countrymen, however, were in favour of retaining India.

On March 13, 1853, a meeting of "The Friends of India" was held in Charles Street, St. James's Square, London, and it constituted itself an India Reform Society, with Danby Seymour as President and John Dickinson as Secretary. Its activities, however, could not materially influence the decision of the House of Commons, which still acquiesced in the retention of the double system of government with all its cumbrous machinery. The anomalous relations of the Board of Control and the Court of Directors also remained practically unaltered. A salutary change was, however, introduced in the Court of Directors. The number of members was reduced to eighteen, of which six were to be nominated by His Majesty's Government from amongst those persons who should have resided in India for at least ten years.

The same qualification was required of a moiety of the twelve members to be elected as before by the proprietors of the East India Stock. All the civil and medical appointments to the Company's service in India were thrown open to public competition.

Such competition was, however, to be conducted in England so that Indians were practically debarred from entering the service.

The result of the agitation, as a whole, was in no way gratifying to the Indian public. It established, however, one point very clearly, namely, that concerted agitation and action had wrung from the British Ministers more than was considered possible.

It illustrated alike the advantages of such discussion and the need for propaganda to dispel the colossal ignorance and apathy of the British public. Dadabhai took these lessons to heart.

Thenceforth, "agitate, agitate, and agitate" became his watchword.

A Preaching Friar

"The desire of my life was to serve the people as opportunity permitted," wrote Dadabhai. With him work was worship; the record of service and sacrifice, even during those early years, was remarkable for its magnitude and variety. We have already seen him at the crest of the wave of reform that swept over society during his youth. Before even he had attained his thirtieth year, his signal services in several spheres raised him to the position of a leader not only of the Parsi community but also of the Bombay public. In that capacity he felt keenly the need of an independent newspaper.

Pioneers of reform are invariably handicapped for want of an organ to expound their views. The Press, as a rule, shouts with the crowd; a cash basis governs the policy of journals just as much as that of any other business concern. There were in Bombay five Gujarati journals, all owned by Parses, but none had the' independence or the impartiality needed for the cause of reform. Dadabhai had the zeal and the will to start and run such a newspaper, but not the means to finance the scheme. He mentioned the difficulties to his public-spirited friend, Kharshedji Nasarwanji Cama, and found in him an enthusiastic counsellor and helper. It was agreed between the two friends that a fortnightly newspaper should be started, named the Rast Goftar, or the Truth Teller, that Kharshedji Cama should provide funds, that Dadabhai should run the paper without remuneration, and that copies of the journal should be distributed among the members of the community free of charge. Whilst Dadabhai was the brain, Cama was the sinews, so to speak, of the journal. That fact was known only to a few; the general public of Bombay looked upon Dadabhai as the sole founder and proprietor of the paper. Even K. N. Kabraji, the famous editor of the paper, showed his ignorance of its origin when, in replying to the toast of the Rast Goftar at a Parsi dinner in London, in 1900, he referred to Dadabhai as its founder. Dadabhai promptly corrected Kabraji and informed the assembly in touching terms of the honourable part Cama had played in launching that journal.

Carlyle speaks of a preaching friar settling himself in every village, building a pulpit which he calls a newspaper, and preaching therefrom what most momentous doctrine is in him for man's salvation. Such a preaching friar was Dadabhai. The public of Bombay in those days required to be educated not only in the principles of social and religious reform, but also in the duties of citizenship. So there he stood, the apostle of truth and exponent of the religion of humanity, in the pulpit of the Rast Goftar, to preach his gospel to the people and to combat the forces of ignorance and conservatism which impeded their progress.

The first number of the new journal saw the light on November 15, 1851, when a thousand copies were printed for free distribution. There was not a single advertisement in it; it was a sheer labour of love. November 15 was an unusual day for launching a newspaper. There was, however, a good reason for ushering it in advance of the new year. A serious local disturbance, which had culminated in a Parsi-Muslim riot, impelled Dadabhai to hasten into the arena of journalism.

Before the catastrophe, the most cordial relations had subsisted between the Muhammadans and the Parses. Some of the most prominent business-houses in the City consisted of partners belonging to the two communities. For instance, Sir Jamshedjee Jejeebhoy, the leader of the Parsi community, and Mahomedally Rogay, the foremost Muhammadan citizen of the day, had been stanch friends and partners in business for a quarter of a century.

At the time of the rupture there was no enmity between the two communities, no cause for any quarrel, but an ill-conceived article in a magazine, edited by a Parsi youth, caused an appalling ferment. This magazine was called Chitra Dnyan Darpan (The Illustrated Mirror); its editor was Behramji Kharshedji Gandhi, the same Sisoti boy whose paper on "female education" had led to practical measures for the education of women. He had arranged to give a series of memoirs of celebrated persons who had influenced and transformed society in different places at different intervals. The Prophet of Arabia found a place in that galaxy, but the account that Gandhi gave of the Prophet's life was wanting in that sentiment of respect and tolerance which is due to a sister community. Not unnaturally, the feelings of the Muhammadans, the most sensitive people on earth in matters affecting their faith, were seriously hurt. The lithographed portrait of the Prophet, which was given with the article, also gave umbrage, inasmuch as this is prohibited by Islam. An undiscovered villain added fuel to the fire by posting a copy of the picture, with ribald and obscene remarks underneath, on the main entrance of the principal mosque.

There could be but one answer to such insane provocation. Islam was up in arms. Large crowds of Muhammadans assembled in the mosques of the town with the Koran in one hand and a knife in the other. The Parses avoided entangling themselves with the infuriated crowd, but the Muslims were bent on vengeance. At a meeting held in the Juma Masjid on Friday, October 7, 1851, they arrived at the frightful decision to proclaim a jihad (crusade) against the Parses. A large crowd rushed out, seething with wrath, and armed with bludgeons, crying "Din! Din!" ("Religion! Religion!") The first thing they did was to fall upon the small police force on duty and to overwhelm it Then they marched triumphantly along the streets to Pydhownie, near the entrance of Bhendi Bazar, which was then a stronghold of the Parses. Sturdy and dauntless though the Parses of the day were, they were numerically insignificant and were belaboured mercilessly by the rioters. For weeks together, that part of Bombay was a scene of pillage and destruction, and the Parses had to put up with shocking atrocities such as defilement of corpses. The police prosecuted a few of the worst offenders, but this had no effect on the hooligans. Only after the editor had been compelled to tender a written apology a truce was declared.

In connection with this disturbance the Parsi community looked in vain to the police for protection. If not altogether hostile, they were indifferent, probably because they held that it was itself responsible for the quarrel. In the midst of grave provocation, the Parsi Press and the Parsi leaders pursued a timorous policy.

Dadabhai felt, along with a large number of Parses, that the leaders had betrayed and humiliated the community. While they sought shelter in their houses in the tranquil locality of the Fort, Dadabhai was living close to the scene of the disturbance and was an eyewitness of the terrorism of the Muhammadans. As the elders did little to protect them, the Parsi residents of Baharkote looked to "Dadabhai Master," as he was then called, to represent their grievances to the authorities. To him they entrusted the task of drafting their memorial, and to him alone they made over the custody of the funds raised for their defence. In the service of his oppressed brethren Dadabhai did not spare himself. Seeing the craven attitude of the Press and the vacillating policy-of the leaders, he felt bitterly the need of an independent and an intrepid newspaper. A truce had been declared, no doubt, but the ferment had not subsided. A fresh outbreak was anticipated. This accounts for the fact that he took the field forthwith with the new weapon, the Rast Goftar.

The paper was thus launched, in the thick of the fray, on a career of stormy usefulness as a fearless champion of truth and justice and as an uncompromising exponent of the forward school of thought. Its young editor was not a novice. His literary output, even at that early date, was considerable and estimable.

He had edited the Dnyan Prasarak magazine and contributed numerous articles on social subjects. No less than eighteen lectures of his on Natural Philosophy and Astronomy had been embodied in that journal. He had also been a regular contributor to the Samachar Darpan, a Gujarati daily, and had written a series of articles entitled "Dialogues of Socrates and Diogenes." As Secretary to the Rahnumae Society, he was editing its publications and had contributed some papers himself. He had also helped Naoroji Furdoonji in editing the publications of the Sir Jamshedjee Jejeebhoy Philosophic Institute.

The first three numbers of the Rast Goftar were almost exclusively devoted to a discussion of the situation created by the riots and their aftermath. In most touching terms the editor showed how unfriendly the police had been towards the Parses, how supine the attitude of the Parsi leaders of the community was, and how humiliating their action in coercing the editor to tender an apology. It might, however, be argued that in his defence of the writer of that ill-conceived memoir Dadabhai was carried away by his ideals of liberty of thought and freedom of the Press. It was not so harmless as Dadabhai, in his anxiety to stand by a brother journalist, took it to be.

Dadabhai's indictment of the police and of the Parsi leaders gives a foretaste of the intrepid spirit which marked his political speeches and writings. The stern critic who, in later years, was never weary of fighting courageous battles against vested interests and denouncing the high-handedness and inequities of the rulers, was not slow in leading a revolt against the leaders of his own community and questioning their authority to speak in the name of the people. Similarly, although he was a Government servant, full of ambition to rise in the service, he did not flinch from criticising in scathing terms the conduct of the officials.

We used to hear (he, observed in one of the articles) of the loathsome conduct of those who assaulted people in the night and fell on their knees on die following morning, craving forgiveness. But in this case the Muhammadan assailers have, instead of bending their knees, forced die aggrieved to make amends to them. We were under die sweet delusion that justice had extirpated tyranny, but during the last two months justice has gone to rest and aggression has had its free innings.

That such injustice should be perpetrated under British rule was a riddle to him. "Are we awake," he exclaimed, "or are we seeing a dream?" Deprecating the action of the officials, who hit upon the idea of extorting an apology from the editor as the simplest means of quelling the disturbance, he asked his co-religionists why they had placed the direction of communal affairs in the hands of a few elders. Was it merely to follow them blindly and to be their slaves ? Did leadership consist in driving comfortably in a carriage and pair and receiving the salaams (salutations) of the poor ? Did it not carry with it the responsibility to treat the poor as their own kith and kin?

On November 26, 1851, a deputation of the Parses waited on the Governor of Bombay. They handed him a petition and prayed that effectual measures might be taken to preserve the public peace. Dadabhai was one of the deputation. From that date "the Promise of India" came to the fore as a recognised leader. There was no sphere of public activity where he was not a leading light; there was no movement for the furtherance of communal or national welfare where he was not an earnest and active worker.

Under his editorship the Rast Goftar became within two months an influential organ of advanced opinion. There was a demand from its readers that its size should be increased and that it should be converted into a weekly paper. Dadabhai thereupon announced that the demand would be complied with, provided there was an adequate increase in the number of subscribers. The rate of subscription was fixed very low—two anas per month—but he hoped that those who could afford would give a larger subscription so as to enable the proprietors to spread the paper among the poorer classes of the population. Subscribers did come forward, and from January 1852 the fortnightly was converted into a weekly, and published every Sunday morning.

From the commencement the Sisoti boys stood by the editor of this organ of reform. It is remarkable that in those days a Government servant was not precluded from running a newspaper. Dadabhai's connection with the Rast Goftar continued even after he left India in 1855 and made England his home. A syndicate was then formed to run the paper. It consisted of Dadabhai himself, Kharshedji Nussarwanji Cama, Kharshedji Rustamji Cama, Dossabhai Framji Karaka, Naoroji Furdoonji, Sorabjee Shapurjee Bengali, and Pestanji Ruttonji Colah. Three years later, Karsandas Mulji, the well-known Hindu reformer, became the eighth member of this group.

When the Persian monarchy was overthrown by the followers of Islam, the national glory and religion of the ancient Iranians received a deadly blow. Early historians have traced the footsteps of the conquerors on the soil of Iran in letters of blood. According to their accounts, the soldiers of the Khalifa of Baghdad traversed the country, sword in hand, summoning the vanquished Zoroastrians to choose either the Koran or death. This story of terrorism, however, cannot be reconciled with the prevalence of the ancient faith amongst a section of the population of Iran to this day. The conversion of Iran to Islam did not take place concurrently with the Arab conquest. Many Zoroastrians, who did not abandon their country, continued to cling to their ancestral religion. They were, however, subjected to various disabilities. For centuries they lived almost like slaves in their fatherland, and for more than seven hundred years they were not even aware of the existence of their co-religionists in India.

Towards the end of the fifteenth century, however, the ties so long severed were renewed.

In the year 1478 a learned Parsi, named Nariman Hoshang, was deputed to Iran by the Parsi settlers in Navsari, Surat, and Cambay to obtain information concerning certain religious questions.

Nariman's visit brought to light numerous inequities. The most galling was the levy of the poll tax. At the time of collection, the tax-gatherer was at liberty to indulge in acts of extortion. The list of the disabilities of the "infidels," as the Zoroastrians were called, was a very formidable one. Only a few items will show how abject their condition must have been. They were not allowed to trade. They could not open schools for their children. The use of umbrellas, spectacles, rings, and various other articles was forbidden to them. They should wear only tight knickers instead of trousers, and their shoes should be of the prescribed pattern, with broad, turned-up toes. Riding on any animal in towns was strictly prohibited; even in the desert they had to dismount if they met a Muhammadan, be he a nobleman or a beggar. Their houses should be so low that the top could be reached by a Muhammadan with his hand extended.

In the middle of the nineteenth century the Parses in India made strenuous efforts to remove those disabilities. An Amelioration Fund was started. Its Trustees deputed Manekji Limji Hataria to Iran as their delegate. So zealously he helped the Irani Zoroastrians that for years afterwards they recalled his name with tears of gratitude.

Hataria was asked to enquire into the social, intellectual, and political condition of the Zoroastrians in Iran. In this enquiry Dadabhai was keenly interested. Hataria sent him pathetic accounts of their impoverished condition and their helplessness in the midst of a fanatical population. At a Parsi meeting, Dadabhai read out the touching letters of Hataria. This led to the opening of a separate fund for helping the oppressed people, for educating their children, and for preparing memorials to the authorities in Iran.

Even after he had settled in England, Dadabhai kept constantly in touch with Hataria, whose letters on important issues went first to him and were forwarded by him to the Bombay Committee with suggestions. Years afterwards, when the Shah of Iran visited England, it was Dadabhai who led a deputation to him and presented to him an address, praying for considerate treatment of his Zoroastrian subjects.

A public meeting was held on September 22, 1852, in the Elphinstone College, to perpetuate the memory of a great philanthropist and patron of education, Framji Cowasji Banaji It was decided that the funds collected for the purpose should be used for the formation of a museum in connection with the Students' Literary and Scientific Society, and that Government should be asked to erect a building for it, to be named the Framji Cowasji Institute. Framji Cowasji had rendered valuable assistance to the Students' Literary and Scientific Society. In gratitude for such assistance Dadabhai collected a sum of Rs. 6,000 and offered it, on behalf of the Society, to the meeting.

A notable feature of the meeting was the presence of several students of the Elphinstone College. Fired by the spirit and example of Dadabhai, they had flocked to the meeting and endowed a special prize fund in the memory of Framji Cowasji.

If it is a teacher's office to lead as well as to teach and by the spark of his personal example to set the heart of his pupil on flame, Dadabhai fulfilled that mission, not only in regard to his college pupils but also in regard to his political disciples throughout his life.

These activities by no means complete the record of Dadabhai's work between the years 1851 and 1855. It was a record remarkable for the range of his sympathies and the versatility of his intellect.

He was an active member of the Bombay Branch of the Royal Asiatic Society and read a paper on "Astrology" before the Philosophic Institute of Bombay. When the first Parsi Dramatic

Society was formed in Bombay in 1853, he took a lively interest in its work and served on the committee of management. He presided at an important meeting when the Trust Deed of the Fort Charitable Dispensary of Bombay was settled and he was one of the Trustees of the Dispensary. Although his means were limited, he gave pecuniary assistance as well as personal service to such philanthropic movements. In 1855 a meeting of Elphinstonians was held to perpetuate the memory of Professor Patton.

Dadabhai was invited to preside over the meeting. In the same year he was put on the Grand Jury. After the horrors of the Napoleonic war there was practically peace in Europe for nearly forty years. High hopes were entertained, particularly after the Great Exhibition of 1851, of permanent peace, but these were doomed to disappointment. Within three years the Czar of Russia claimed recognition of his rights as Protector of the Christian subjects of the Turkish Sultan.

This claim was repudiated by the "Sick Man of the East," who, despite all his infirmities, declared war upon Russia, fully relying on the support of England and France. The astute Ottoman was not wrong, England and France soon found themselves drawn into the fray. The theory then current was that Russia on the Danube meant Russia also on the Indus. No wonder when the Patriotic Fund was raised in connection with the war, there was great enthusiasm among the people of India to mark not only their sense of loyalty to the British Crown but also their gratitude for the endeavours of the rulers to keep the Russian wolf as far away as possible from their frontiers. A public meeting was held in Bombay on January 31, 1855, in furtherance of the objects of the Patriotic Fund. Lord Elphinstone presided; Dadabhai was one of the speakers. He saw in the conflict a struggle of liberty against tyranny and prayed for the success of Great Britain and her allies because, he believed, they were on the side of justice and freedom.

> "A very pertinent question has been asked," said he, "why the natives of Bombay should join in contributing to the Patriotic Fund, and the question has been very ably answered by Dr. Wilson, who has pointed out to us that the interests of India are bound up with those of England."

From College to Counting House

Dadabhai, what a fall!" said Principal Harkness when he learnt that the Professor had decided to exchange mathematics for merchandise.

What could have induced Dadabhai to take such a step in spite of his indifference to wealth and his earnest desire to consecrate his life to the service of humanity? The explanation is afforded in some stray notes he has left behind. There he states that he accepted the offer to join the commercial firm of the Camas (the first Indian firm established in London in the year 1855) as he was "desirous of seeing an intimate connection established between England and India," and "particularly to provide a home for young Indians so that they might freely go to England and compete for the Indian Civil Service and other services." "India for the Indians" was his slogan even during those early days, and this great aim he steadfastly kept before his eyes in the midst of all die allurements of business. Indeed, business was but a passing phase; pleading at the bar of the British public for the redress of India's wrongs was his permanent mission in England. Thus what seemed at first sight to be a fall turned out to be a rise, an indispensable step for Dadabhai's elevation to the unique position he afterwards attained as the greatest patriot of his day.

Before the year 1855 there was not a single Indian mercantile firm in England. The Camas were pioneers in the line. They decided to open a business-house in London with a branch in Liverpool. It was a venture in which they required the cooperation of a partner of high ability and integrity; they invited Dadabhai to join the firm. The Professor agreed, but he was not so sure of his success as a business man. Nor could he be certain that he would not soon be tired of the humdrum life of a merchant.

He requested Government that he might be granted leave and allowed to keep his Hen on his post, but the request could not be granted. The die was cast; he resigned his post.

In a farewell address, the students of the Elphinstone Institution expressed their sense of the great loss to the college.

Amongst them were Ramakrishna Bhandarkar and Bal Mangesh Wagle who became one of Dadabhai's lieutenants during the time when he was Prime Minister in Baroda. The Students' Literary and Scientific Society also placed on record its deep sense of the valued services rendered by Dadabhai as a member of the Society. A deputation consisting of the Society's representatives waited upon him and presented to him its resolution eulogising his services "in connection with female education and the diffusion of knowledge among the Parsi community by means of popular lectures on Natural Philosophy and the publication of a cheap periodical literature."

Thus honoured and blessed, Dadabhai started on his first voyage to England on June 27,1855, in the P. and O. Navigation Co.'s boat Madras. She took as many days to reach Aden as are now taken to land passengers at Marseilles. At Aden the passengers were transferred on July 9 to the Calcutta steamer Oriental, bound for Suez. Thence, proceeding overland, they joined the Sultan at Alexandria and arrived at Southampton on August 22nd.

With Dadabhai went Muncherji Hormusji Cama and Kharshedji Rustamji Cama to found the new firm, under the name Cama & Co. These three were to form a triumvirate. No action was to be taken unless they were unanimous in their decision; matters in dispute were to be referred to the Head Office in Bombay. A more unbusiness-like arrangement could not have been devised. Numerous occasions arose when the triumvirate found it impossible to come to a unanimous decision.

There were also strong differences of opinion concerning fundamental principles and policy. Dadabhai felt he was called upon to lay in England the foundations of success not merely of his firm but also of the business enterprise of Indians generally.

On the credit of his firm and the confidence which it inspired in the London market would depend the chances of development of India's trade with the Continent. Kharshedji Cama shared his idealism in business, but it often startled Muncherji Cama. He complained to the Head Office that it had given him as a colleague a philosopher who did not mind sacrificing the interests of the firm to what appeared to be quixotic principles of commercial morality.

On one occasion Dadabhai suspected that the manufacturers with whom his firm had placed an order for reel-threads, on behalf of a Bombay firm, had not supplied reels of the specified length.

He therefore took the bundles of thread to his bedroom and sat up till midnight, measuring the thread. Some reels measured eighty yards instead of a hundred, which was the stipulated length.

"We shall have to reject these reels," said Dadabhai to his colleagues.

"Why?" asked Muncherji Cama.

"Because of the shortage."

"That is not our concern," urged Muncherji. "Such discrepancies are not unusual; if our Bombay friends feel aggrieved, they may prefer a claim for damages."

Dadabhai was, however, obdurate. "What you say may be true," said he, "but having discovered the shortage, how can I be a party to the transaction?"

Kharshedji Cama agreed with Dadabhai. The matter was referred to the Head Office; sharp came peremptory instructions not to make any more fuss about the shortage. Dadabhai was prepared for this rebuff. Often had he been overruled in this fashion, and a continuance of the business alliance after the expiry of his agreement with the firm seemed undesirable and impracticable.

Amongst the varied commodities handled by Cama & Co. in the course of its business were opium, wine, and spirits. Dadabhai could not persuade himself to pocket the earnings of dealings in articles which led to the degradation and ruin of thousands of human beings. In a letter written to Kharshedji Nassarwanji Cama in the Gujarati language, which was then the medium of communication between them, he informed his more practical partners that he had decided not to accept his share in the profits accruing from such transactions.

Will you tell me (asked Cama in reply) from what sources Government get funds for the payment of salaries to professors of colleges and other officers ? Did you not receive your salary as a professor from revenue derived from the traffic in opium and liquor? If you retire from business and revert to Government service, will you not once more live on the tainted revenue obtained from the same business that stinks in your nostrils?

If our firm ceases dealing in opium, will it put a stop to the traffic in that commodity ? Will not others deal in what you taboo?

Nothing, however, could induce Dadabhai to change his mind.

The result of all such differences of opinion was that Dadabhai severed his connection with the house of Camas. Kharshedji Rustamji Cama also retired from the firm before the termination of the agreement. Although his biographer does not specifically refer to it, there is an allusion to the reason in the following sentence of the memoir: "At the end of 1858 or early 1859 he decided, for personal reasons which did credit to his honesty, to resign his partnership."

The Camas, as we have already noticed, were his best friends.

They warmly sympathised with his ideals of service and sacrifice and shared his enthusiasm for the betterment of the condition of his countrymen. To them he looked confidently for moral and material support in his work of social and religious reform, and from them he always derived inspiration. One can realise, therefore, the feelings of regret with which he must have severed his business connection with such friends. The dissolution of partnership, however, left no rancour behind. Each side appreciated the point of view of the other, and their relations continued to be as friendly and cordial as before.

During his association with the firm, Dadabhai did not fail to inspire some of the young scions of the Cama family with his ideals of personal as well as commercial morality. A remarkable instance was that of H. R. Camajee, who wrote to Kharshedji Rustamji Cama on April 4, 1859, from Liverpool:

Papa has at last given to Dorabjee the management of the China firm and he is to make me and Dorabjee general partners when my term expires. Do you recommend me to join with Papa in China business? I do not really like Opium Trade because I have seen with my own eyes the result of such trading and the effects on the consumers.

Dadabhai returned to India, his mind more enriched than his pockets. To have lived in England for three years during that era was in itself a liberal education. It was an era when such great figures as Gladstone, Cobden, and Bright were breathing a new spirit of liberalism into British politics, and such authors as Herbert Spencer, Mill, and Carlyle were revolutionising society with new theories of social reconstruction. In such an atmosphere Dadabhai realised vividly the contrast between the social, political, and economic condition of the people of the West and that of his own countrymen. Where could he have studied political theory, the working of democratic institutions, and the parliamentary system of government better than in the country universally recognised as the "Mother of Parliaments" ? What indeed, could have been a better school for the study of international Commerce, banking, and currency than London, the heart, the brain, the nerve centre of the British Empire? While growing more and more conscious of the faults of the British administration in India, Dadabhai learnt to appreciate more and more the sense of justice and fair play in England. The study of the strong and weak points of British character stimulated in him the desire to have India's battles fought not only on the floor of the House of Commons but throughout Great Britain, In March 1856, Dadabhai was nominated Professor of Gujarati in the University College, London. He held that office till the year 1865-66, when he retired. He was also a member of the Faculty of Arts and Laws and a member of the Senate of the College. The following entry in the University Calendars for these years shows what his duties were and the books he read with his pupils: "Monday and Thursday, from six to seven o'clock, Grammar and Exercises, Green's Sentences, and Bal Shastri's History of British India."

What information, however, have we about the life which Dadabhai led in England ? Where did he live and in what style?

Whom did he meet ? Whose friendship did he cherish ? What did he think of them and they of him ? In vain have we tried to glean information on these points. Only a few particulars could be gathered from personal enquiries made of Dadabhai's nephew, Framji Rustamji Desai, who was one of the batch of students whom Dadabhai took with him to England in the year 1859.

Unlike the other Camas, Muncherji Cama was very conservative in his views and habits. The three partners, therefore, lived in London in Parsi style. It appears, however, from Dadabhai's correspondence with K. R. Cama that Dadabhai lived mostly in Liverpool, where the bulk of the cotton business was transacted.

They had a Parsi cook and Parsi waiters, as Muncherji insisted on all the Zoroastrian rites being rigidly observed. As he had no objection to knives and forks, he might well have reconciled himself to the use of finger bowls, but he insisted on the Parsi butlers going round the table, at the end of each meal, with a jug of water in one hand and a basin in the other. Whether their English guests joined in the customary ablutions is not known.

In those days Dadabhai went about in Liverpool and London dressed in a costume of his own invention—a long broadcloth coat, buttoned up chest high, a white silk handkerchief round the shirt collar passed through a plain gold ring, black trousers to match and a light black velvet cap, from which flowed a blue silk tassel. Pherozeshah Mehta, Hormusji Wadya, J. C. Cama and other proteges, and office assistants of Dadabhai, all used to be attired in the same Dadabhai Naoroji fashion. Later, however, he decided to do in Rome as Romans did, but whenever he returned to India, he reverted to the orthodox Parsi costume.

Though absent from Bombay for three years, Dadabhai had not lost touch with the problems of social reform. On August 20, 1855, the Parses of Bombay submitted a petition to the Legislative Council for reforms in the laws relating to Parsi marriages and succession. Bigamy was allowed by the elders of the community in special cases in those days. Social reformers railed against the custom as a gross perversion of the doctrines of Zoroastrianism. Wordy warfare was, however, of no avail.

Monogamy could be enforced only by the legislature. Those in favour of reform, therefore, carried on a crusade for an enactment specifically prohibiting bigamy. Dadabhai, though away from the scene of the contest, took lively interest in it and supported the advocates of reform with a lengthy memorandum.

Dadabhai's stay in Bombay was a short one; the Parsi Prakash chronicles two events. On December 15, 1858, a public meeting was held in the city to celebrate the opening of the Victoria Museum and Gardens, as a mark of the feeling of love and loyalty of the citizens of Bombay to Queen Victoria. We find that Dadabhai supported a proposal requesting Government to give a suitable site for the erection of a building for the purpose.

Pestanji Ruttonji Colah, Dadabhai's colleague, published in 1859 a journal called Stri Gnyan Mala, which aimed at enriching the knowledge of women. Dadabhai contributed articles to the first number of the journal, dealing with several social topics of feminine interest.

On January 9, 1859, Dadabhai embarked on his second voyage for Europe, accompanied by Jamshedji Palanji Kapadia, who afterwards won renown as a Persian scholar and historian, and Pestanji Ratanji Colah. He also took with him, as his proteges three students—his nephew Framji Rustamji Desai, and two youths of the Cama family, Jamshedji Kharshedji Cama and Hormusji Dorabji Cama. Arriving at Liverpool, he wrote to K. R. Cama (March 7): "I expect to move into my house, 63, Oxford Street, next Thursday."

Soon afterwards Dadabhai started business on his own account under the name of Dadabhai Naoroji & Co. and took Kapadia and Colah as his partners. Edulji Nasarwanji Master joined him in the middle of the year 1860 as an assistant. There was none now to stand between him and his principles. The course of business ran smooth. It was established beyond doubt that successful trading was in no way incompatible with the principles of ethics; a thriving tradesman could remain a high-souled man, as did Dadabhai.

One day, when he was in his office room, a visitor was announced.

"Hello, Ardeshir, what brings you here?" asked Dadabhai, warmly embracing the visitor.

"Business," replied Ardeshir, "and excellent business too!"

Ardeshir's services had been specially engaged by a firm in India trading with China. He was sent to England to make all necessary arrangements for obtaining four big vessels required by the firm. He decided to place the order with some shipwrights, through the house of Dadabhai, who had done him a good turn and to whom he was longing to show his gratitude.

Conscientious Dadabhai invited tenders for the work. One of the quotations included an item, "Commission to Dadabhai Naoroji & Co." at the rate of 5 per cent on the amount of the tender. It was not the lowest tender, but had the amount of commission been omitted, it would have been the lowest. Dadabhai sent for the representative of the firm.

"What is the meaning of this item?" he asked.

> "It is the usual practice," replied the representative. "We allow a certain percentage to all firms through whom we receive orders."
>
> "If it is the usual item, why have the other firms not shown it in their quotations ?"
>
> "If they have not specifically mentioned it in their estimates, probably one of the young Camas, they must have made provision for it under some head or another."
>
> "But this would make it impossible for my firm to accept the tender," said Dadabhai. "If you give us commission, how can we be expected to supervise the work conscientiously? I am paid for the work by the buyer; I cannot accept payment from the seller as well!"
>
> The representative did not know what reply to give. He must have felt as though he had been suddenly transported from a commercial house to the pulpit!
>
> "You must delete the item," continued Dadabhai, "if you want us to accept your tender."

The item was deleted, and the tender was accepted. Little could the representative of the manufacturers have then thought that the elimination of that item was to cost his firm a good deal more than five per cent! Scrupulous to a fault as he was, Dadabhai's supervision entailed additional work, which in fact meant extra expenditure of thrice the amount that they would have paid by way of commission, had Dadabhai been a "normal" business man.

Dadabhai's firm was then in its infancy, but he appears to have earned enough to keep him in fairly affluent circumstances during those days. He was a Director of the Queen Insurance Company and a guarantor of the Industrial Exhibition of 1862. Ever willing to help a good cause, he cheerfully rendered substantial financial assistance to several projects of public usefulness, among which were the movements to raise funds in Bombay for perpetuating the memory of Mountstuart Elphinstone and Jugannath Shankar-sheth, for an address and purse presented to Principal Harkness on his retirement, and for the provision of a Library of Sanskrit books for the Elphinstone Institution. Handsome also were his contributions to the Zoroastrian Fund raised in Europe in 1861 for the Parsi community in London and to another Fund raised in Bombay for giving English education to Parsi girls.

How varied and manifold were his activities in England about this time may be realised by a mere recital of the institutions with which he had been associated. He was an active member of the Liverpool Literary and Philosophic Society, the Philomathic Society, the Council of the Liverpool Athenaeum, the Royal Institute of London, the Royal Asiatic Society of Great Britain and Ireland, the Ethnological Society, the Anthropological Society, the Society of Arts and of the National Indian Association. Highly respected as a mason, he was one of the founders and the treasurer of the Lodge, "The Marquis of Dalhousie."

The British public knows little about the Parsi inhabitants in India. In Dadabhai's days it knew much less. He, therefore, read papers before the meetings of the Literary and Philosophical Society of Liverpool on the manners and customs of the Parses and on their religion, giving two distinct accounts, one of the old or orthodox school of Parses and the other of the new and reform school. In the first part he described the incidents in the daily life of a Parsi of the old school, from the moment he got out of bed to the hour of his going to rest, and the principal ceremonies from the hour of his birth to the last moment of his exit from this world. Although one could gather from the tenor of his speeches that he was a reformer, he spoke of the orthodox school with his usual fairness and forbearance. This made so favourable an impression on Professor Max Muller that he made a special reference to Dadabhai's fairness in his Chips from a German Workshop?- "There is no sneer," says he, "no expression of contempt anywhere, even when . ... the temptation must have been considerable."

It was Dadabhai's conviction that Indians should study the business methods of the British. Interested in the cotton trade, he became a member of the Manchester Cotton Supply Association; and while himself benefiting from the available opportunities to study the organisation of the cotton trade in that district, he also read before the members of the Association instructive papers on the supply of Indian Cotton. Likewise, he repeatedly impressed the Bombay millowners and cotton merchants that they could not successfully compete with Lancashire in the London or Liverpool market, or in the Bombay market, until 1 Vol. I, London, 1867, p. 165, they had carefully studied the methods and devices of the Lancashire merchants and manufacturers to secure India's raw material at the lowest price and to sell manufactured articles to the best advantage.

In Liverpool Dadabhai came in contact with Samuel Smith, one of the most trusted business men with whom Dadabhai Naoroji & Co. dealt in cotton. The business acquaintance soon ripened into lifelong friendship. Smith was keenly interested in Dadabhai's struggle for the emancipation of India, and whole-heartedly supported him in all his political activities when he was in a position to do so as Member for Liverpool from 1882 to 1885 and for Flintshire from 1886 to 1906. He was a pillar of strength to the temperance movement in England, and in that work Dadabhai was his enthusiastic coadjutor. He went to India in 1906 to preside over the All India Temperance Conference and attended the historic session of the Indian National Congress at Calcutta when, for the first time from the Congress platform, Dadabhai as President demanded self-government. On the fourth day of the Congress (December 29) the delegates heard with grief that this true friend of India had suddenly passed away and they placed on record their deep sense of the loss sustained by India in his death.

In the midst of all his literary and commercial pursuits Dadabhai seldom missed an opportunity of voicing the grievances of Indians. Indeed, he became an unofficial ambassador for India in England. In 1859 commenced his campaign of agitation concerning the injustice inherent in the system of recruiting the Indian Civil Service. Open competition for the Service had not long been established when, all of a sudden, the India Office announced a reduction in the age limit from 23 to 22. This change debarred the very first Indian student, Rustamji Hirjibhai Wadia, from appearing at the examination. Dadabhai submitted a protest to Lord Stanley, Secretary of State for India. The change in the age limit, he urged, should have been notified beforehand, and he asked that in justice all candidates otherwise eligible should be allowed to appear at the examination.

Dadabhai then asked Sir Erskine Perry to take up the matter on behalf of India. Sir Erskine's friendship was for Dadabhai an unfailing source of inspiration and strength. It was a friendship resting on the union of two hearts drawn by mutual attraction to each other, and it endured till the last days of that noble-minded Englishman.

Sir Erskine interested John Bright in young Wadia. That steadfast friend of India cheerfully accepted the brief. Before, however, he and other friends could raise the subject in the House, the American Civil War broke out. It engrossed the attention of Parliament completely; the Indian Civil Service question had to be shelved. Dadabhai, however, continued his correspondence with the authorities, until an assurance was given by the Secretary of State in a letter that "no further changes in the Civil Service Regulations would at any time be made, without due publicity being given to them at the earliest possible period."

To Dadabhai this was a question of vital national importance. Macaulay had said years ago that no yoke was more oppressive than a foreign yoke. Dadabhai was convinced, after his critical examination of British policy and administration in India, that unless Indians were given an increasing share in the administration of their own country, the British yoke would become more and more galling. The upheaval of 1857 made him very pessimistic about the future, but the transfer of the administration from the East India Company to the Crown and Queen Victoria's memorable Proclamation, promising equality of treatment to her Indian subjects, buoyed him up. That Proclamation became his Bible. He quoted it repeatedly with as much reverence as a Christian divine would have quoted the Scriptures. All his political preaching resolved itself in its ultimate analysis to the root idea that by the pledges solemnly given the Government and the people of Great Britain were bound to give fair treatment to India and to extend to her children the rights and privileges of British citizenship. It was not, however, easy for the rulers to fulfil the pledges implicit in that charter of liberty. They tried for years to circumvent it, but growing tired of that game, during the Viceroyalty of Lord Curzon, they sought to ride off on a new and narrow interpretation of the promise. The words "so far as may be" in the Proclamation gave them, they contended, the discretion to set a limit to its application. Lord Morley, however, vindicated the honour of England.

> I do not believe (said he) that the Ministers who advised Queen Victoria in framing one of the most memorable documents in all our history meant those words to be construed in a narrow, literal, restricted, or pettifogging sense. I do not believe that Parliament ever intended this promise of the Queen's should be construed in any but a liberal and generous sense.

The grievances of the people were many, but in the opinion of Dadabhai the fountainhead of discontent was the denial to the people of their share in the administration. Increased association of Indians in the administration of their own country was the very foundation of progress. It was this broad aspect of the problem that impelled Dadabhai to conduct lifelong agitation on the subject. The same consideration impelled him, two years later, to raise a controversy concerning appointments in the Indian Medical Service. This controversy also had its origin in an arbitrary decree by which the doors of the Service were closed to Indian students. The aggrieved youth in this case was Mancherji Byramji Colah, who was shut out from competition for the post of Assistant Surgeon to the Army Medical Department. There was, it was contended, an altruistic motive underlying that decree.

His Majesty's Government feared that Indian youths would not be able to stand the climate of the different places to which they would have to be posted from time to time!

As advised by Dadabhai, young Colah submitted a memorial to the Secretary of State for India. The reply was disappointing. Nothing daunted, Dadabhai had another memorial submitted separately to the War Office, to the House of Lords, and to the House of Commons, signed by several Indian residents in London.

The ban was removed. Meanwhile, however, young Colah had passed the age limit and was disqualified. Subsequently, owing mainly to Dadabhai's exertions, he was admitted to the service and rose to a high position in it.

The number of Parsi students in England was growing; there was also a steady increase in the number of Parsi residents engaged in commercial pursuits or employed in business-houses in London and in other cities of England. With his usual foresight Dadabhai thought of providing for them a centre of social intercourse.

A club would not have answered the end he had in view. He was aiming at an organisation which might grow with the growth of the Parsi community in England and cope with all the problems concerning their welfare. The outcome was the London Zoroastrian Association, which has during the last eighty years rendered valued assistance and advice to Parses resident in the United Kingdom, particularly to Parsi visitors and students.

From the inception of the Association in 1861 till the date of his retirement from England in 1907, Dadabhai was its President.

To the youths sent to England he was a sort of guardian-general. He had a wonderful gift of drawing them to him and giving a turn to their minds and their hearts which made them useful instruments of public weal. For several years there was under his supervision a group of students who profited by his unrivalled knowledge of the affairs of the world as well as by the example of his simple and methodical habits and high ideals.

To help them to qualify themselves for high offices in the State was the first step towards the goal of Indianisation of the services.

The next step was agitation. In regard to that step Dadabhai found himself invariably thwarted by official high-handedness.

"Defeat" and "Despondency" were, however, words not to be found in his vocabulary. Taking the pledges in the Queen's

Proclamation as his birthright, year in and year out, he continued to preach the gospel of "India for Indians" and lived to see a steady and substantial improvement in the opportunities available to rising generations to occupy higher positions in the service of the State.

Domestic Troubles

It is time now to glance into the home of Dadabhai. A pathetic feature of the life of almost all leaders of thought in India, during the middle of the nineteenth century, was the lack of intelligent fellowship and cooperation of their wives. In no case, however, could the situation have been more poignant than in that of Dadabhai. Into the details of that chapter there is no need to enter. In order, however, to follow the course of events that impelled him to return to Bombay post-haste, in September 1863, it is necessary that the veil should now be partially lifted.

If marriages were made in heaven, as many a good Parsi believed in those days, the selection of Gulbai as a bride for Dadabhai was a heart-rending illustration of the inscrutable ways of Providence. Besides labouring under the disabilities common to the illiteracy of the age, Gulbai was far from being prepossessing, and awkward in speech and manners. Dadabhai tried his best to teach her, but she showed not the least aptitude for study. She could not even read or write, Dadabhai resigned himself to his lot. In no way did the infelicity of this union ruffle the serenity of his mind or alienate his affection; on the contrary, it served to elicit the highest and the noblest that was in him. However ill-matched, he was not found wanting in tenderness or fidelity. He took her out, whenever possible, and with rare patience and self-renunciation played the husband and the teacher in turn to widen her outlook on life and render her as happy as one could be in her position.

Dadabhai was, no doubt, reconciled to, if not quite content with, his lot. Not so, however, his mother. As her son arrived at man's estate, she began to realise the enormity of the mistake she had made in thoughtlessly marrying him in his early boyhood to one incapable of being his better half. What an elevated position in society he was occupying! What higher positions and distinctions awaited him in the future! Such a talented young man required the inspiring company, intelligent cooperation, and cheering assistance of an accomplished partner in life.

Could she not yet repair the mischief done? By this time, however, Dadabhai was the father of a boy, born in 1859. Even so, his mother thought it was not too late to mend the mistake!

It was not then quite uncommon for a Parsi to take a second wife. Bigamy was repugnant to the teachings of Zoroastrianism, but the religious prohibition was not rigidly enforced.

During the days of dictatorship of the Parsi Panchayat a Parsi could marry a second wife with the permission of the elders, given in exceptional cases. Towards the middle of the nineteenth century, however, when the Panchayat had lost all its authority, particularly on the eve of the passing of the Parsi Matrimonial Laws which made bigamy penal, many a Parsi took unto himself a second wife in the lifetime of the first. Dadabhai's mother wished her son to follow suit, but he instinctively shrank from what appeared to be a revolting proposal.

Painful though it was to him to disregard her wishes, he could not help thinking that she was in this respect unreasonable and unjust; she, on the other hand, thought he was dense and obstinate.

Saintliness and self-abnegation were virtues, but every virtue carried to excess is converted into a folly, if not a crime; and Dadabhai, she believed, was not justified in sacrificing his life in this manner. At last she appealed to her brother, Rustamji Desai, to prevail upon Dadabhai not to allow his sentiments to overpower his reason. The uncle tried to induce his nephew to pay heed to his mother's advice, but in vain. It was an example of sheer renunciation—a case of factum valet, however hard and disagreeable. He made a final appeal to his mother in the name of humanity. "Put me," he said, "in the place of my wife. Suppose I, your son, am suffering from the disabilities from which she suffers. Would you, in that case, ask my wife to marry a second husband?" After this his mother dropped the subject.

That was the position when Dadabhai had gone to England for the second time. In front of his residence there was the house of an English medical practitioner, Dr. Archer, who had three educated and intelligent daughters. Dadabhai used to visit them frequently.

Muncherji Cama could not brook such familiarity. Rumours were soon set afloat that Dadabhai had become a convert to Christianity and wished to marry an English woman. These reports reached the ears of his mother. She sent piteous protests, imploring him to desist from taking such a step. "I tried to persuade you," she said, "to take a second wife, but you would not listen to me. Now you think of marrying an English woman and bringing disgrace to our family".

Dadabhai was greatly hurt. Not only his honour, but also the happiness and peace of mind of his wife and mother were at stake. He went straight to the P. and O. Company's office and booked his passage to Bombay.

It was twelve o'clock midnight (September 9, 1863) when a visitor knocked at the door of Dadabhai's family house in Bombay. Manekbai and Gulbai were fast asleep, but a friend and major-domo of the family rushed to the door.

"Who's that?" he asked.

"It is Dadabhai," was the reply.

> "What?" thundered the man inside. "You villain, how dare you take Dadabhai's name who is in England ? Get away, otherwise I will break your bones!"
>
> "Maku," said the visitor, gently calling the man by his name,
>
> "please open the door."

These words had a magic effect on Maku. Recognising the familiar voice, he joyfully threw the door open and held Dadabhai in his arms.

Then met the mother and son; and then the husband and wife;

"This letter was written by me," said Framji Rustamji Desai to the author, "as dictated by Dadabhai's mother" their eyes wet with tears. Within a few minutes Dadabhai cleared all misunderstandings. He was still the same spotless son of his beloved mother, the same faithful husband of his afflicted wife.

Life in Bombay was as full as ever for Dadabhai. Social reform and literary work kept him fully engaged. There were some amusing incidents also. In October 1863 he went with Ardeseer Cursetji Cama and Hormusji Wadya to Purandhar Sanatorium, twenty-five miles from Puna. One evening, whilst he and Cama were walking on a public road, Wadya, who was a few yards in front of them, riding a pony, said poke to a party of two Englishmen and a lady, who were walking ahead of him. That expression was generally used to call upon pedestrians to give way to horses and carriages, but it nettled one of the Englishmen. He struck the pony on the head with his stick. Before the rider could say anything, the animal bolted, and the indignant pedestrian entered into the gateway of a bungalow close by, showering abuse on the rider. Dadabhai and Cama, who could not realise what all the noise was about, came up running to the Englishman and asked what the matter was.

"D...n the rider and the pony also," exclaimed the man.

"That beast had nearly trodden on my wife's heels."

"You might speak more politely," said Dadabhai on hearing some other coarse invectives.

"D...n you and your politeness. I will not allow you or anyone else to tread on my wife's heels."

"Such conduct is most ungentlemanly," interposed Cama.

Greatly incensed, the man rushed out of the compound and said, "You are as great a cad as your friend."

"Thank you," retorted Cama, "that's very polite of you; we are much obliged."

This roused the ire of the man still more. Brandishing his stick, he threatened to assault Cama. Then, turning to Dadabhai, he asked, "What's his name?"

"The fact of the matter is —"The calm and collected professor tried to soothe him, but was not allowed to proceed further.

"I don't want facts. I want your name"

Dadabhai took out a card from his pocket. Having written with a pencil, "Mr. A. C. Cama," under his own name, he handed die card to the indignant Sahib, and said, "And may I have your name ?"

"It is not necessary," was the curt reply. "I am Commandant of the Military Post of Purandhar."

Returning to his lodgings, Cama wrote a letter to the Commandant, Captain Morgan, demanding an apology. An acrimonious correspondence ensued, resulting in the expulsion of the three Parses from the Cantonment by order of the Commandant.

The incident had its sequel in the law courts. Cama filed a suit against the Commandant, claiming damages. The gallant officer repeated in the court all the choice expressions he had used and added that he had shaken his fist about six inches from Cama's face and had said, "If you were not such a contemptible little snob—or brute I forget which—I would knock your head off your shoulders for your insolence." He justified the intimidation on the ground that Cama's ironical "Thank you" was pro vocative and said that he had expelled the Parses from the hill, as they had not obtained his permission to enter the Cantonment. The Sessions Judge gave judgement in favour of the defendant with costs.

Cama appealed to the High Court, which reversed the decree of the lower court. The learned Judges held that the acts complained of amounted in law to an assault, but that the plaintiff was entitled to only nominal damages, as he had in no way suffered in reputation. They gave a decree for him with nominal damages of one rupee, observing at the same time that Cama was "fairly entitled to the credit, the value of which his residence in England and his apparent adoption of English views as to the points of honour in conduct will have taught him to appreciate, of having behaved with some show of spirit in the whole affair."

Another exciting incident took place at a public meeting held on February 25, 1864, at Sir Jamshedjee Jejeebhoy's Casde, where it was proposed by Dadabhai that a statue should be erected in honour of Jagannath Shankarsheth in the Victoria and Albert Museum in recognition of his public-spirited services. Edwin Hancock seconded the motion; Dr. Birdwood, the Sheriff, and some other Europeans supported the proposal. A discordant note was, however, struck by Chisholm Anstey, the famous barrister of the day. He contended that the Sheriff had convened a meeting of all the inhabitants of Bombay, whereas those who had sent a requisition to him had asked for a public meeting to consider a method for expressing the gratitude of "Mr. Jagannath.

Shankarsheth's countrymen" towards him. Although he was an inhabitant of Bombay, he was not a countryman of that gentleman. It was, therefore, officious on the part of the Sheriff to have called him and the inhabitants at large to that meeting. He might have stayed away, but he was there to enter his protest so that the meeting might not be made into a precedent by silly and designing men. He went on to say that there were about half a dozen signatories to the requisition expecting similar tributes to their work. He referred pointedly to Robert Knight, editor of the Times of India, "who had been promised a heavy purse." This was the unkindest cut to the "Bayard of Indian Journalism," whom the Bombay public had spontaneously decided to honour, on the eve of his departure from India, as one of the very few English journalists who had striven consistently to promote good feelings between Indians and Europeans. Despite the thunder of the irate lawyer, however, it was resolved to appoint a Committee to raise funds for the statue. Dadabhai was one of its active members.

There was a distribution of prizes and scholarships to the girls of the Students' Literary and Scientific Society's schools in Bombay on December 12,1863. At this gathering Dadabhai was a welcome visitor. Sir Bartle Frere, Governor of Bombay, who occupied the Chair, paid him a warm tribute as being "one of the first promoters of female education in Bombay in its earliest infancy. It was a matter for gratification, he added, that Dadabhai was then amongst them "after a number of years usefully and profitably spent in England," to observe 'with satisfaction the progress made in the schools.

A notable achievement during this short visit to Bombay was the inauguration of a Society of Parses who took an oath not to dine without having the ladies of the family at the same table.

This "revolutionary" social organisation marked the beginning of the emancipation not only of Parsi but also of Hindu women from the tyranny of a social usage which enjoined restraints on their liberty little different from those associated with the purdah system. Among the promoters of the organisation the two most conspicuous figures were Manockji Cursetji and Dadabhai Naoroji. They held each other in great esteem; both stood head and shoulders above their peers in intellect and zeal for social reform. Whilst the orthodox section of the community was deriding the innovation, Dadabhai sought to justify it by giving an account of the condition of women in different countries in the past and of their elevating influence wherever they had attained their real status in society as their husbands' partners in life.

The cultured members of the family of Manockji Cursetji were the life and soul of the movement for social reform. Their relations with Dadabhai were most cordial and intimate. Dadabhai was a frequent visitor at their residence, Villa Byculla, in Parel Road.

Manockji Cursetji left his sons Cursetji and Jehangir, who were students in England, under Dadabhai's care. He saw to the payment of their school fees and other matters. Manockji Cursetji had started a fund in the middle of the year 1863 for a school to teach the English language to Indian girls. Dadabhai contributed Rs. 5,000 to the fund, and gave the Cursetjis all moral support.

Manockji Cursetji sailed for Europe with his two daughters on April 14, 1865, a fortnight in advance of Dadabhai. To Miss Serene Cursetji, Dadabhai was an affectionate friend and counsellor—she always addressed him as "Dadabhai Master" and she had no more true and disinterested friend. In her diary for the day, she wrote: "It is seldom that one meets with such a friend, as this world is a vile one; consequently I am proud of him—and thankful to God that he has given me a good, pious, and virtuous friend."

Dadabhai left Bombay for England on April 29. On this occasion he took with him, for the first time, his mother and wife, and his son Ardeshir and daughter Shirin. Where they put up, there is no family record to show, but we learn from Miss Cursetji's fascinating diary that he rented a house in Hornsey, with a splendid garden, and named it "Parsee Lodge." Among young Cursetji's reminiscences of the period there is one concerning Dadabhai's affection for his children that deserves mention:

It was a sight at once charming and delightful to see him, when off work, unbend himself, squatted on the drawing-room carpet, playing with his little boy and girl. His conversation was always interesting, informative, and instructive, decked out with anecdotes and stories, and flashes of friendly fun and ready wit. His voice had a singular charm; I have it still in my ears.

Before he sailed for Europe Dadabhai had offered to the Bombay University, of which he had been nominated a fellow in April 1864, a sum of Rs. 1,75,000 for the endowment of a Fellowship to perpetuate the memory of Lord Canning. The amount was contributed by several donors, Dadabhai himself having subscribed Rs. 50,000. The proposal, however, fell through as, before the amount was paid, the commercial crisis which supervened on the termination of the American Civil War spelt the ruin of many a business concern and also of many an individual in England and India. Before the war England used to buy huge quantities of cotton from the Southern States of America; after the outbreak of hostilities the supply was cut off and the Lancashire spinners had to look to Bombay for the raw material. There was thus a boom in the cotton trade in the Bombay markets, followed by speculation, which drove the entire population of Bombay crazy and brought about the ruin of numerous merchant Princes and commercial houses in India.

For Dadabhai's firm the war was a windfall. During the period of hostilities it received large consignments of cotton, and he amassed a fortune. He had, however, dealings with several firms in England and India, which owed him large sums of money.

Their collapse inflicted severe losses on him, but the chief cause of catastrophe was his own good nature, his sheer self-effacement in helping others. Although the times were critical, he had tried to extricate a friend from embarrassment. This friend had established himself in business in England. Speculation during those giddy days had brought him to the verge of insolvency. When Dadabhai heard the tale of his woes, he bestirred himself to avert the crisis. Against the warning of friends he stood surety for the man who had incurred losses to the extent of £30,000 and was practically bankrupt. He thus saved the friend's firm, but imperilled the stability of his own. The creditors of the insolvent firm flocked to his doors, brandishing their books of account and demanding immediate payment. Dadabhai quickly met all his obligations as a surety, but saw his own firm go under.

Another friend to whom Dadabhai extended a helping hand was Karsandas Madhavji, through whom he had large dealings with Bombay houses. Even during the hectic days of the share-mania Dadabhai gave credit to Karsandas's constituents, relying on the recommendations of this friend. Karsandas soon found himself in deep waters and asked Dadabhai to honour his bills to the extent of £60,000. Dadabhai's friends in Bombay, particularly Jamshedji Kapadia, who had an inkling of the impending bankruptcy of the Hindu merchant, cautioned him not to incur any such liability. Kapadia had retired from the firm and returned to India in 1865. The warning, however, came too late. Dadabhai had already informed Karsandas that he would accept the bills; and, true to his word, he honoured them all. It was such single-heartedness and readiness to help a lame dog over the stile that meant his own undoing.

Even in the midst of failure Dadabhai's credit for integrity stood as high as before. Much sympathy was expressed for him in England as well as in India. Within a week he placed his accounts before his English creditors. Impressed by his integrity, they released him from his liabilities and engaged his own services in connection with the liquidation proceedings. They also showed their confidence in him by offering him fresh loans to set him up in business again.

Referring to the crisis of 1866, the writer of Dadabhai's obituary in Investor's Review (July 17,1917) wrote:

Many years after, when his character and attitude happened to come up in the Bank of England Discount Office, its chief, while as a conservative pooh-poohing and sneering at Mr. Naoroji's utterances, told us that he knew him to be a man of strict integrity in business and as proof added, "he met all his engagements in 1866, a thing comparatively few in the East were able to do."

Another story is related, indicating how highly Dadabhai was respected in banking circles. Some of the banks in England refused accommodation against documents which Cama & Co. were prepared to honour, and insisted on the firm drawing bills and getting the recognised brokers' acceptance. Dadabhai raised a controversy and eventually had his way. The Governor of the Bank of England, it was reported, called on Dadabhai at his office and complemented him on "his spirited resistance and the justness of his contention."

Ever cool and collected, patient and contented, Dadabhai took his misfortunes calmly and philosophically. Miss Serene Cursetji, who was then a guest of the family, refers in her diary in touching terms to the troubles which he faced with his characteristic calm during those unhappy days. Writing on Tuesday, June 26, 1866, she observes:

Poor Dadabhai has truly a deal of patience and his troubles he bears marvellously. I learnt from papa that his affairs will have to be wound up in a day or two: this will be done more through the misconduct of his creditors, many of whom have behaved shabbily, very shamefully towards him, but I feel sure God will reward him for his righteousness.

By Friday, June 29, it was all over. Miss Cursetji's diary for the day opens with these words:

None could think from the unshaken calmness and patience that reigned in Dadabhai's face as well as action that his affairs were in such a dreadfully painful condition. As usual he took his breakfast—but poor Dadabhai's mother was sad and kept crying for the whole day and speaking in more than harsh terms to poor Mrs. D. All this was very painful.

After the failure of his firm it was impossible for Dadabhai to keep with him the proteges whom he had been supporting in their studies. The family, however, stayed with him for a year more. On her return from England, Dadabhai's wife gave birth to a second daughter, in Bombay, on October 10, 1868. The girl was called by the pet name Maki, I which clung to her ever afterwards. Abbreviation of Manekbai.

Educating the British Public

The gloom of JL reverses in business was dispelled by the brilliance of Dadabhai's success in other spheres of public usefulness. Pursuit of commerce in England was not an end but a means to an end, namely, work for the economic and political well-being of India. To that end he now bent his whole energy, resorting to means more congenial, more direct and more promising.

Dadabhai's first impulse, when he went to England, was to obtain first-hand knowledge of the cultural and political institutions of England. Whilst studying those institutions, he felt more and more convinced that if the British people were true to themselves, true to their inbred sense and traditions of equality, justice, and fair play, they would help India to obtain freedom.

The policy of the Government of India was certainly not such as to stimulate such hopes; the arrogance of the British officials of the day and their unfeigned contempt for Indian intellect and character were positively destructive of such optimism.

But who were the real rulers of India? The Government of India 3 Certainly not. Their masters in England ? Yes. But who held the reins of government in England? The bureaucracy? Certainly not. The Crown? Not at all. The Ministers? Nay, despite the fact that they held the reins of office, not even they ruled England and India. It was the people of England that governed both. To call the Government of England a limited monarchy was a misnomer; it was a republic, limited only in name, a commonwealth where the electors were really and truly the sovereign. It was their will which, subject to constitutional limitations, was law. The destinies of India were linked with those of such a commonwealth; their interests were identical; united they stood; divided they both must fall. If the policy of the Government of India had not been directed in the past towards the end visualised by Dadabhai, it was, he felt, because the British public were not kept well informed of the true state of affairs in India. If their ignorance were dispelled, their insular prejudices removed, and the mists of misunderstanding cleared away, the ties between the two countries could be strengthened, to the lasting advantage of both. "We Indian people believe," he used to tell English audiences, "that, although John Bull is a little thickheaded, once we can penetrate through his head into his brain that a certain thing is right and proper to be done, you may be quite sure that it will be done."

Such being his reading of the English mind and English character, it became his lifelong mission to awaken the British people to their responsibilities concerning the administration of India. Already he had launched his campaign for the removal of certain wrongs and had succeeded. It was, however, impossible for him, single-handed, to rivet the attention of the British public on the diverse neglected problems affecting the welfare of India.

For the diffusion of the knowledge of Indian affairs and for the creation of a healthy public opinion in England it was necessary to have a group of workers. Without British allies and their cooperation the need for Indian reforms could not be adequately impressed on the House of Commons in whom rested the ultimate authority. Dadabhai, therefore, started, in collaboration with W. C. Banerjee, the London Indian Society, with the object of bringing Englishmen and Indians together at social gatherings and exchanging views on subjects connected with India. There were two interesting self-denying ordinances. The Society could not discuss "any purely religious subject," nor could it at any time pledge itself to any party, political or social, in India or in England. Thus protected from pitfalls, the London Indian Society carried on useful propaganda for more than fifty years, with Dadabhai as its President until his retirement from England in the year 1907.

How he fought on behalf of candidates for admission to the Services we have seen. That struggle, however, merely marked the commencement of a war that was to last for thirty years. The question of the Indian Civil Service again came to the front in 1865, owing to a change in rules adversely affecting Indian aspirants for the Service. Sanskrit and Arabic used to be included in the optional subjects for the examination; most of the Indian students found it easy to take up one or other of the languages.

It was, however, proposed to reduce the number of marks that could be secured in this way. Dadabhai raised his voice against the proposal. In addressing a meeting of the London Indian Society, he stressed the importance of the two classical languages, and of the precious store of knowledge enshrined therein. The Society thereupon sent protests to the Secretary of State, and the controversy ended in Dadabhai's triumph.

Skirmishes of this sort were almost a normal feature in the life of Dadabhai. Not only for defending the economic and political rights of the people of India, but also for vindicating their intellect and their character, he had to enter the arena of public controversy from year's end to year's end. In February 1866, John Crawford, President of the Ethnological Society of London, read a paper in which he sought to establish the intellectual and moral superiority of European races over Asiatics. Not only the President of that learned Society, but almost the whole of Europe was then under this ethnological illusion, which was the result of a superficial study of races according to the divergences of their cephalic index, colour, facial angles, and other peculiarities.

Dadabhai would not allow such a libel to go unchallenged. He was not out to demolish all the sociological fallacies underlying the paper; he was anxious merely to vindicate Indian intellect and Indian character. He, therefore, came forward the very next month with a crushing rejoinder, tearing to shreds all the specious arguments in Crawford's thesis. It was a spirited and cogent appeal to history and science which only a student of the history and literature of Europe as well as of Asia, ancient as well as modern, could have put forward within so short a time.

It was stated by Crawford, as an illustration of the mental inferiority of the Asiatics, that in the seminaries at eighteen the Indian youth was left far behind by the European and that he never after recovered his lost ground. Dadabhai explained that the principal object of the Indian boys who joined English seminaries during the early years of the East India Company was to acquire a knowledge of the English language. The fact that they discontinued their studies on attaining that object was no justification for the assumption that the Indian youth was incapable of progress after eighteen. Since those days there had been such a rapid advance in university education that the Friend of India had remarked that university examinations had been "assuming a Chinese magnitude" and presenting a spectacle at once curious and gratifying.

The dearth of great names in Asiatic literature was another disparaging comment of Crawford. Dadabhai cited several famous works in ancient Persian and Indian literature. With pride he recalled the tribute paid by European savants to the unsurpassed achievements of the Brahmins in grammatical analysis and Sanskrit works abounding in every branch of science.

Quoting Horace Wilson, he pointed out that in fiction much of the invention displayed on the revival of letters in Europe had an Indian origin, while in spiritual and philosophical speculations Hindus had traversed the very same ground trodden by the philosophers of Greece and Rome. In astronomy and metaphysics, too, they had kept pace with the most enlightened nations of the world, while in medicine and surgery they had attained as much proficiency as was practicable before the study of anatomy was rendered possible by the discoveries of later research.

As regards character, Dadabhai quoted testimony after testimony of authors, travellers, and administrators, to refute the sweeping denunciation made on imperfect information. What would an Englishman have to say to the following picture of English character drawn by a Parsi who was disgusted with the bad name given to Indians by European writers of the type of Crawford?

Look at all the mass of untruths in the daily advertisements and puffs. . . how much swindling is there in the concoction of companies for the benefit of the promoters only. . . . Look at the number of immoral haunts in London, read the account of Life in Liverpool, see the social evil and street immorality, cases of unfaithfulness in domestic life. . . . Studying the English character in this superficial manner, that critic had formed the opinion that the English were the most hypocritical, the most selfish and unprincipled people. "If," said Dadabhai, "such evidence as Mr. Crawford relies upon be conclusive as to the character of the natives of India, I do not see how the Parsi gentleman's conclusion cannot also be admitted as proved." Why, the principal argument that he and his colleagues had to encounter in their efforts to promote female education in India was that it had corrupted English society!

When we left India in 1855 to come over here to open the first Parsi firm (said Dadabhai), the principal advice given by our European friends was that we should be exceedingly careful in our business in the city against the many rogues we should meet with there. "In India," said one, "we keep one eye open; in England you must keep both eyes wide open."

Was evidence of this sort to be allowed to traduce whole nations 2 Differences in the condition of different people and their various peculiarities required careful study, and due allowance had to be made before attributing any result to innate differences.

Repeated misrepresentations brought home to Dadabhai the need for an organisation, more broad-based than the London Indian Society, which could bring together Englishmen and Indians on a common platform not merely for the ventilation of Indian grievances but also for the removal of erroneous impressions. Once more, therefore, we find him working on a project for the formation of an association to lay solid foundations of mutual understanding and friendship between England and India. The outcome was the East India Association, inaugurated on December 1, 1866, in collaboration with a committee of retired English officers with whom the idea of acquainting the British public and the British Government with matters pertaining to the East Indies appears to have originated. Its membership was thrown open to all who were interested in the welfare of India.

Independent and disinterested advocacy of the interests of India and promotion by all legitimate means of her welfare was its object. As an institution it aimed at providing a Library and Reading Room, and affording Members of Parliament and the public generally information and assistance on Indian subjects.

It was, however, not to take notice of complaints of individuals against the Government of India or their Civil and Military Servants unless a question of public importance was involved.

Nor was it open to it to undertake to act in matters that could be decided by law courts, or by an appeal to the Judicial Committee of the Privy Council.

During his stay in England Dadabhai had succeeded in rousing in English friends such deep sympathy for his country and such high regard for his disinterested labours that a large number of eminent English politicians, statesmen, ex-governors, and ex-officials resident in England readily joined the Association. The first President was Lord Lyveden, son of Robert Smith, Advocate-

General of Bengal, whose fame among the people of India was, to quote the words of James Mackintosh, the philosopher-lawyer of Bombay, "greater than that of any Pandit since the days of Manu." Lord Lyveden was born in Calcutta. This circumstance, coupled with his connection with the Board of Control, first as its Secretary and then as its President, had given him an interest in the welfare of India almost as keen as his interest in England.

Dadabhai was at first only a member of the Committee, but the duties of Secretary of the Association soon devolved on him.

The platform of the Association provided a forum for all possessed of any special information or views on Indian and Colonial subjects. At its meetings was always to be seen a brilliant assemblage of prominent Englishmen, Indians, and Anglo-Indians, exchanging views on Indian affairs, uniting in voicing Indian grievances, and stimulating, so far as possible, the British public and the British Government to take a deeper interest in India than they had previously evinced.

Dadabhai was the outstanding figure at these gatherings. At the very first meeting held on May 2, 1867, he read a paper on "England's Duties to India." He raised three main issues. Was British rule in India a benefit to India and England ? If so, what were the best means to make it endure for the longest possible time ? Were such means adopted ? Acknowledging the benefits of law and order under the British regime, he gave figures showing enormous contributions made by India towards England's wealth and strength. Then he referred to the annual drain of the wealth of the country to England and the total exclusion of Indians from the administration of their own country. Nevertheless, India wanted her connection with England to endure.

Why 2 The explanation was to be found in a parable taken from a vernacular journal. A fox entangled among some creepers was pounced upon by a swarm of flies. Seeing them sucking his blood, a crow asked the fox whether he might drive away the flies. "No," replied Renard, "these flies are now satisfied, and if you drive them away, another hungry swarm would take their place."

What about the means to ensure solidarity between the two countries? Some people maintained that India was conquered by the sword and must be retained by the sword; some advised a policy of benevolent despotism; others, however, stressed the wisdom of a policy of justice, of "equality among all Her Majesty's subjects and honesty with the Princes of India." Reviewing the three policies, Dadabhai observed that the third, "the policy proclaimed to the people and the Princes of India in the name of the Sovereign, was the hope of India and the anchor of England."

It is gratifying and hopeful to find that the statesmen who rule and the thinkers who guide the policy of this country have distinctly seen and clearly enunciated that India should be ruled for India's sake; that the true and only tower of strength to the English rule is not a hundred thousand English soldiers, but the willing consent and grateful loyalty of the people themselves; and that when the time comes for a separation, and which I trust is far distant, die world may rejoice in a glorious chapter added to its history, of the regeneration of an old, but long unfortunate, race, and India may for ever remember gratefully the benefactors who restored her to more than her ancient splendour and civilization.

If this was the right policy, what were the right means adopted of implementing it? Now followed a formidable list of grievances. Neglect of education, denial to qualified Indians of a share in the administration, repeated famines, lack of irrigation and means of communication, these and other woes of India were brought vividly to the notice of the audience, with an exhortation to the British people to be "true to their nature and genius," and to apply themselves honestly to the discharge of their duties.

In another paper read by Dadabhai, on July 5, on "Mysore" he gave documentary evidence to show that the British Government were bound to acknowledge a separate Government in Mysore and the continuance of a "native rule" in that territory.

On November 25 Dadabhai came forward with yet another paper on the "Expenses of the Abyssinian War," demanding that India should not be saddled with any portion of the cost of wars fought in the interests of the British Empire. It was argued by official apologists that India had lost nothing because it would have had to pay the troops even if they had not been transferred.

Dadabhai's examination of this argument was devastating. "What is it that die troops are kept in India for e Whatever that was, India lost by the transfer of the troops. If it was nothing, then the army should have been reduced. If it was something, then how could it be said that India lost nothing ? If the troops were required for security, then it was unfair that India should have been deprived of that security and yet have been made to pay for it.

Dadabhai's enthusiasm proved infectious. Member after member came forward to read papers on important subjects, On June n General Sir Arthur Cotton read a paper on "Irrigation and Water Transit in India." The unprecedented succession of drought and famine was then filling India with distress and discontent. The authorities seemed to favour the construction of railways more than canals as a remedial measure.

Sir Arthur had some caustic remarks to make with regard to the published papers on the subject, all filled with writing, but with not one word about doing anything. If India could be irrigated with ink, the famines would have been stopped long ago; but he should have preferred a Governor-General, or head of the Public Works Department, "who would irrigate one acre, or cut one mile of navigation, to one who would write a whole Blue book full of frothy declamation about the necessity of irrigation, and the terrible difficulties attending it."

On August 13, 1867, Dadabhai raised the question of admission of Indians to the Civil Service and proposed that a memorial be sent to the Secretary of State for India, demanding that competitive examinations should be held in India as well as in England.

Through the kindness of Sir Erskine Perry he had come to know of a minute of a Committee of the Council of the Secretary of State for India which had recommended, in the year 1860, that examinations should be held simultaneously in both countries for all the, Civil Services. He was asking nothing more. Sir Herbert Edwards suggested that the Association should also call attention to the desirability of establishing scholarships so as to enable students to go to England to complete their education. After having heard the members of the deputation, Sir Stafford Northcote expressed himself favourably disposed to both the suggestions.

The next step was to interest members of the House of Commons in this subject. Dadabhai approached several M.P.s and succeeded in getting Henry Fawcett to give notice of motion to the effect that the House of Commons deemed it desirable that the examination should be held simultaneously in London, Calcutta, Bombay, and Madras. He then read another paper on April 17, 1868, and moved that die Association should support Fawcett's motion.

Hostile critics often questioned the fitness of Indians for offices of trust. They were under the illusion that Indians were deficient in ability, integrity, and physical power and energy.

Dadabhai did not wish to go over the ground he had already covered in his paper on European and Asiatic races, but, he said, he asked those who spoke scornfully of Indians not to forget how some Englishmen in India, in former days, were suddenly transformed into rich Nawabs; how after selling their power and influence in India the Company bought their power in the English legislature by bribery; how the Company's servants cheated their own masters; and how their conduct furnished some of the most remarkable instances upon record of the power of interest to extinguish all sense of justice and even of shame. It was natural for educated Englishmen drawing high pay or profits to feel indignant at the bribery and corruption of the poor people with low education, low pay or profits, and low prospects, but Dadabhai asked them to look round and observe the amount of fraud and "doing" in London and to remember that several Englishmen, drawn from the lower classes, were not behaving creditably in India.

The real question was, when Indians were as highly educated as Englishmen, did they attain to the same character for integrity or not ? Holding in his hand a pamphlet of ninety-five pages, entitled Evidence relating to the efficiency of Native Agency in India, Dadabhai said he had collected a large volume of testimony "as to the efficiency and integrity of die educated natives employed in the various departments of the Indian Service in office of trust and responsibility."

It was an interesting symposium of opinions given by eminent authorities. Retired governors, civilians, and military officers, having experience of varied provinces, all testified to the intelligence of Indians; a few of them, however, thought that integrity was not yet a strong point in Indian character. Dadabhai did not keep back from his audience a single adverse opinion; he left it to them to draw their own conclusions. Some of these opinions served to clarify the situation. For instance, Sir Bartle Frere observed:

> In India, as in Europe, we find a great difference in capacity between different races; between different classes in the same race; between the same race in different stages of civilization; between the children of an intellectual and a non-intellectual family; between the rich and the poor; between members of different religious schools; and, in fact, we find that every variety of circumstance in the origin and training of a man makes some difference in what I may call his original intellectual capacity.
>
> And after making allowance for this difficulty in instituting any comparison between the two groups of nations, I should say that there was no perceptible difference between the children of the two groups, save that the children of the warmer climate were more precocious in the early development of their intellects, and paid for their advantage in lacking somewhat of the stamina and strength of the more slowly ripening children of the colder climate.
>
> Of this I feel pretty confident, that, if a million children could be taken at random, so as to represent every variety of nation, rank, and religion in Europe, and another million taken in like manner in India, there would certainly be no inferiority observable in the intellectual capacity of the Indian million. I believe that many of the prevalent differences of opinion as to the actual result, as shown by experience, arise from our forgetting, in almost every comparison we make, many of the main elements which ought to enter into our calculation and comparison.

Nobody supposed, said Chisholm Anstey, that the natives of India were deficient in ability. He believed in their integrity, in their capacity, and in their fitness for government. Nevertheless, he was against the clamour to "thrust a certain proportion of natives every year as eligible for high office" upon the Secretary of State, the Viceroy and the Commander-in-Chief. He would not employ an Indian any more than an Englishman in a particular district or province in which his household gods were set and his worldly fortunes were cast. Why? Because he was an Indian?

No, because he would not appoint anyone to an office in a locality in which he had for some time resided.

Dadabhai was ready with a rejoinder. To say that there should be no Indians in the Civil Service of India was like saying that there should be no Englishman in the Civil Service of England.

The localities of appointment were mere matters of detail. The main question was to put Indians and Englishmen on a footing of equality as regards entrance into the service. Dadabhai's motion was carried, the learned counsel being the only dissentient.

Within two years of its existence the Association had demonstrated what a wide field of useful work lay before it. It set Dadabhai thinking how the efforts of its members could be reinforced if it had branches in India at the capital cities, and if it were helped financially by the Princes and the people of India.

This idea commended itself to his colleagues. It was decided that he should proceed to India and establish branches of the Association in selected places and collect funds.

A deputation of the Association, including Dadabhai, had presented to the Secretary of State a memorial soliciting immediate attention to the necessity of irrigation works in India. It needed, however, not one or two, but a volley of memorials before the authorities could be roused to set the official machinery in motion. On the eve of Dadabhai's departure to India, it was proposed that another representation should be made to the Secretary of State. In a minute which Dadabhai left behind and which was placed before the Association's meeting, held on December 8, 1868, he gave a historic survey of the devastating famines with which the population was periodically afflicted.

Why was the work of irrigation culpably neglected? Was it a question of cost ? If so, he urged, the question should not be considered mainly as one of profit and loss. Even if it were certain that the expenditure would yield no return, the State would, in his opinion, "be bound by the highest sense of duty to undertake them".

In 1870 it was decided by Government to spend an additional amount of £100,000,000 on railways. Sir Arthur Cotton challenged the wisdom of that decision, and the East India Association devoted no less than three evenings to an examination of the issues raised by the "Grand Old Man of Irrigation," as he was called.

Soon afterwards the Duke of Argyll moved the second reading of the Governor-General of India Bill in the House of Lords. The Bill contained a clause empowering the Governor-General to nominate qualified Indians to the Civil Service under a system of selection instead of by examination. It was, in a way, a triumph of Dadabhai's prolonged agitation. He was, no doubt, an advocate of free competition and had suggested that a competitive examination for some of the appointments to the service should be held -in India and that the selected candidates should be required to go to England and pass further examinations. The Secretary of State had, however, endeavoured to meet the wishes of the Association by a system of nominations under which nine out of sixty appointments would have gone to Indians, whilst the doorway would have remained open for an Indian candidate to enter the service by open competition at the examination held in England.

As a compromise, Dadabhai was prepared to welcome the concession, trifling though it was. It produced, however, a strange ferment in India. The Bombay Branch of the East India Association condemned the system of nomination as humiliating to the country. Moreover, where was the guarantee that the enactment of 1869 would not remain a dead letter as did the Act of 1863 and the Royal Proclamation? Even if its provisions were implemented, where was the guarantee that selection would be based on merit?

Dadabhai, therefore, sent from India a paper on the subject, which was read at a meeting held on July 7, 1869. "I do not suppose," he observed, "that anybody would be disposed to blame Indians for this suspiciousness, especially when their fears are based on past experience. Yet, justifiable though the reasons were for doubts, Dadabhai considered that they might have reliance upon the distinct pledge given by the Secretary of State.

Until the system of nomination was abolished in 1886, there was a constant uproar about the appointments made by Government.

To purge recruitment of the abuses inherent in the system and to ensure the selection of the most deserving candidates by competitive examinations in England and India, a decisive battle had to be fought, and was fought, as we shall see, on the floor of the House of Commons, one of the combatants being Dadabhai himself.

A Fruitful Mission

With his heart and soul deeply engaged in the work of W the East India Association and his mind full of plans for strengthening its position and extending its operations, Dadabhai arrived in Bombay, On May 5, 1869, he gave his first lecture explaining the objects and work of the Association. Like the lion, a very appropriate symbol of English character, the English public could not be roused easily, but, said Dadabhai, when once roused, no obstacle could stop it. All that was necessary was to make out a good case. "A kind of Providence," wrote Edmund Burke, "has placed in our breasts a hatred of the unjust and cruel in order that we may preserve ourselves from cruelty and injustice." Probably Dadabhai had these words in mind when he told his audience: "The Englishman is incapable of despotism.

He might, and often did, carry things with a high hand, but the instinct and love of liberty, the constitutionalism which is born with and ingrained in him, made him at the time of trial recoil from being stigmatised a despot."

Many of us are anxious (he observed) that we should have representative institutions, a Parliament in India. That is the goal we must all work to. But can we say that we are at present prepared for such institutions? ... Is it not necessary for us, especially the educated, to set ourselves to work to educate the people in this important matter e While doing this on one hand, preparing a public opinion, a public voice, and a body of public men, is it not necessary that in. England a Society should exist which should have, by its judicious and proper advocacy, by the weight and influence of its conduct, acquired an influence so as to be prepared, when wanted, to fight the last and greatest battle of representation in or for India?

The lecture evoked great enthusiasm. It roused the energy and quickened the imagination of the citizens of Bombay. At a large and influential meeting of representative citizens, held on May 22, the Bombay branch of the Association was formally inaugurated.

Dadabhai then went on a lecturing tour, particularly with a view to enlisting the support of the ruling Chiefs. Some of his Bombay colleagues, such as Dr. Bhau Daji and K. T. Telang, however, fought shy of those potentates who, they believed, were intellectually, morally, and traditionally incapable of sharing the aspirations of young India or of furthering the objects that Dadabhai had in view. He was, however, of opinion, and that opinion is held even today by no less eminent a politician than Mahatma Gandhi, that if leaders of society in British India excluded the Princes from their political activity, they would be letting a very useful power run to seed. Men of ability and influence in British India should place their advice and services at the disposal of the feudatory chiefs, and they in turn should lend their financial strength in support of the activities of such leaders for the advancement of India. It was this belief that had prompted him, during the time he had been in England, to help Indian Princes, on several occasions, to tide over their difficulties. It was this belief that prompted them, too, to participate in the arduous work of national progress.

The result of his tour in Kathiawar justified Dadabhai's faith. The Princes received him kindly. Particularly from Cutch, Junagadh, and Gondal he received handsome donations. His Highness, Maharaja Shri Bhagvat Sinhji, Thakore Saheb of Gondal, who was an ardent admirer of Dadabhai and befriended him all his life, convened a public meeting of his subjects to hear the Indian patriot. His address, breathing ardent love for his country, thrilled the good people of that State, who had seldom heard a discourse on problems such as those presented to them, nor listened to such a lucid and saintly speaker.

Within a few months branches of the Association were established in Calcutta, Madras, and other cities, and substantial donations poured in from the Indian States. Thus, for the first time in history, one might say, Dadabhai was able to arouse a distinctly national feeling in India.

Caustic in his comment on public affairs, trenchant and unsparing in his criticism of the system of government and of the hauteur and indifference of officials, Dadabhai eschewed bitterness. His intense earnestness, his transparent sincerity and selflessness, and his sweet reasonableness and moderation, lent a peculiar charm to his appeal and extorted admiration even from members of the resident English community, intensely sensitive though it then was to criticism of the British administration.

There was a consensus of opinion that this ardent patriot, who had dedicated his time and talents to the sole mission of educating the people of India as to their rights, and the people of England as to their responsibilities, was rendering a national service.

About this time Pherozeshah Mehta had returned to Bombay from England. He was one of the proteges of Dadabhai whose sage counsel and inspiration (to quote Mehta's own words) had formed his character and elevated his ideals whilst he was studying law in England. Having been an eyewitness of the efforts made by Dadabhai in arousing the interest of the British public in Indian affairs, he told his countrymen, in his own impressive way, what sacrifices had been made by Dadabhai in discharging that patriotic duty. Seeing how a wave of enthusiasm had spread over the entire province and how the patriotic sentiments of the people had been stirred by Dadabhai's speeches, Mehta also started a movement for publicly appreciating the eminent services rendered by Dadabhai. Endorsing a suggestion made in the Bombay Gazette by a correspondent that the Sheriff of Bombay should soon give the public an opportunity of expressing their grateful appreciation of Dadabhai's work, he said in a letter to that journal (January 21, 1869):

I can personally testify to the high esteem and regard in which Professor Dadabhai is held and the value set upon his assistance and advice by not a few of the leading Indian Officials "at Home."

Indeed, if I were called upon to point out the man most deserving to be styled the Sir Philip Sidney of Indian Renaissance,

I would unhesitatingly single out Professor Dadabhai, and that after a close and personal knowledge of and intercourse with him. In his characteristic simplicity and unostentatiousness he may forget himself in rendering services; let us not forget him in acknowledging them!

The public of Bombay responded cheerfully to the call. Since the days of Rammohan Roy, observed the Native Opinion, no Indian had achieved a more distinguished reputation both in India and in England. Rammohan Roy's reputation was chiefly confined to his own presidency of Bengal, but, said the writer, Dadabhai's name was welcomed by his compatriots in all the provinces, and most by the Indian Chiefs. This was all the more honourable to Dadabhai, as he had been able to achieve that distinction without in any way gratifying their vanity or pandering to their prejudices.

Some of the leading citizens took counsel together, and it was resolved to present an address and a purse to Dadabhai. Why a purse ? Because they knew that in his devotion to the cause of his countrymen he had neglected his own interests. They also knew how the genius of eminent politicians was often painfully humiliated and impeded by the straits of embarrassed circumstances. Dadabhai was not the man who would open his lips to anyone about his private troubles, but they felt it was their duty to spare him such embarrassment. A sum of thirty thousand rupees was accordingly collected. Whether Dadabhai would accept such a testimonial to his public spirit was doubtful, but his fellow-citizens had discharged their duty.

Never before or after was a popular demonstration in India in honour of a "political agitator" so vitalised by the participation of the European population as it was on this occasion. In the homage paid to the national hero the heart of the European resident beat in unison with the heart of the populace. There was a unique assemblage of the inhabitants of the City, European and Indian, at the Framji Cowasji Institute, on July 3, 1869, to do honour to Dadabhai. The address recalled the fact that wherever he had been, whether at home or abroad, he had disinterestedly devoted his time, talents, and energy to the promotion of social, political, and moral welfare of the people of India. It also referred in felicitous terms to his efforts in the cause of popular education and diffusion of useful knowledge, for the spread of vernacular literature and the creation of a taste for reading in the Gujarati-speaking population of the Bombay Presidency.

Dadabhai was overwhelmed with joy when he heard his early activities recalled, one after another, with appreciation and warmth of feeling, but the purse handed to him as a "small token" of his countrymen's esteem and affection was a source of great uneasiness to him.

I accept the testimonials (he observed), which are more proof of your kindness than of my deserts, with great thankfulness.

If I could consult my own feelings, I should hesitate to accept the purse. But certain circumstances with which I need not trouble you have made it necessary for me to avail myself of it. I hope, however, I shall not give any reason for dissatisfaction to those kind friends who have particularly wished me to accept the purse, when I may be able to devote the generous gift to some purpose of public usefulness.

Out of the subscribed amount a sum of Rs. 25,000 was presented to Dadabhai, and the balance was kept for the cost of his portrait, which it was proposed to present to the Framji Cowasji Institute later. The greater part of the purse soon went to the East India Association. Owing to a defalcation on the part of an office-bearer of the Association, its financial condition had become so critical that Dadabhai took over the liabilities of that officer. There was not a ray of hope of recovering even a farthing, but there was the satisfaction that he had given a new life to the Institution.

There are men (observed The Times of India) whom, if we can feel sure of not spoiling them, the community does itself good by publicly honouring—and there are times, very few, indeed, we admit—when it is suitable and in the true sense profitable to emphasise a unanimous public sentiment by a substantial gift.

The conditions which render the testimonial of a community sincere and suitable, and which make appropriate a gift of money for private use, given to a man while yet in the midst of active life, are, we think, to be found in the circumstances which have resulted in the presentation to Mr. Dadabhai Naoroji. If there be any who have looked askance on Mr. Dadabhai's recent lectures and agitation because of their political character, we may remind them that there is very much in connection therewith in which the most conservative and timid can rejoice.

Dadabhai was yet in his prime; he was exposed to all the temptations strewn in the path of men in active public life. The testimonial was, therefore, a test of his moral fibre. It entailed on him new responsibilities and enjoined greater self-denial.

With the satisfaction that his mission on behalf of the East India Association had been crowned with success, beyond expectations, Dadabhai embarked on his fourth voyage for England. Little did he then realise that besides instilling new aspirations and hopes in British India his political propaganda had created an awakening among the Indian Princes. Much less did he realise the extent to which the sphere of his influence had been extended during those few months and the warmth of feeling of respect and admiration which his ability, integrity, and patriotic fervour had evoked from the Feudatory Chiefs whom he had set thinking as to the extent to which his propaganda could be helpful in adjusting the relations between their durbars and the Paramount Power. Still less could he have dreamt that the contacts thus established would give quite an unexpected turn to his own career and bring him back to India to offer advice and assistance to several Princes and to be installed on the seat of Prime Minister of Baroda.

Arriving in England, Dadabhai attended a meeting of the Association, held on October 29, 1869, at which a paper on the question of means of transport in India was discussed. Welcoming die decision of Government to construct railways in future by raising loans instead of by giving concessions to private enterprise and guaranteeing payment of interest on their stock, he pointed out that under the system of giving companies a guarantee, all the losses arising from waste fell upon the State, while the profit mostly went to the guaranteed companies.

The question of adulteration of cotton in Bombay, the Cottonopolis of India, then came under discussion. The Bombay Cotton Act of 1869 contained penal provisions for preventing adulteration. In a paper on the subject, Dadabhai contended that no case had been made out for such stringent and hampering penal provisions as were embodied in that Act. The discussion on the paper had the desired effect; the obnoxious measure was dropped.

During the years 1870 and 1871 the principal topic of discussion was Indian Finance. Within six weeks, between June 15, and July 28,1870, no less than four papers dealing with the subject in all its bearings were read and discussed at great length; one on "Indian Finance" by I. T. Prichard, another on "Public Works in India.'" by Sir Bartle Frere, another on "Wants and Means of India" by Dadabhai, and the fourth on the "Finance of India" by Sir Charles Trevelyan. All these papers had a direct bearing on the subject which Dadabhai had most at heart—the impoverishment of India—and their importance demands separate treatment.

In the year 1871 the number of members of the Association ran into four figures and its influence began to be felt in Parliament.

At Dadabhai's instance, Henry Fawcett, dubbed "the Member for India," had begun what became the annual custom of moving a resolution in the House of Commons favouring "simultaneous examination" for recruitment to the Indian Civil Service. Moreover, whenever Indian questions were discussed in Parliament, several M.P.S prompted by members of the Association, or inspired by its discussions, spoke with knowledge of the wants and wishes of the people and brought informed criticism to bear on the solution of Indian problems.

The Civil Service question loomed large in the proceedings for the year 1871. Amongst the other subjects dealt with during the year may be mentioned "Popular Education in India by William Tayler; and "The Means of ascertaining Public Opinion on Indian Affairs" by Sir Bartle Frere, a paper which was discussed at three sittings. In the year 1872 I. T. Prichard raised the question of "Representation of India in Parliament." This was followed by papers on "The Progressive Capabilities of the Races of India in Reference to Political and Industrial Development" by Hyde Clarke, "What the True Interests of Manchester really are in India" by Dr. George Birdwood, and on "Trusteeship as the Basis of Imperial Policy" by Major Evans Bell.

The work of the Association was growing apace; it needed a centre; it had to equip and maintain a library; it had to build up an endowment fund to ensure its stability. The funds brought by Dadabhai from India were not sufficient for these requirements.

He was once more proceeding to India; would he be good enough to send the hat round Dadabhai cheerfully undertook the begging mission. Immediately on arrival in India, he made arrangements for placing the branch of the Association at Bombay on an efficient footing. He then toured Kathiawar and Rajputana to collect funds and to interest the Princes and the people of the States in the cause of the Association.

The City of Bombay was then convulsed by the powerful agitation of the people for reform in the machinery of municipal administration. Dadabhai threw himself into the movement, presided at a great meeting of the Bombay Ratepayers, and headed the deputation to the Governor of Bombay to present a memorial adopted at the meeting.

The Council of the East India Association was warm in its acknowledgment of the assistance rendered by Dadabhai at all times and in the most critical circumstances. It was stated in a minute that without such assistance it would have been almost impossible for the Association to carry on its work. The Council also placed on record its gratification at the large accession to the list of life members, which Dadabhai had been able to secure.

Even so handsome an acknowledgment could hardly have conveyed to the public an adequate idea of the infinite pains taken by the hard-working Secretary in approaching people to join the Association. Stenographers were not then to be had: Dadabhai had to carry on his voluminous correspondence and to write his minutes and contributions to the Press in his own hand. Likewise, he addressed numerous appeals to friends, prominent citizens, and Princes, asking them to help the Association in its work of national importance.

Another glowing tribute was paid to Dadabhai at the annual meeting of the Association on July 17, 1872. In moving a vote of thanks to him, the Chairman of the Council, E. B. Eastwick, observed:

In respect of the Council's remarks regarding the Covenanted Civil Service, I cannot help thinking that in Mr. Dadabhai we have a gentleman who could have reflected honour on the Indian Government, had he been in their Service. Indeed, I can honestly say that I have never met a man who showed greater ability and more pure love of his country than Mr. Naoroji.

The Drain

Sunk in abject poverty, India had the costliest and the lordliest administration in the world in the 'sixties of the past century. The inevitable consequence of a foreign rule everywhere is persistent transfer of wealth from the country of the people to that of their rulers. In the case of poor India the extravagance of the authorities intensified the drain. A very large portion of her revenue was carried away annually to England, depleting the national capital. Of that fact people in England had no conception. Dadabhai, therefore, set himself the arduous task of proving the appalling poverty and distress of the people and the astounding indifference and extravagance of their rulers.

It demanded patient study of details, intelligent research, and exceptional knowledge, skill, and reasoning in marshalling facts and figures. Fortunately for India, he had the requisite qualities, including a voracious appetite for work and inexhaustible energy to explore every avenue of research. Pursuit of commerce had now been subordinated by him to the quest of means to provide food for the half-starved millions of his country; the ordinary business man's casual contemplation of the world's output and trade statistics had been superseded by the critical publicist's close scrutiny of the data concerning the production of the country and the income per head of population. The whole foundation of administration, financial and general, rested upon that one fact—the produce of the country, the ultimate result of all capital, labour and industry.

To work out the result was then equivalent to making bread 'without flour. Official information on the subject was inadequate and misleading; Blue books were compiled without the least idea of providing information on the issues with which the expert mathematician wished to come to grips. The sources of non-official information were practically dry. The Universities in India had not yet popularised the study of political economy; and books on the subject were a novelty. In the year 1870, the only journal in India which gave statistics concerning the agricultural, mineral, and other sources of national wealth was the Indian Economist, edited by Robert Knight. It, however, did not give Dadabhai the information he wanted. Detailed classification of the cultivated area was not available; nor were there estimates of the average yield per acre for all the different crops. There were price statistics, but incomplete, and scarcely accurate for minor crops.

Not only was information lacking, but there were also handicaps in the approach to the sources of information. Not all the barriers could, however, keep the indefatigable explorer off the track. Toilsome and tiresome though the journey, and doubtful the chances of reaching the goal, he dedicated all his energy to the uphill task. Being an adept at ferreting out the truth for himself, he gathered from far and near all possible information bearing on the question, subjected the evidence thus collected to a minute analysis, and came to the startling conclusion that the yearly income per head of the population was only 405., roughly equivalent to Rs. 20.

The gross land tax for 1870-71 had been estimated at £21,000,000. On the basis of one-eighth of the gross produce, the gross production was estimated at about £168,000,000. To these were added receipts for opium, salt, coal, and other sources of revenue, and the total of the raw produce of the country raised to £200,000,000. To this sum Dadabhai added £100,000,000 to include the proceeds of manufacturing industries, and of excise on spirits, augmenting the total to £300,000,000. The population of British India being 150,000,000, it gave 40$. per head.

This preliminary analysis of the economic situation formed the subject-matter of a paper on "Wants and Means of India," read before the East India Association on July 27,1870. It was only the first step in his memorable investigation and exposition of the difficult problem. He knew it demanded more detailed study and scrutiny, but it was not necessary for that reason to withhold from the public the results of his enquiry such as he could then put forward.

Dadabhai's paper was, however, only one of a series of papers on Indian Finance. To put the case in the perspective that is needed, it is necessary to recall a few broad facts concerning the position in India, during those days, as regards the financial resources of the country, the machinery of administration, and the system of control. In the history of public finance no Chancellor of the Exchequer was set a task more difficult than that which fell to the lot of the Finance Minister for India during the years following the assumption by the Crown of the responsibility of governing India. None was so shackled as he in confronting the tremendous difficulties involved in the governance of a vast country—the sixth in extent and second in population in the world. Before the administration of those territories was taken over by the Crown, it was in the hands of a business corporation pecuniarily interested in the efficient management of the estate.

The spirit of commerce governed their policy. They did not consider it their duty to provide amenities, but to furnish a clean balance sheet was their bounden duty. The new trustees were not so keen on keeping a watchful eye on the profit and loss account; they had many other affairs of State to look after; so they made over the management to their nominees. Responsibility divided meant no responsibility.

Under the new regime, a legislative measure, after it had passed the Council in India and had been confirmed by the Viceroy, could be lightly vetoed in England. Within the experience of the East India Association, a child as it was of five summers, there was an instance in which a budget had been rejected by the Home Government and flashed back to Calcutta to be recast.

The Indian Chancellor of the Exchequer had to serve two masters, the Local Government and the Home Government, and he had to prepare a budget which both could relish. Both would fling their platters in his face, if the meal was not to their taste.

As, however, the Home Government had the last word in the matter, he preferred to follow the menu likely to agree with his masters in England.

Under such a system of patchwork, lacking unity of design, the financial administration of India could hardly be expected to give satisfaction. During the days of which we are speaking, India enjoyed unprecedented immunity from internal and external disturbances; nevertheless there were deficits necessitating enhanced taxation. The revenue had increased, but the expenditure had grown in still greater proportion. Lord Mayo had to deplore the fact that from the year 1866 to 1870 the Government of India had been plunged in a chronic state of deficit.

The confusion of the Government of India afforded a good reason for demanding an enquiry into its finances. Under the inspiration of Dadabhai and Naoroji Furdoonji, the Bombay branch of the Association took the lead. It sent a petition to the Secretary of State, praying that the finances of India might be placed on a satisfactory footing. It also sent Naoroji Furdoonji to England to enlist support in favour of the petition. The memorialists protested against the increasing burden of taxation and asked for the abolition of the income-tax. It does not appear to have occurred to them that the class bias underlying this proposal was scarcely befitting champions of the poverty-stricken millions of India!

The parent Association had at the same time embarked on a complete survey of the situation. After Dadabhai's paper was read, the President, Sir Charles Trevelyan, gave a very illuminating discourse on the subject. Twelve years of his life had been spent in the administrative service of India and nineteen more years in the British Treasury. He was then appointed Governor of Madras, and finally Finance Minister in India. Speaking, therefore, with unrivalled experience, he expressed his concern that a real crisis had arisen. He welcomed the petition of the inhabitants of Bombay; they had approached Parliament in the most dutiful and constitutional manner and were at least as well entitled to a respectful hearing as any English constituency would have been. The doyen of Indian finance could not, however, accept Dadabhai's description of the Home charges, as "tribute," "drain," and "political remittances," nor would he subscribe to the Indian critic's observations concerning the "impoverishing effect of foreign rule." What were the Home charges ? Mostly stores supplied to India; interest on money borrowed in England and pensions. Were they not legitimate charges for goods supplied and services rendered? Was there anything objectionable in their nature, although there were, he admitted, certain evil tendencies of foreign rule?

There was, no doubt, lavishness in respect of salaries and leave allowances, and in the immense gathering of civil and military officers from all parts of India at the hill stations during nearly half the year. The ever-growing military expenditure, which absorbed nearly a third of the gross revenue, was more than the ordinary military expenditure of the great military monarchies of Europe, more even than the expenditure by which England maintained the security not only of the country but also of the whole of the British Colonies, including Canada. Even the Controller-General of Military Expenditure had remarked that military history presented "no instance of any army so constituted, or of one so costly."

The Public Works Department was another illustration of unparalleled extravagance. Public works were excellent things, but there were other things equally good or better—financial integrity, for instance. When the choice was between more or less of public works and bankruptcy, they might well pause and consider. The ex-Finance Member then related a pathetic story:

When Lord Auckland returned to England from India, he selected Colonel Irvine of the Bengal Engineers for the Office of Director of Works at the Admiralty. Colonel Irvine had not been in office many months before he came to me at the Treasury, and said, with real distress, "I cannot get on here; they care no more about spending a crore of rupees than we do a lac." He died within three days. I do not say that was the cause of his 1 One hundred lacs, i.e., 10,000,000 death, but no doubt the harassment arising from that state of things had something to do with it.

One of the causes of the unsatisfactory state of Indian finance was the imperfect nature of the accounts. There was, moreover, no periodical review of the administration, as was the case when the East India Company had to appear every twenty years before Parliament as a suppliant for the renewal of their Charter.

After the transfer, the auditor and the accountant had become one. The only control that could be exercised was self-control.

So far as Parliament has exercised any influence in the matter, it had facilitated and increased the interested pressure upon the India Office, for, until the conscience of Parliament is roused by a formal public proceeding, powerful interests are always more or less able to use it as an organ for their designs. Departmental rule has not proved strong enough to protect the public interests of India against great class-interests, such as the army, trade and manufactures, and native Princes.

Reform, however, never came anywhere from within. It was time, urged Sir Charles, that Parliament should resume the function of auditor and judge. The Association resolved to present a memorial to Parliament, praying for the appointment of a Select Committee of both Houses to enquire into the general administration of Her Majesty's Indian territories both at home and in India, especially in relation to the conduct of the Finance Department.

Before the decision was taken, Dadabhai had to make a personal explanation. A member of the Association had sent him a letter, in which, while agreeing with him as to the main principles embodied in his paper, the member had criticised some portions as "having a possible seditious and mischievous tendency."

First of all I say (said Dadabhai) no native from one end of India to the other could be found more loyal than I am to the British rule; because it is my sincere conviction, which I have expressed often, that the salvation of India, its future prosperity, its civilization, and its political elevation, all depend on the continuance of the British rule. It is because I wish that the British rule should be long continued in India, and that it is good that the rulers should know native feeling and opinions, that I come forward and speak my mind freely and boldly.

Reverting to the subject under discussion he observed:

The misunderstanding which I want to set right is simply this.

Here is a foreign power ruling over India, producing certain social, moral, political, and economic effects. I want to draw the attention of the English nation to the economic effects of its rule.

I certainly should never be so absurd as to ask English gentlemen to go out and serve India and take nothing for it; but when a country comes under a foreign rule, certain economic results must follow, one of which is, that a drain must necessarily take place from the country ruled to the country ruling. Now the question is, whether the economic injury of this drain (no matter how legitimate this drain may be as far as the recipients are concerned) in the case of India is made up or not by the management of British rule. If it is, it is very necessary that the natives should see that, and the sooner this question is fairly settled the better for England as well as for India.

William Tayler said that lie could see nothing either seditious or mischievous in the paper. It seemed to him to be a sound, practical, and sensible exposition of what Dadabhai sincerely believed to be the difficulties and embarrassments of India, arising out of the fact that India was under a foreign Government, and that there was a drain from year to year upon its resources. All his observations were quite legitimate and were only what they would have wished an independent Indian gentleman to lay before them.

Thus encouraged by British friends, Dadabhai took every opportunity throughout his life to bring home to the British public the avoidable drain on the resources of his motherland, and to plead for redress. In the intensity of such pleading his own vitality was drained to the last drop.

Soon after the resolution of the Council of the East India Association a Parliamentary Committee was appointed to enquire into the financial condition of India. It was another feather in Dadabhai's cap. He promptly submitted for its consideration "a few remarks"—just sixteen thousand words!

The financial administration of any country, like all other human institutions, required four important elements: material, head to design, hand to execute, and sound principles of design and execution. As regards material, the question was: "Did India produce enough to supply, without hardship or privation, both her ordinary wants as a nation and her extraordinary and peculiar want to remit to a distant country a portion of her produce as the natural result of a foreign rule e" The answer was an emphatic No. She did not produce enough even for the daily food of her children, much less for all other needs.

If the India Office should prove that Dadabhai was wrong, well and good; if not, said he, "no ingenious device of even ten

Wilsons or Temples will relieve the Financial Administration of its difficulties unless the Indian legislators and financiers possess the divine power of creating something out of nothing."

Once more he urged arguments in justification of his rough estimate of the total production of India. The proportion of distribution varied from province to province and between district and district. On the whole, therefore, the average income per head of the poor labouring population of all the provinces, excepting the more favourably situated Bombay and the Punjab, could hardly exceed 25$. Complacent assertions of officials to the contrary were worth nothing; he had taken his stand on facts and figures such as he could obtain.

For testing his conclusion, detailed statistics were needed, which it should be the duty of compilers of Administration Reports to give. How minutely he wished the subject to be enquired into and what a multiplicity of data he asked for, can be seen from a single illustration. In order that the average estimate of the income of the unskilled labourer might be correctly estimated, he suggested the compilation, of an annual return showing the number of people living upon unskilled labour, and rates of wages, with details; the number of adults (male and female) capable of work, say between twenty-one and fifty years of age; the number of children under twelve years of age; the average wage earned by males and females of the above-mentioned different classifications (calculating the average on the correct principle of taking the number of labourers earning each rate into account); the number of the sick and infirm; and the number of days during the year that the different rates of wages are earned.

The poverty of the country once admitted, the question of remedy resolved itself into the following heads: 1. Provision of capital necessary for all public works of a permanent character required to increase production and to facilitate distribution; 2. A just adjustment of the financial relations between India and England so that the political drain might be reasonably diminished; 3. The best way of attracting capital and enterprise to utilise the vast cultivable waste lands; and 4. The best way of increasing the intelligence of the people by a comprehensive plan of national education.

The head which designed the financial legislation was the supreme Legislative Council, while social legislation was designed by the Local Councils. All these Councils had a controlling head in the India Office Council in London. The question was: "Could any legislation ever do its work satisfactorily where the opinions, feelings, and thoughts of the people paying the taxes were not freely represented?"

Dadabhai then asked: "Could the Services be efficient without a proper proportion of Indians in all grades ? Could the English officials, no matter how clever, manage Indians as well as Indians of the same standing, ability, and integrity?" The question had also to be considered in the light of the financial implications involved. The mere fact that all the earnings of the Indian officials remained in the country was in itself a financial advantage to the country.

Finally, as regards principles of design and execution, the questions for consideration were: (i) whether the burden of taxation was equally distributed over the shoulders of all classes of people; and (ii) whether the expenditure was not capable of being largely curtailed without impairing the efficiency or strength of British rule. For a solution of these questions it was necessary that the Committee should examine the principle and necessity of each item of receipt and expenditure. For instance, in dealing with the land revenue, the principles on which the rates of assessment were based should be examined. Were the principles sound? If so, were the rates such as to encourage increase of cultivation, to lead to increase in capital, and there by to increase in production and prosperity?

"Was the burden of taxation on the cultivator equitable, compared with the burden borne by other classes ?" Government claimed the rights of a landlord; did that mean that Government must have a certain portion of the produce, "even though the exactions were inequitably higher than those from other classes of people?" Or, was the Government demand upon land to be adjusted on the principle that land should contribute its equitable quota with all other industries towards the revenue required for state purposes ? Because richer interests could resort to agitation and make themselves heard, should the poor labourer and cultivator, who could not, be squeezed more than the agitators?

Was the machinery for the collection of the land revenue economical? Whilst instituting a comparison between the burden of taxation in India and that in other countries, Lord Mayo came to the conclusion that the burden was not "crushing." What idea His Lordship attached to the word "crushing," Dadabhai could not say, but he observed:

His Lordship seems to forget the very first premiss that the total production of the country is admitted to be 403. per head ... so that living from hand to mouth, and that on "scanty subsistence" (in the words of Lord Lawrence) the very touch of famine carries away hundreds of thousands. Is not this in itself as "crushing" to any people as it can possibly be? And yet out of this wretched income they have to pay taxation as well.

Then he introduced his drain theory. Whatever revenue is raised by the other countries, for instance, the £70,000,000 by England, the whole of it returns back to the people and remains in the country; and therefore the national capital, upon which the production of a country depends, does not suffer diminution; while, on account of India being subject to a foreign rule, out of £50,000,000, of revenue raised every year, some £12,000,000 or more are carried away to England, and the national capital—or, in other words, its capability of production—is continually diminished year after year.

The method adopted by Lord Mayo, continued Dadabhai, was not the "fairest way" of comparing the taxation of one country with that of another. One should ascertain "the proportion of the amount which the Government of the country took for the purposes of administration." If that test were applied, the result would show that England raised £70,000,000 out of the national income of about £100,000,000—that is, about 8 per cent, or about £2 10s. per head, from an income of about £30 per head; whereas the Government of India raised £50,000,000 out of a national income of £300,000,000—that is, about 16 per cent, or 6s. 8d. per head, out of an income of 405. per head.

Without the data concerning the population and national income of the countries mentioned by Lord Mayo, Dadabhai could not say from what income per head they met their burden of taxation; he could, therefore, only make the general observation that while a ton might not be a burden to an elephant, a few pounds might crush a child. The capacity to bear a burden was not to be measured by the percentage of taxation, but by the abundance, or otherwise, of the means of income to pay it from.

Though an expert at figures, Dadabhai was yet a novice in matters concerning the procedure of parliamentary committees.

When, therefore, he appeared as a witness before the Select Committee, together with Naoroji Furdoonji, on behalf of the East India Association, he could not carry the Committee with him on the first day of the evidence. It is best, however, that he should relate the story himself. Speaking at a meeting, held in Bombay on September 21, 1885, to consider the question of raising a memorial to Professor Fawcett, he gave his personal reminiscence of that incident:

When I appeared before the Finance Committee in England in 1873, I had perhaps die rashness of writing a letter beforehand of what I wanted to give my evidence upon. What I said there, somehow or other, did not suit Mr. Ayrton, the Chairman of the Committee, and he hindered and hampered me in every way.

Before I went to the Committee I saw Mr. Fawcett, who was always sympathising with us, and I laid before him the notes which I wanted to submit to the Committee. He considered them very carefully and told me that that was the very thing that ought to be brought to the Committee. But, strange to say, when I went before the Committee Mr. Ayrton chose to decide that that was just the tiling that was not to be brought before the Committee.

On the first day I was hardly able to give evidence of what I wanted to say. But the next day, when it came to Mr. Fawcett's turn to examine me, in a series of judicious and pointed questions, he brought out all that I had to say in a brief and clear manner.

The report of the Select Committee was eagerly awaited, but the sudden dissolution of Parliament, early in 1874, owing to the defeat of the Government on the long-disputed question of higher education in Ireland, led to the Committee's extinction.

It had not even completed the enquiry. Meanwhile, finding the country sinking under chronic deficit, Lord Mayo, as Viceroy, strove strenuously for financial solvency. Mainly by decentralisation on a provincial basis, subject to central control, he succeeded in leaving a firmly established surplus. It was, however, merely the first step along the path of financial reform. Dadabhai had yet to write many a minute, ask for many an enquiry, and himself sit on a Royal Commission, not only to examine the real wants of the people of India, but also to suggest an equitable adjustment of relations between India and Britain.

Calcutta Congress

The time for the twenty-second session of the Congress was drawing near. It was an occasion for stock-taking. With the coming of age of the national political organisation of the country, had India obtained her birthright ? If not, did not the "mendicant policy" of the elders stand condemned as barren?

That, at any rate, was the opinion of young India. A conflict, therefore, arose over the question of the ideals and methods of work of the Congress. Young India demanded a proper Constitution and a vitalising programme for the Congress—a reconstitution of the political life of the country. The "old-world politicians," who had been carrying on the Congress work in their own way for twenty years, paid no heed to this demand.

It was, however, not a mere emotional conflict; nor was it a personal conflict for ascendency; it was essentially an intellectual conflict, a conflict of ideology. Self-government under British paramountcy was the goal of the old school; the ideal of the new school was national autonomy, freedom from all foreign control.

This antithesis between the viewpoints of the two sections showed a revolutionary change in the mind of the people. Indeed, for the rulers, it marked a dangerous phase in the political education of the country, and it caused no little concern among official circles and the European community generally. For a long period the British and the Anglo-Indian Press had affected supreme unconcern about the manifestations of political unrest in India, but they could not now ignore the striking change that had come over the country. The ranks of the national party had been reinforced by discontented youths as to whose temper there could be little doubt. The fulminations of the Congress, though provoking, had been practically harmless. Despite twenty-one years of hard and apparently vain patriotic toil, its leaders and members as a class had amazingly adhered to its fundamental principles of loyalty and constitutional methods. In that sort of agitation there was no menace to British supremacy.

But the young rebels were determined to give a blow to that supremacy.

There was, however, no desire as yet, except among a handful of revolutionaries, to appeal to force. That would have been suicidal. There was, however, such a weapon as boycott to which, thought the young enthusiasts, they could safely resort boycott of British goods and, if need be, of the Councils. They believed they could, without going beyond the law and the Constitution, bring the authorities to their knees by refusing to associate with Government and by withholding from it all voluntary and honorary service; and they defied any one to say that their ideal was not legitimate or that their method was not constitutional.

Such was the conflict between the two sections—the moderates and the extremists, as they were called, during the year 1906.

The question which then agitated them most was, who should be the President of the Congress for that year ? The elders were in danger of being swamped by the Bengal delegates, a large majority of whom and the extremists favoured the selection of Bal Gangadhar Tilak, who had suffered imprisonment in his fight for freedom. The Bengal leaders, Surendranath Banerjee and Bhupendranath Basu, however, forestalled the Tilakites by asking Dadabhai by cable whether in the event of his being elected as President, he would accept the office. They were confident that even the most rabid extremist would not think of opposing the nomination of one whose life had been given wholly to the country, who had stirred the hearts of his countrymen for two generations, who had the knack of bringing together conflicting forces and making them operate towards one end, whose word carried unequalled authority, and who was revered throughout the land. The weather-beaten pilot, over whose head the storms of no less than eighty-one years had swept, did not for a moment pause to consider the hardships of the voyage, the danger to his health, or of the much greater risk of offending one party or the other, or both, and damaging his reputation as the Nestor of Indian politics. He was loved and revered as the Grand Old Man of India, but he had not yet ceased to be the ideal young man of India. With the ardour and optimism of youth, he promptly replied that he would accept the office.

The Tilakites saw that they were outwitted; whilst acquiescing in the selection, they condemned the action of the two leaders as unconstitutional. They, however, justified their action on the ground that the Congress had not laid down any definite procedure for the election of President and that there were precedents in favour of the procedure followed by them. Be that as it may, their action was ratified by a formal resolution passed unanimously by the Reception Committee.

Even from the point of view of the extremists, no more felicitous selection could have been made. Not merely because in Dadabhai the Congress had secured a President of ripe experience, possessing sweetness of temper and infinite patience and tact, but also because he occupied a position much nearer the advanced wing of the Congress than any one of the moderate party. He was neither a moderate nor an extremist, he had never hesitated to speak freely in the language of his heart and he was not the man to lower the standard with a view to placating one side or the other.

After the repressive regime of Lord Curzon, his words invariably breathed fire. He had already asserted and could assert over again what the extremists had been urging with double the force and effect with which any one of them could have done. True, he was one of those who still believed in a constitutional struggle for progressive expansion of political freedom and whose ambition stopped short at placing India on a level with the self-governing colonies. But he was no longer the same submissive supplicant that he was in his earlier years, praying for justice before the bar of British public opinion.

We have already noticed the tone of his latest speeches and letters. Let us recall one or two more utterances. Speaking at the Newington Reform Club, Walworth, he said:

One of the arguments put forward in defence of the system was that the British prevented the different peoples of India from plundering each other. That was only a half truth; the whole truth was that they prevented the different peoples from plundering each other in order that they themselves might plunder all.

Then they were told that the British had introduced security of property, but only in order that they might carry it away with perfect security. As to the security of life, it was said that the old mental despots used to kill thousands and thousands, and harass the people. If that was so, the British Government, with great ingenuity and scientific precision, was killing millions by famines and plagues, and starving scores of millions. . . . The Anglo-Indians, or the British, were like clever surgeons who, with the sharpest scalpels, cut to the very heart, and drew every drop of blood without leaving a scar.

Again, in a letter to the Daily News, dated April 21, 1905, he asked an English correspondent the following question:

Suppose, by some mischance England came under French or German or some alien despotic government, in the same condition and under the same circumstances as India is at present, will he not, as an Englishman, do his utmost to throw off "the heaviest of all yokes," the yoke of the stranger, even though all Englishmen were full of all the faults which the Anglo-Indians, rightly or wrongly, ascribe to the Indians? Will he not as an Englishman at once tell me, "Corrupt or not corrupt, faults or no faults, a Briton shall never be a slave" ? And yet he coolly justifies and assumes the right divine of making other people slaves!

An Urge for Self-government

In the course of several speeches Dadabhai had urged, for more than three years, that no palliatives for the "draining and bleeding" could do any good and that the only remedy was self-government which alone could bring prosperity to any country.

Once more in his message to Gokhale, on the eve of the 1905 Congress, he had summed up his demands in these words:

We require, on the one hand, to inspire the people of India at large with the desire of attaining and enjoying their birth and pledged rights and the absolute necessity of freedom and self-government like that of the colonies for their material and moral development, progress and prosperity. . . . No palliatives of any kind whatever, no mere alteration and tinkering of the mechanical machinery of administration can or will do any good at all. ...

Self-government is the only remedy for India's woes and wrongs. For this purpose, we must strengthen the Congress, to go on making every possible effort to accomplish this end, which is quite practicable.

If Dadabhai had gone so far in 1905, the extremists might well have entertained the hope that he might go a step further in 1906.

All opposition to his election as President was withdrawn. Those who were canvassing for Tilak (wrote Surendranath Banerjee to Dadabhai on October 25, just before his formal election) have given us the assurance that they will unanimously join in electing you as President and have authorised me to communicate the fact to you. Reuter has wired out to this country that you have booked your passage provisionally for the 30th November. You have saved us from a great crisis.

Simultaneously with the official invitation, Dadabhai received a letter of welcome from Motilal Ghose—rather tear-stained, for with the note of welcome was blended a wail concerning the woes of Bengal:

So you are coming (he wrote). You are welcome, thrice welcome. You are aware that a change has come over the people.

The Congress as it is, cannot satisfy them. The method must be changed and you yourself latterly acknowledged it in many of your speeches. . . . The Indian people want a practical scheme from you, so that the Congress programme may be an all-year-round affair and keep the entire nation interested in it. Now it is an organisation of the upper five, the lower millions knowing nothing and caring nothing for it. Some such direction should, therefore, be given to it as to make it really a national thing and an object of attraction to the highest and the lowest.

Ghose then gave a recital of the arbitrary acts of Government and related in what an excited state of mind the people of Bengal were at the moment. He also pointed out how sharp the deplorable cleavage between the two factions was. It required considerable courage to step into the breach; the chances of reconciliation were remote, but Dadabhai had already agreed to enter the arena of the strife in obedience to the imperative call of his countrymen. He definitely arranged to leave London on November 29.

A complimentary breakfast meeting of friends of India was held at the Westminster Palace Hotel on November 20 to bid him Godspeed Addressing the gathering, Wedderburn, who presided, observed:

> The repression and reaction of the last twenty years has undoubtedly driven many to despair and, deeming constitutional agitation a failure, some think passive resistance was the only available policy. India thus stands at the parting of the ways and, by universal consent, Mr. Naoroji is the man born to set things right. He goes out as a perfectly free hand and not as the leader of any party.

Speaking as a friend of fifty years' standing, Samuel Smith added:

> A more single-minded man was never born, and though I did not quite agree with Mr. Naoroji on all points, we have learnt to respect each other, each believing that the other was doing his best for the cause. Mr. Naoroji would go out as a peacemaker in somewhat anxious and troubled times, which were causing much concern to those who were friends of India. The people of this country were earnestly desirous for the well-being of their Eastern Empire. If mistakes were made, it was not with their consent or knowledge. There was a period some years since when a bastard Imperialism prevailed in this country—a period of reaction. But now we have passed from that. ... If our Indian friends would only exercise a little patience, they will find one reform after another come easily and naturally. The seed has been sown. The fruit is ripening and will soon be garnered and I hope that our guest will live to partake of some of it.

The Honourable Mr. Justice B. J. Wadia, who was then in London as a law student, gave a charming etymological epigram of Dadabhai's name. His very name, he said, carried with it the attributes of a great patriot: Dada (father) of all India by universal consent, and Bhai (brother) of those who suffer and live under suffering, the first of India's sons working for the Naoroz (New Day) of India's liberty and emancipation. This epigram might perhaps have gained in brilliance if, taking cognizance of the *suffix ji* (Lord), the speaker had designated Dadabhai as the Lord of the New Day (Naoroz) of ampler life.

In a brief reply, Dadabhai hailed the activity which had produced differences of opinion in India. It spoke of life. During the first fortnight of December, the whole of India was following in thought the progress across the seas of the P. and O. Company's steamship Arcadia, which was carrying on board the President-elect of the Congress. He landed in Bombay on December 14, where he received a markedly demonstrative welcome. In Calcutta, too, there was a personal warmth and spontaneity in the demonstration of people's love and reverence for him, recalling the scenes during his triumphal march in 1893.

The Calcutta Congress was the largest political gathering witnessed in India. The address of welcome delivered by Dr. Rash Behari Ghose was typical of the views of the advanced section of Congressmen. He stoutly defended Swadeshi and Boycott and reminded the audience that the wounds of partition were still as sore as ever.

The keynote of Dadabhai's address was Swaraj. He had been claiming it for some years past and others, notably Tilak, were reinforcing the demand, as the only solution for the ills of India, but this was the first occasion when the demand was made from the Congress platform, and it thrilled the audience and the whole country from end to end. It was the first session of the Congress after its coming of age, and it was time, said Dadabhai, that they should carefully consider what the position of Indians then was and what their future should be. He did not intend to repeat his lamentations over the past. He would look only to the future.

What position did the Indians hold in the British Empire? Were they British citizens or not? The moment Indians came under die British flag, they became free British citizens and their rights as such were beyond question. They had every reason to claim all British rights as their birthright and also as rights solemnly pledged to them. Just as the administration of the United Kingdom in all services, departments and details was in the hands of the people of that country, so should it be in India, As in the United Kingdom and the Colonies all taxation and legislation and all power of spending the taxes were in the hands of the representatives of the people, so should it be in India, and the financial relations between England and India must be adjusted on a footing of equality.

We do not ask any favours (he added). We want only justice. Instead of going into any further divisions or details of our rights as British citizens, the whole matter can be comprised in one word—"Self-government," or Swaraj, like that of the United Kingdom or the Colonies.

The next important question was whether it was practicable to grant Indians the rights of self-government at once and, if not, when and in what way. The whole machinery of Indian government could not certainly be broken up and the system of self-government introduced all at once. The time had, however, arrived for the transfer to begin.

The peasants of Russia are fit for and obtained the Duma from the greatest autocrat in the world, and the leading statesman, the Prime Minister of the free British Empire (Campbell-Bannerman), proclaimed to the world, "die Duma is dead, long live the Duma!" Surely, the fellow-citizens of that Empire, by birth- right and pledged rights, are far more entitled to self-government, a constitutional representative system, than the peasants of Russia.

I do not despair. It is futile to tell me that we must wait till all the people are ready. The British people did not so wait for their Parliament.

Dadabhai then proceeded to deal with the most crucial question regarding methods:

I have been, for some time past, repeatedly asked (he said) whether I really have, after more than half a century of my own personal experience, such confidence in the honour and good faith of British statesmen and Government as to expect that our just claim to self-government as British citizens will be willingly and gracefully accorded to us with every honest effort in their power, leaving alone and forgetting the past.

Proceeding to give a full and free answer to this question, he related how his faith in British justice had sustained him for so many years, but how, owing to the non-fulfilment of solemn pledges, a change had taken place in the mind of the educated:

Since my early efforts I must say that I have felt so many disappointments as would be sufficient to break any heart and lead one to despair and even, I am afraid, to rebel. . . . But I have not despaired.... You may think it strange. I stand before you with hopefulness. I have not despaired for one reason and I am hopeful for another reason. I have not despaired under the influence of the good English word, which has been the rule of my life. That word is "persevere." ... As we proceed, we may adopt such means as may be suitable at every stage, but persevere we must to the end. Now the reason of my hopefulness after all my disappointments. And this also under the influence of one word "Revival"—the present revival of the true old spirit and instinct of liberty and free British institutions in the hearts of the leading statesmen of the day. . . . Within the short life that may be yet vouchsafed to me, I hope to see a loyal, honest, honourable, and conscientious adoption of the policy of self-government for India—and a beginning made at once towards that end.

Turning then to the burning questions of the day, Dadabhai condemned the Bengal partition as a "bad blunder for England." He hoped it would yet be rectified. Swadeshi was not a new thing. It had existed in Bombay for many years past. "I am a free trader," he added. "I am a member, and in the Executive Committee of the Cobden Club for twenty years, and yet I say that Swadeshi is a forced necessity for India in its unnatural economic muddle. As long as the economic condition remains unnatural and impoverishing . . . the talk of applying economic laws to the condition of India is adding insult to injury."

Then followed a fervent appeal for a thorough political union among people of all creeds and classes. I do not know what good fortune may be in store for me during the short period that may be left to me, and if I can leave a word of affection and devotion for my country and countrymen, I say: Be united, persevere, and achieve self-government so that the millions now perishing by poverty, famine, and plague, and the scores of millions that are starving on scanty subsistence may be saved, and India may once more occupy her proud position of yore among the greatest and civilized nations of the world.

It was meant to be, and was really, a conciliatory speech. There was not a word in it which was in any sense inflammatory.

Strongly controversial topics such as the question of Swadeshi were disposed of in a few sentences; the boycott was not even mentioned. For once, the usual language of the heart was not there.

The air was, therefore, loud with debate as to where Dadabhai stood and how far he would allow, the advanced party to proceed. That party had by no means got what it wanted. There was scarcely anything in the address to bridge the gulf between the two parties. Instead of recommending any change in methods and tactics, the President had once more adjured his countrymen to put their faith in the British people's sense of justice and fair play, and to tread the same old path which, it seemed, led nowhere.

He had held out hopes resting on the revival of Liberalism in England, whereas India had despaired of obtaining justice even at die hands of the Liberal Party. On the other hand, the moderates were pleased. The demand for Swaraj under British paramountcy, tempered with advice to persevere in the same old path of constitutional agitation, vindicated the attitude taken up by the members of the old school. The Bengali hailed the Presidential address as the political gospel of the new era, while Bande Mataram shed tears at "the great refusal."

What about the Anglo-Indian journals ? So far as the extremists were given a cold shoulder, they were pleased; but the unequivocal demand for Swaraj introduced a new element in the political struggle, which spelt disaster for the European community. The Presidential address was, therefore, condemned as a surrender to the extremists. In echoing the indignant outburst of that community, one of the journals observed that the contention that the inhabitants of India were entitled to all the political rights, privileges, and franchises which the inhabitants of England enjoyed had no more root in history or in law than it had in common sense. "We have won India by the sword," it added, "and it is well for the small and highly educated classes, which are alone represented at the Congress, that the British sword stands between them and their native enemies. That is the fundamental fact in the whole situation which makes all claims for full self-government in India absurd."

But for the moral to be drawn from it, it would not have been now necessary to refer to the levity with which such a problem of far-reaching significance to the British Empire was discussed by the Anglo-Indian Press at that time. Before the representative element was introduced in the municipal bodies and legislative councils, journals of this type had simply refused to believe that representative institutions could ever flourish in India. In 1852 the demand for such institutions was likened to an attempt to assimilate the natural productions of the two hemispheres. When, to their dismay, such institutions were established and the people proved their' capability to run them efficiently and asked for self-government, even Anglo-Indian papers of high standing ridiculed the demand. Within ten years, however, responsible government had to be proclaimed by the Secretary of State for India as the goal of British policy.

Thereafter, when India demanded "Dominion Status," once more the critics ejaculated "impossible," forgetting that the world moves. Soon afterwards, when a section of the people expressed its determination to strive for and die for Independence, some of those journals came forward with the assurance that Dominion status was implicit in all the declarations made since the year 1917 and that the question was only one of ways and means and stages. Dadabhai, who was charged with talking nonsense, pernicious nonsense, at the Calcutta Congress, had asked for nothing more.

There were violent scenes at the Subjects Committee meeting over the refusal to submit resolutions for extending boycott all over India. Some of the extremists left the meeting, headed by Bipin Chandra Pal and Khaparde. There was, for a while, jubilation in the anti-Congress camp, but those who welcomed the split were amazed to find a display of unanimity at the Congress session. There was heated discussion, no doubt, on the resolution moved by Ambica Charan Mazumdar, seconded by Pal, that the boycott movement, inaugurated in Bengal, by way of protest against the partition of that Province, "was, and is, legitimate." The extremists put their own interpretation on the resolution, claiming that it applied to the whole country, and the moderates interpreted it as confined to Bengal only.

A united front had, however, to be presented. Tilak had the patriotism and the statesmanship to realise it. Despite his disappointment, he struck a refreshing note of unity. Supporting the Swadeshi resolution, he said he was glad that they had arrived at a satisfactory solution, because their Anglo-Indian friends had predicted that the twenty-second Congress would meet with premature death immediately after the attainment of the age of majority. The prediction, however, had been falsified under the able, impartial, and judicious guidance of the veteran leader in the Chair. All differences, continued Tilak, had been squared; both parties had approached the question in a spirit of conciliation and met halfway.

On the closing day of the Congress, Surendranath Banerjee presented to Dadabhai, on behalf of Mr. Kambli, of Puna, a Swadeshi umbrella. Everything in connection with it, he said, was Swadeshi, with the exception of the wire. He expressed the hope that under the home-made umbrella all India might stand united. Dadabhai remarked:

> The labours of the past fifty years have not been in vain. If Congress has had no other result, it has placed before us the "clear star," as Sir Campbell-Bannerman would say, of self-government. I regard it as the best result of the political work during the past fifty years that we have now decided upon a goal.

Return to Home

Split in the Congress camp was for the time being healed, the Congress session was brought to a peaceful termination. It was the general opinion that the difficult mission, courageously undertaken by Dadabhai, had been creditably accomplished. With that satisfaction he returned to London, on February 8, to continue his fight for freedom, but the strain had been too great for a frame enfeebled by the wear and tear of more than fifty years of strenuous public life. He was no longer the same young man at eighty-one that he was before he had embarked on that mission. He then looked such a picture of health that hopes were running high that he would live to be a centenarian. An echo of these hopes was heard in the following stanzas which appeared in India:

> A harvest full, its seed long sown
> Be yours ere life be done!
> Hopes never proved vain that steadfast hold
> At fourscore years and one.
>
> In heart and mind unchanged, the past
> Life's full allotted span,
> We wish an honoured century
> For India's Grand Old Man!
>
> BIG BEN

> "I am in the best of health," was Dadabhai's reply to a question put to him by a representative of the Tribune who had called on him on his birthday on September 4, 1906. "I am a little uncomfortable at having to wear a Russel-cord coat when I would prefer a muslin jacket, with a shirt of the same material. Otherwise I should love this heat, which is reminiscent of my own country."

To what do you attribute your good condition? (asked the journalist).

To lifelong abstinence (said Dadabhai), to avoiding tobacco, to eschewing spices and condiments and to working hard. I breakfast at 8.30. Then I write at home until it is time to go to the office. From n until 7.45 I labour there, after which I dine.

I walk for about an hour and then continue my work until midnight. My correspondence with India is enormous.

That youthful vigour and energy had gone—gone never to return again. Soon after his arrival in London he was prostrated by an attack of bronchitis, which caused great anxiety to his friends. His granddaughters Gosi (afterwards Mrs. Maneck Captain) and Nargiz (afterwards Mrs. Dorab Captain), who were in England, ran up to London to look after him. There was a slight recovery in the first week of March; on April 26 India announced the cheering news that the patient had greatly improved in health. A change at Bexhill-on-Sea led to further improvement. His medical advisers were, however, of opinion, and it was also the wish of his British friends, that he should retire from public life and spend his last days in his motherland, for the good of which he had spent the best strength of his life, there to be supported by the tenderness and care of his dear ones and cheered by the love and blessings of his countrymen.

And it is in India you should die (wrote Birdwood). That will give the necessary dramatic unity to your life, that dramatic emphasis to your life's work—that returning to die, and dying in your motherland—in the arms of your Earth Mother—that set the seal to your service, devotion, and inflexible loyalty to India.

Dadabhai, however, felt that his work for his country had not yet been completed. He had just launched a fresh crusade for obtaining self-government, and he was loath to leave his place in the fighting line before a single decisive battle had been won.

The advice of friends was reinforced by an appeal from home. It was a letter from Homi Dadina (July 20), in which he said:

Judging from what you write—this last Indian visit of yours has completely shattered your health—and it is only fair that you should give yourself complete rest for a long time. We are informed on all hands that your medical adviser is also of the same opinion, and though he has pressed you very much to retire for good, you decline to do so. Dr. E. Treasurywalla is about to return soon to India—cannot you see your way to bid goodbye to England and come and settle down to enjoy a little quiet rest in this town of your birth ? You have served your country and rulers nobly, and this country can well afford to give you a little holiday. In fact the public think that your advice and counsel would be more beneficial to them here in this crisis through which the country generally is passing.

In August there was a setback. Indian astrologers were busy studying the horoscope of the sage, who appeared to have had one foot in the grave. One of them gave him a further lease of life for seven years. Fram Dadina duly conveyed the forecast to

Dadabhai. Soon afterwards, there was a marked improvement in his health. The astrologer was right, but he was to prove wrong at the end of the seventh year when Dadabhai seemed to be good for at least seven years more.

It was arranged, when the patient seemed fit to undertake the long journey to India, that he should leave London towards the end of September. The members of the London Indian Society met at the Holborn Restaurant to give a sendoff to their retiring general. Indians of all creeds and English friends of all shades of political thought attended the reception, but Dadabhai was not well enough to be present. The departure from London was postponed.

Dadabhai was removed to a nursing home in South Norwood. Here he gradually gained strength and was bearing up as well as he could for the long journey. The strong willpower, serene disposition, and buoyant spirit, which had sustained him in all his struggles, displayed themselves at their best during this illness. On October 11, the day fixed for commencing the journey, the weather-gods were exceptionally propitious.

Whereas during the preceding days the weather had been stormy, chilly and changeable, on the day of departure the sun shone brightly with the warmth of a mid-September day. Dadabhai was taken in an easy running motor car to Tilbury, and transferred to his berth in the S.S. Moldavia under the care of Dr. Treasurywalla and a trained nurse. The members of the London Indian Society had assembled there to present to him a farewell address. Although Dadabhai had stood the fatigue well, it would have been an ordeal for him to receive and reply to the address.

It was, therefore, received by his grandson, Jal Naoroji, on his behalf. Although Dadabhai was leaving England for good, the members of the Society wished that he should continue to be its President. Dadabhai would not consent. They then asked him to allow his name to be associated with the Society as Honorary President. Dadabhai agreed, but not without hesitation. He had seen young Indians in England drawn into something like a spirit of revolt. He had met in Calcutta several ardent young exponents of the gospel of violence. They looked upon outrages as the only effective weapon of political protest. Dadabhai feared that that gospel would spread throughout India and that it would also captivate the Indians resident in England. It was quite possible that youths stirred by the new doctrines, subversive of the policy of non-violence he had always advocated, would capture the Society.

He unburdened his mind to his successor, Mr. J. M. Parikh, and told him that the moment the Society countenanced violence, his name should be removed from its roll. "My honour," said he, "is in your hands."

With these parting words quietly disappeared from English public life the illustrious Indian who had spent himself in his country's service. During half a century he had incessantly grappled with hard facts and figures concerning the woeful condition of his country and presented them to the British public, as none before him had done, and had done everything possible to bring England and India together. A glowing tribute paid to him by Wedderburn on the occasion was accorded a prominent place in the Daily Neivs of October 17:

Last Friday, at the age of eighty-three, Mr. Dadabhai Naoroji said goodbye to England for the last time, and sailed for India.

The sands of life running very low, his heart worn out with many wars and eyes grown dim with gazing on the pilot stars.

What his feelings now may be I know not, but for half a century he has kept alive among Indians the belief that in the end England will be true to her own best traditions; that she will make of India a trusted partner, instead of a bond slave, . .. Like Edmund Burke, he has never lost faith in the "ancient and inbred integrity" of the British people.

Birdwood also took the opportunity to give expression to his admiration of the work accomplished by Dadabhai, in a letter which he wrote to the London correspondent of The Times of India:

Dadabhai Naoroji is a man in whom mind has the complete mastery of matter and who, it might be said, cannot be killed until he no longer desires to live. ... In all my visits to him he has shown no thought of himself; all his thoughts, with all their clearness, insight and interests and play of dialectics and fancy, have been on his life's work, which seems ever before him, as not knowing a past or a future, but only an abiding present. And so, sitting and talking with him, one feels of him that even in the article of death, it would not be the death of what was really and truly Dadabhai Naoroji, but translation—a quick shift to immortal conditions.

After a fairly comfortable voyage, Dadabhai reached Aden on November 8, where he had a conversation with the leading citizens of Aden who were delighted to find him much better than they had expected. His health, however, seemed to give way during the voyage from Aden to Bombay: all demonstrations to greet him at the Apollo Bunder had, therefore, to be abandoned, and he was taken quietly from the docks to his residence at Versova. Here he was taken charge of by his granddaughter Meherbanoo, under whose loving care and skilful treatment he regained his health and strength within a very short time. She was relieved subsequently by Dadabhai's daughter, Manekbai, who gave up her medical appointment in Jamnagar to be near her father.

The first greeting Dadabhai received, as soon as the steamer entered the Bombay harbour, was from the Governor of Bombay, Sir George Clarke (afterwards Lord Sydenham). It cheered him up. During the second week of January the people of India heard with great satisfaction that Dadabhai had completely recovered from his illness. With the return of bodily strength his mind became active and alert as before. He did a lot of reading throughout the day, insisted on attending personally to all correspondence and pored over newspapers for hours together to keep himself acquainted with what was happening in the world generally and in India particularly.

The eighty-fourth year of the Grand Old Man was an occasion for special thanksgiving. The veteran who had passed through a critical illness had been spared to spend the closing years of his life in his native land, surrounded by members of his family and friends. He was in excellent health, was receiving visitors in the afternoon, going out for a drive every evening and enjoying reading books and newspapers and writing letters to his friends in India and England. "Dadabhai Day" was, therefore, celebrated with more than usual enthusiasm all over India. On this occasion also, the first to send him his greetings was Sir George Clarke. "I hope," said he, "you will be spared to see the passing of some of the clouds which darken the Indian sky and threaten the peaceful progress of the people." Dadabhai in return expressed his belief that the clouds would disperse and that a change for the better would take place if the necessary reforms were undertaken in time, restoring that faith in British justice which he always had and which he prayed India might "always have good cause to cherish."

"My correspondence is enormous," said Dadabhai when interviewed in England by a representative of the Press. It was scarcely less cyclopean when he was supposed to have retired from active life. While he was in England, he had to carry on ponderous correspondence concerning his varied activities, on behalf of his country, with various individuals and political and social organisations in the United Kingdom and India. None can read the immense mass of letters and memoranda which he wrote personally without being astounded at the energy and agility it attests. Besides the daily political and business letters, every week he received from his daughters, grandchildren, and sons-in-law, scattered over different places in India and England, their weekly budgets of news concerning their studies, or other avocations, their needs and their amusements, their hopes and aspirations, accompanied, in the case of the grown-up children, with statements of accounts, and he replied to them regularly, expressing his joy or concern regarding the progress made by each or other incidents in their lives. In addition, he carried on a lengthy correspondence with the teachers of his grandchildren from whom, too, he received periodical returns and reports giving in detail the progress made by their pupils in different subjects. Such domestic correspondence was, however, nothing compared with the miscellaneous correspondence entailed by enquiries and appeals, congratulations and greetings, coming from individuals and institutions from the four corners of the world. So long as the poor and the improvident are with us, so long as there is unemployment among people who are willing to work, so long will people in public life, particularly the soft-hearted, be flooded with piteous appeals for pecuniary help or work. Of these Dadabhai had, probably, the largest share, considering the unique position he occupied as the unofficial ambassador of India in England and considering the reputation he had for service and self-sacrifice. Young men desiring to go to Europe from India or Africa for study or business, students stranded in England or other parts of Europe, parents of young men who after or before completing their studies were in no mood to return home, Indian women deserted by Indian husbands, European women who had married good-for-nothing Asiatics, fathers and mothers horrified at the news of conversion of their sons to Christianity, all sought his help. Similarly, Englishmen and Englishwomen in distress, or interested in welfare work, approached him almost daily for help.

Dadabhai had made it a point to acknowledge all communications, and he complied with as many appeals as he could. Even if he could not render any assistance, he would put in a word of sympathy. Prisoners sentenced to death, or imprisonment, on charges of arson or murder or cheating, dismissed employees, ill-treated workmen, hard-worked postmen, dissatisfied contractors, duped business men, European and Indian, all appealed to Dadabhai for redress. The petitions of several of them were presented by him, or through his good offices by others, to the Home Department, or to the Colonial Office, and even questions were asked on their behalf in the House of Commons. Each case entailed wearisome correspondence, but Dadabhai never grudged the time, trouble and expense involved. Among such cases there was one concerning a man in Teheran, who complained that he had been wrongfully dismissed from the telegraph service and asked Dadabhai to approach, on his behalf, John Morley or Edward Grey for justice!

Any request, emanating from any quarter, concerning the higher education or industrial training of Indian youths, or the political education of old or young, was welcome to Dadabhai.

Knowing his willingness and readiness to help in such cases, people demanded all sorts of information and assistance from him. One student asked for particulars concerning available posts in banks; the father of another informed Dadabhai that "the nuptial ceremonies in connection with the second marriage" of his son had just been consummated at Ahmedabad, and he wished to know the way in which assistant engineers were recruited for service. There was, however, nothing frivolous about most of the requisitions. They satisfied the patriotic impulse of the man to whom they were addressed. For instance, the Government of Travancore sent two graduates for Associateship in Geology and Mining, and asked Dadabhai to help them and to keep an eye on them. Indians in South Africa and Indian students in Japan asked for Congress literature and other particulars. There was a constant flow of appeals for "some clement showers of generosity and benevolence," most of which he was obliged to turn down, but not infrequently young Indians succeeded in borrowing from him small loans which were advanced with practically no hope of recovery.

The following amusing illustration of Dadabhai's innate good nature to rush to the succour of anyone in trouble, deserving or undeserving, was given to the writer by C. M. Cursetji.

A Parsi doctor who had made something of a name in Bombay proceeded to London with his wife and children to practise there. He took a fine house in a fashionable locality, kept a smart brougham, liveried servants, and looked forward to lucrative business. But within no long period of time, living much beyond his means, he soon found himself in deep waters. Decreed debts, default and claims followed, till, one day, court bailiffs got into the house. He made a pressing appeal to Dadabhai, who promptly arrived, looked into the trouble, settled and paid up the debts and so rescued the worthy doctor, who was, of course, profuse in thanks and promises, and by way of showing his gratitude finished up by inviting Dadabhai for the next day and treating him to a sumptuous lunch!

Till the end of his life the pressure of daily correspondence was considerable. An undergraduate from Agra College, a son of a rich zamindar, but a victim of a stepmother's wiles, wrote to him: "A sum of Rs. 300 will easily enable me to pass my B.A. Half of the above sum I can easily manage by selling my mare, which was given to me on my marriage, but for the remaining half I must depend upon you"

Another, who described himself as "a native of Bombay, who has received a liberal education and is acquainted with the theory of carriage-building,' wished to be enlightened on several points regarding facilities in London or any province in India to learn the trade. A journalist in Mirzapur wanted answers to more than fifty queries regarding the balances kept by Government in England and India, the creation of a Central Bank in India, the reasons for and against its establishment, the conditions under which it should operate, the methods of meeting capital expenditure, the sale of Council bills, the exchange value of the rupee and level of prices, gold standard reserve, paper currency reserve, purchases of silver, hoarding, and "financial organisation and procedure generally." To all such communications, replies, however brief, were sent, and they were mostly in Dadabhai's hand. Authors sent him their books soliciting his opinion, editors of journals asked for articles, and not a few individuals wrote long letters merely to air their views on current political and economic problems. To one such dilettante from North Kanara Dadabhai had to write (December 13, 1913):

> As in the present state of my age and condition of health I am not able to devote much attention to public questions, you need not trouble yourself to write to me about diem, especially in matters of details of existing administration.

Several people who sent him letters of congratulation on his birthday from different parts of India, China, Japan, Africa, and England, also appeared to have given little thought to his advanced age. They wrote sheets and sheets about themselves or public affairs. Till the last moment, however, until disabled, Dadabhai attended to all such correspondence personally, as may be gathered from the office copies of replies left behind in his own steady, unweary hand.

Not a small portion of his correspondence was, however, of his own seeking. After a few months' rest, the recluse of Versova had plunged once more into the whirlpool of politics. Those were stirring days. Things were moving rapidly. With the change for the worse in the attitude of the Indian mind towards British rule, the attitude of the British mind appeared to be undergoing a change for the better towards the people of India. Undeterred by anarchical activities on one side and angry cries for stern reprisals on the other, Lord Morley and Lord Minto were bent on meeting, as far as possible, the new aspirations which had sprung up among the people. Reforms were on the anvil. Dadabhai heard about it from Wedderburn and others; how could the father of the agitation for reform remain silent at such a juncture?

Radiant in Retirement

Throughout the year 1908 the bark of Indian politics was drifting in stormy waters. There was a definite split in the Congress camp, and the national organisation was in imminent danger of being completely captured by the extremist section. Two different types of unrest combined to unnerve the authorities—one, the unrest of loyal subjects dissatisfied with Government for their failure to discharge their obligations to the people; the other, the unrest fomented by doctrines subversive of order and threatening the basis of constitutional society. It is unnecessary to refer to the outrages that followed one upon another. Those outbursts of violence on the part of the young rebels of the day were met by Government with repression.

Repression, however, failed to repress and engendered new forces of disorder. The grim monster of anarchism followed in its wake, compelling Government to take further repressive measures.

The Radical of one generation is apt to become the Tory of the next and to look askance at the forward movement of that generation. This could not be said of Dadabhai. While the other political leaders disowned and denounced the forward section, his sympathies were with them. His hopes were centred not so much in his immediate followers as in the youth of the country stirred by national consciousness and patriotic fervour. At the same time, he stoutly deprecated violence. In his message of thanks to his countrymen for the numerous proofs of their goodwill he stated:

> I take this opportunity to entreat that all resort to violence should be avoided. Our grievances are many and they are just. Maintain the struggle for essential reforms, with necessary endeavours and self-sacrifice, peacefully, patiently and perseveringly, and appeal without fear or faltering to the conscience and righteousness of the British nation.

This message marked the opening of a new chapter in the story of Dadabhai's life. It heralded, so to say, the rebirth of his political life. He was now blest with sufficient physical and mental vigour to follow with interest, almost as intense as before, the progress of events in the country and once more to express his views and exert his influence thereon. The announcement of the Morley-Minto Reforms called to memory Morley's own words: "Every single right thing that is done by the legislature, however moderate may be its area, every single right thing is sure to lead to the doing of a great number of unforeseen right things." That instalment of reform, insignificant as it might appear today, was the fruit of his "long and untiring labours, as Wedderburn put it in his letter to Dadabhai (January 1, 1909).

What has now been accomplished, and what we trust must follow, is the result of persistent constitutional effort, and there is no one who has done as much as you have during all these dark years, to keep your countrymen in this safe path of progress.... It is interesting to look back to our Minority Report, and to see how many of our recommendations (which Lord George Hamilton did not even deign to notice!) have now been adopted.

The Reforms marked the first step of the authorities along the path of justice and rectitude. The best way to accelerate the pace of progress along that road, thought Dadabhai, was to encourage the statesmen who had taken that courageous step. He, therefore, wrote a personal letter to Lord Morley and Lord Minto, stating that their declaration of the Reforms had justified his faith in British character and had strengthened it "after many a cruel disappointment bordering on despair."

The general hope now is that you will be able to complete early the adoption and practical application of these reforms successfully, with any reasonable and beneficial modification that may be suggested by yourselves and the public opinion. I do not discuss details. ... I wish only to remark that the Viceroy's council may also be left without an official majority, and that some consideration had been given to that unfortunate blunder—the partition of Bengal.

He had written that letter, he added, with mixed feelings of gratification and disappointment, for the fundamental reform, the holding of simultaneous examinations in India and in England for admission to the Civil Service, had been overlooked. He, however, did not wish to trouble them on the subject, when they had enough arduous work to get the reforms adopted by the Imperial Legislature. Within a short time, however, he took the opportunity to revert to the question. In his letter of April 3, offering to Lord Minto and Lord Morley "most grateful thanks for the appointment made of an Indian to the Viceroy's Council," he observed that India had not yet obtained "the absolutely necessary reform without which all other reforms would be more or less ineffective." There were two sides of the policy of British Government in India—one good, the other evil. In a lengthy appendix he gave extracts from the speeches and writings of English statesmen and administrators from 1764 to 1903. The consequences of the evils inseparable from the prevailing system of administration, about which the reader may now justifiably refuse to hear anything more, were then enumerated. He next dealt with the question of the Civil Service examination and expressed the hope that "the right beginning now made" would lead evolutionally "to the complete remedy of the inseparable evil by self-government, to England's glory all its own."

The letter and its appendices consisted of eighty typed sheets. But this was not all. In the following year (April 23, 1910) was issued from the sanctum of the "political recluse" another communication, dealing with the financial aspect of the problem and giving tables made up from official records, "to further illustrate the aspects and consequences of the evils complained of." These tables indicated the gross revenue of India per head of population. Three months later, a further letter, giving trade statistics and other details, was sent to complete the picture of the condition of India under foreign domination. These epistles and the appendices attached to them made up, one might say, an abridged edition of Poverty and Un-British Rule in India, revised up to date and annotated in the light of events subsequent to its compilation!

Despite such manifestations of his zeal and vigour and arduous effort in the cause of his country, this period of Dadabhai's life may be said to be one of comparative quiet and tranquillity. The only incident that marred his happiness was the death of his wife in the month of May. She had been absolutely unable to share his intellectual pleasures or to cooperate in his patriotic work. But their life was, nevertheless, one of unclouded harmony and affection. Messages of condolence came to Dadabhai from all quarters of the earth; the Governor of Bombay, Sir George Clarke, who was then in mourning over the death of his own daughter, being one of the earliest. "I can so perfectly feel for you," he wrote, "in the picture of my own sorrows."

The political situation grew worse and worse. The extremist section regarded the reforms as a concession to violence. Further reforms could only be wrung from unwilling hands by further violence. In his eighty-fifth birthday message, therefore, Dadabhai reverted to his counsel of non-violence.

Last year I entreated my countrymen "that all resort to violence should be avoided." Since then a most deplorable outrage has taken place in the assassination of Sir Curzon Wyllie—who was, moreover, a friend to Indians, and that when we were already beginning to obtain reforms. It is only a sad consolation that another Indian, D. Lalkaka, redeemed the Indian character with his life. Those who resort to violence inflict the greatest possible injury to the Indian cause.

In the Bombay citizens' address, tendered to Dadabhai by a deputation appointed at the public meeting held on the occasion, it was stated that they would strive to do their duty with courage and self-sacrifice and would always "endeavour to keep within constitutional limits." That assurance was very gratifying to Dadabhai. He was hopeful, he told them, that by that method and with self-sacrifice and persevering work their goal of reforms would be reached.

Twelve more months rolled by. The spectre of anarchism was still stalking the land. Dadabhai had, therefore, to reiterate, in his manifesto of 1910, his appeal to the anarchists to desist from violence.

Among the letters of congratulations received on his eighty-sixth birthday there was one from Dadabhai's grandson Jal, in which he said:

> I fear that this will arrive a week later, but the wish itself will arrive in time by telepathic means. I do not remember whether you have any belief in such things as telepathy, but if Mr. W. T. Stead is to be believed, there is much truth in it. Your mathematical mind will probably give it a very short shrift. . . various people send you messages and greetings through me, all of which you will have to presume, as I am not capable of the mental gymnastics necessary to remember all the messages and the donors thereof.

A melancholy interest attaches to this letter. Just as the writer was handling it on June 28,1938, he received the distressing news that Jal's quiet but useful life, brimful of love for his country, had been prematurely cut off. Only a few months before, in a vivid dream, Jal had seen Dadabhai walking along the Victoria Embankment in London, somewhat worried. "Hullo, Dad! What are you doing here?" asked Jal. "I am working here," replied Dadabhai. "I live in a hotel near by. I want all my papers edited. You had better do it." "Why don't you come back home with me?" asked Jal. Dadabhai agreed. Then Jal saw that they were both on the high seas. When they were nearing Bombay, Dadabhai appeared to have changed his mind. "I don't think I shall land with you," he said, "there will be too much fuss and noise. You take charge of the papers and I shall dictate the marginal notes."

Another notable letter received by Dadabhai during this rime was from Jal's sister, Gosi, in which she said:

I met the South African Mr. Gandhi last summer. I found him an extremely interesting and sincere man. He simply worships you. I had a very long talk with him about the organisation of the agitation in South Africa and all he said about it was that they had your example before them and they were following it with perfect faith.

Dadabhai wrote in reply that he was very glad she had met "Mr. Gandhi, a very good man," who had been "fighting a great patriotic battle."

No detail concerning the Congress escaped Dadabhai's notice. He was pleased with the success of the 1909 session which met at a very critical period in the history of the national movement.

> "My congratulations," said he in a letter to Lala Harkisanlal (January 6, 1910), "for the success of the Congress. Punjab has vindicated its character for stalwartness."

Similarly, in connection with the Congress session, he wrote to Surendranath Banerjee (October 10):

I am glad you have exhorted for large attendance at the next Congress. Mr. Wacha sent me a message from you when you were in Bombay about simultaneous examination. Write to me fully what it is. I hope you will do your utmost at the Congress to give prominence to the reform for simultaneous examinations for all the Indian services. In the Congress of 1906 in Resolution 9 it was section (a) which is still not attended to by Lord Morley.

Even at that age he must take pains to quote chapter and verse! Another interesting letter—one from Dadabhai's solicitor, Frank Birdwood (February 3)—gives a further glimpse of the study of the political recluse.

I am sending by separate post the USA statistics. They are dull reading to most of us, but I know that you will be able to extract pleasure and profit for all.

There is another letter, written by Dadabhai, to the Thakore Saheb of Gondal (January 31), showing the stuff with which he was feeding his mind:

> Thanks for sending me the Administration Report for 1908-9. Kindly send me also of the two previous years. I have been sending cuttings from the Press as I come across them. Surendranath Banerjee, on his return from England, once said to a friend: "Dadabhai is living in a sea of Blue Books." This was as true of his retreat at Versova as it was of his active life in England.

J. N. Gupta asked Dadabhai to give some reminiscences of Romesh Dutt, whose biography he had undertaken to write. Dadabhai replied that his papers had been all packed up and were in England. He was not, therefore, able to give him Dutt's letters. But of "personal interests" he recollected two. "When Dutt was invited by an Eastern England constituency (Yarmouth) to become a candidate for the House of Commons," he said, "I was very glad and readily agreed to give him a loan for immediate expenses. He did not, however, require it, as he did not contest.

Once we met at a dinner when he told me that after all he was satisfied and agreed with me that the chief cause of all the difficulties of India was the drain to England." Dutt was laying great stress on the defects in the Land Revenue system. Dadabhai feared it would divert attention from the fundamental cause of Indian poverty—the drain—and its remedy, self-government. In his letter of July, 1903, Dutt pointed out that in reality there was no difference between his views and Dadabhai's on the question of the drain.

I have never lost a single chance of urging that the drain from India is the cause of her poverty, I have said this again and again in my Economic History (1837-1900), which will appear next year. But this drain will not be stopped until you stop its main source—the land revenue, and therefore by endeavouring to restrict the land revenue I am doing exactly the same work which you are doing in endeavouring to stop the drain. Curiously enough, I am doing now exactly the same work which you were doing thirty years ago. I am reading your evidence before the Parliamentary Committee of 1873, and I notice how eloquently you pleaded against the excessive land assessment of some Talukas of Puna. If die Government had listened to you in 1873, the Puna Riots of 1875 would have been avoided. If you were right in combining the land revenue question with the drain question in 1873,I am right in doing the same in 1903.

Early in the year Valentine Chirol of the Foreign Department of The Times came to India to study the political situation on the spot and particularly to gauge the degree of satisfaction or dissatisfaction with which the "Reforms" had been received. He brought with him a letter of introduction to Dadabhai from George Birdwood.

It may happen (wrote Birdwood) that you may feel able to see Mr. Valentine Chirol and yet be unable to converse with him.

If so, simply see him for a moment only; he will be grateful to have the opportunity of saluting you in homage to the disinterestedness and honesty of purpose and devoutly inspired enthusiasm with which you have devoted your whole life to serve, to the best of your intelligence and ability and sense of duty, the material and moral interests of India.

It is surprising that not only his friends in England but also those in India should have thought Dadabhai was then an invalid. When Sir George Clarke had expressed a desire to see him at his residence, Dadabhai's friends warned him that it would be too great a strain on Dadabhai and would involve great risk. The idea was abandoned for two years. Two years later, Hormusji Wadya informed him that Dadabhai was in such good health that he would enjoy receiving visitors and even discussing politics.

Dadabhai had a long interview with Chirol on April 23. What transpired no one knew. A laconic note in Dadabhai's own hand merely tells us, "gave copy of correspondence with Lord Morley and Lord Minto when he called to see me, also copy of extract from letter to Lord George Hamilton."

The work of propaganda was thus continued even during his declining days.

Nothing could suppress India's demand that England's obligations to her should be fulfilled. Day by day it became more and more vocal through the expanded Legislative Councils. The policy initiated in 1909 had to be carried out to its logical conclusion. The announcement that Kong George V intended to revisit India to make known in person to his subjects his succession to the Imperial Crown of India stimulated hopes for a peaceful settlement of the political conflict. In his birthday message for the year 1910 Dadabhai recalled the King's previous visit and stressed the hopeful prospects which the contemplated visit opened out for India.

Among their precious and gracious words and acts (he said) we have first the speech at Bombay on 9th November, 1905, when His Majesty as Prince of Wales declared "Love" and "Affection" for the Indian people and an increased and abiding interest in India's wants and problems.

Then followed a string of quotations from the King-Emperor's messages and declarations to the Indian people in which he had proclaimed from time to time his desire to abide by the spirit of the noble declarations of Queen Victoria and Kong Edward VII. Next, he raised the question of reforms for training Indians for self-government and placed simultaneous examinations for the Indian Civil Service first in his list of reforms.

On his arrival the King-Emperor saw on every side the stirrings of new life. The interests of the people, he said, would always be as near and dear to him as those of his subjects in other quarters of the globe. Six years before, he had sent from England to India a message of sympathy. On this occasion he gave to India the watchword of hope. "Reading between the lines," said Dadabhai in his manifesto of September 26, 1912, "of all the incidents, despatches, and events of this ever-memorable visit of Their Majesties, it seems that there is thought out and determined upon a new evolution to secure the prosperity of the Indian people."

Thus through those passing phases his buoyant faith perceived the larger movements and changes that were to follow. But how to accelerate the pace towards the goal visualised by him?

Dadabhai submitted that the King-Emperor's desire to give the Indian, people the blessings of peace and prosperity could only be attained by giving self-government to India. It was only natural for him to expect that, while political conditions were changing all over the world and while the internal conditions in India were also changing, the Government of India could not alone refuse to move with the times. The fault, he believed, was in the head, not in the heart. Lord Hardinge had brought about a change in the mind; already a friendly policy was being evolved, leading to complete autonomy in provincial affairs.

The fates, however, appeared to be against a peaceful approach to the cherished goal. To his horror Dadabhai heard of an attempt on the life of the good and great Viceroy and of Lady Hardinge at Delhi. It had a very depressing effect on him, but the appointment during the year of a Royal Commission on the Services in India filled him with hope. "I pray," said he, in his birthday manifesto, "that its work may result in securing to our country the justice that has been long delayed. It has been my lifelong conviction that simultaneous examination will furnish the only remedy for a great and just grievance."

The question of treatment of Indians in South Africa was not overlooked.

The situation of our countrymen in the Colonies, and particularly in South Africa (he observed), stirs us with deep emotion.

They have suffered long and suffered much and have so borne their misfortune as to entitle them to the better regard and protection of His Majesty's Government. I have viewed with deep concern the indifference of the Imperial Government in regard to the recent Act in South Africa. But I shall hope for justice and action.

By this time Versova had become a place of pilgrimage, not only for loving and admiring Indians and Englishmen, but also for the highest authorities in India. After Sir George Clarke, Lord Hardinge, and then Lord Willingdon, honoured Dadabhai with a visit and profited by his exposition of the hopes and aspirations of the people. Such intercourse was not confined to exchange of courtesies or to sharing domestic joys and sorrows of one another.

Whenever the economic or the political situation demanded it, Dadabhai carried on a vigorous correspondence with them.

On February 21, 1913, a letter was addressed jointly to Lord Crewe and Lord Hardinge, asking that the Public Services Commission then conducting its enquiry should be supplied, before it made its report, with "information about the aspects and consequences of the economic factor of the public service" so that they might be able to realise "how much of the moisture which ought to give sustenance to the people of British India was sucked up by Europeans under the existing system of public service."

In one of his Council speeches Lord Hardinge had inferred from certain trade statistics that India's material condition and progress compared favourably with that of any other principal country in the world. Though bowed with the weight of four score years and eight, Dadabhai lost no time in pointing out in a long letter (October 8, 1913) that the interpretation put on the figures was not correct. The subject had been dealt with by him before. He repeated all those arguments and said India's exports brought no gain to India; it was all loss, loss, loss.

The outbreak of the Great War elicited a stirring message from Dadabhai (August 10, 1914):

The War in Europe. What is our—India's—place in it? ...We are above all British citizens of the Great British Empire. Fighting as the British people are at present in a righteous cause for the good and glory of human dignity and civilization, and, moreover, being the beneficent instrument of our own progress and civilization, our duty is clear to do our—every one's—best to support the British fight with our life and property.

This message struck the right note at that critical moment in the history of the British Empire. Lord Willingdon was extremely pleased with it. "We are here all citizens of our great Empire," said he in a private letter written to Dadabhai (August 11), "and shall show by our attitude our determination to stand shoulder to shoulder in the great struggle before us. Truly, India by her loyalty and devotion to the King Emperor, which will be proved during the war, will gain her rightful place in the future in the 'sun' of the British Empire."

Lord Hardinge also wrote to Dadabhai (August 13):

> There is a simplicity and sincerity about the words you have addressed to them which will appeal directly to their hearts, and not the less forcibly that you have at times been a fearless critic of Government.

The events that followed form one of the brightest chapters in the history of Indo-British relations. A wave of loyalty spread over the whole country. By handsome contributions of men to the Army and money to the War Fund, and in several other ways, the Princes and the people of India helped the British Empire, to the best of their ability, to wage and win the war.

Exchanging Christmas greetings with his friend W. H. Owen, who regularly corresponded with him from England, Dadabhai wrote:

As I have already said, India has now been able to show its sincere loyalty to the British Empire, and I fully hope that the British people will not fail to be true to the British character of faithfully performing their promises and making the grand British

Empire a true Empire of free and happy humanity and equal right to all subjects.

Two very interesting letters were received by Dadabhai during the Year. One of these was from Dr. John Pollen, famous Civil Servant of his day and a very old friend of Dadabhai. Congratulating Dadabhai on his ninetieth birthday and stating that his message to the people had certainly helped to nerve the nation's heart and was "in itself a deed," Pollen wrote:

Now I have a great favour to ask. You know I am struggling to carry on the good work you commenced nearly half a century ago in connection with the East India Association. Pennington and I contemplate writing a history of the Association to appear on its forth birthday, and as you are really the Father, I want you to send me a few words of blessing. It would be too much to ask you to recall any details of the birth of the Association.

These we can gather up from your excellent speeches of the day, but if you could send us now a few words of encouraging preface, we could doubtless make a start at once. As I write, I have before me your picture published by the Times of India, and it would form a good frontispiece to the history of our Association.

There are moments when even the best of friends have to be displeased or disobliged. This was one. Pleased and grateful as he was to receive the letter, Dadabhai could not help refusing the "favour" asked for. "Unfortunately," he replied, "I have some unfavourable opinion about the present Association, and I should not like to write at present anything unpleasant. I thank you for your kind opinion about my work in the Association."

Although he said little about it, Dadabhai was sick at heart till the end of his life that this organisation that he had reared for the good of India did not lend a helping hand in the struggle for the political elevation of his countrymen. Recently, however, the activities of the Association have been renewed, and it may be hoped that it may yet play an honourable part in the final stages of the political evolution of India.

A very cheering reminder of the early days spent in England was a letter (October 10) from Miss Annie Archer, one of the members of the family with whom Dadabhai had been on intimate terms, a friendship which, as we have seen, was viewed with disfavour by his orthodox partner, Muncherji Cama.

I read with great interest (she said) your excellent letter in The Times and since then, how many of your people have given their practical evidence of goodwill, and I am sure England values it very highly, especially in these terrible days, one can think, talk and read of no other subject but the war. The loss of life has been enormous and the amount of sufferings not only of our men but the poor women and children is heart-rending....

I felt I should just like to send a word of remembrance to you, and I very often picture you sitting in "Mr. Dadabhai's Chair," which is still as good as ever, in my dining-room; how often you have sat in it, and told us such interesting details of your religion and customs, and how we all enjoyed your visits.

What a fine unexpected pleasure (replied Dadabhai) to receive it from one of my earliest and best friends in England! I remember well the days of my visits, spending my evenings among the kind family of Dr. Archer, sitting in "Mr. Dadabhai's Chair" (good chair), with Annie with a kind sisterly interest tenderly seeing to my comforts.

Dadabhai's next birthday synchronised with one of the most sensational incidents in his life. Mrs. Annie Besant, who had then switched off to politics from metaphysics, was trying to form a Home Rule, League in India. It was announced in September 1915 in her organ, the Commonweal, that it had been decided to start the League with "Home Rule for India" as its only object, as an auxiliary to the National Congress in India and its British Committee in England. "Its general aim will be," it was stated, "to educate the people and to give to the demand of the Congress for self-government... the strength of a nation which has realised itself, and which, through its national organisation, has voiced its claim for years, only to see it rejected." Then followed the sensational news that Dadabhai had consented, to be President.

In the quiet of Versova, Dadabhai was a moral and spiritual force. Placed as he was on a pinnacle, above all earthly strife and turmoil of politics, and adored by the whole of India, irrespective of class, or creed, or party, none expected that Dadabhai would once more descend from that pinnacle to the slippery path of active politics. His friends and admirers were, therefore, amazed to read the announcement. Most of the Congressmen considered it outrageous that another organisation should be brought into being, to pursue the same object which formed the principal plank in the Congress programme, namely, self-government. They suspected that the extremists would utilise it merely to wreck the Congress. Besides, the majority of the people were not enamoured of the methods of the gifted but volatile lady who, it was understood, would be at the helm of affairs of the League. Others, however, thought that while the Congress remained a deliberative body, there should be an organisation to do the day-to-day, active, propagandist work for securing Home Rule.

What about your Presidentship of the Home Rule League (asked Wacha) which Mrs. Besant is broadly advertising? ...We do not approve of the methods of Mrs. Besant who late in the day has come forward to support the Congress movement.... We are alarmed that the way in which she is going about on her own responsibility, supported from behind by the extremists, is a distinct menace to the peaceful progress of our country.

Not merely Congress colleagues but all the world seemed anxious to know whether Dadabhai had really accepted the presidentship. He therefore announced publicly (September 28) that it was true that he had given his consent to be President on certain conditions.

How did it happen ? Mrs. Besant wanted not only Dadabhai, but also S. Subrahmania Aiyar and Wedderburn to join the League, as she believed that the counsel of such veterans, holding in old age to the ideals of their youth, and looking hopefully and confidently to the Promised Land, veterans who could inspire as well as lead, would be invaluable. Subrahmania Aiyar had agreed to be President of the Indian Division, and it was hoped Wedderburn would accept the Presidentship of the English Division of the League. To induce Dadabhai to agree to be the head of the movement, Mrs. Besant, with her lieutenant, Mr. B. P. Wadia, paid him a personal visit. She had stood beside him in his memorable fight for election to Parliament in 1892. Dadabhai recalled that fact in his very first words of cordial greeting. She implored him to be at the head of the League. "We are all getting old," she said; 'let us combine to give a strong lead to the younger people and guide their energy into wisely chosen channels."

> "You old!" exclaimed Dadabhai, with eyes beaming with kindness, "you old! Why you (seventy) are as far away from me (ninety) as Homi (pointing to Dadina, who was sitting next to diem) is away from you!"

In the course of the conversation the veteran champion of Home Rule for Ireland and the standard-bearer of self-government for India welcomed the idea of forming a League. He also expressed his warm approval of the way in which New India (Mrs. Besant's paper) claimed self-government for India as a right, not as a boon.

> "I read New India daily," he added. "England understands plain speaking and does not resent it. Appeal to the English sense of justice and fair play and take it for granted that England will do justice, when she understands. I have always done so."

With clear political insight Dadabhai consented to be the President of the League, although he anticipated that some of his lifelong friends would disapprove of what they might regard as an alliance with the extremist section. One of the conditions lie imposed was that he should not be called upon for any active work or for speaking or writing, as he was not competent to undertake any such work at his age. He also asked, and Mrs. Besant agreed, that the League must not be turned against the Congress.

Not knowing in detail how the existence of the Congress was threatened during those days, Dadabhai did not realise the danger inherent in starting an all India institution with the same methods and ideals as the Congress had and with young rebellious blood infused in it. All his thoughts were then centred in the fulfilment of his dream—Swaraj. What objection could there be in having a new auxiliary organisation to press forward the claims of the country for home rule ? India had bought admittance into the world-war with her best blood. Her brave sons were then laying down their lives with the sons of the British Empire in defending the common flag. Could they, after the termination of hostilities, be denied any longer their rights as British citizens?

He, for one, saw no reason why Mrs. Besant should not go forward with her project. She herself, however, realised the strength and the significance of the opposition.

About this time Wedderburn issued jointly with Sir Krishna Gupta a note in which were summarised the practical steps to get India placed in a position analogous to that enjoyed by the self-governing colonies. He informed Mrs. Besant that it appeared to him and to his friends whom he had consulted that as he was Chairman of the British Committee of the Congress, it was undesirable that he should be the local head of another political association not directly affiliated to the Congress. As regards objects, there was no difference of opinion between the two bodies, but there was a difference as regards tactics.

Though we wish an authoritative scheme to be prepared (said he), we are not in favour of public action until peace is in sight, whereas you propose a vigorous agitation in the Press and on the platform. At the present moment such a popular agitation in this country is not possible. No newspaper would support it, and we could get no one to come to public meetings. I had a long talk with Lady Emily Lutyens this morning, and explained to her the difficulties and danger of the situation. It will be disastrous for the cause of self-government if there is conflict among Congress supporters. Already our opponents contend that self-government for India is impossible on account of the enmity between Hindus and Muhammadans, and it will strengthen their case if they can say that even the reformers cannot agree among themselves. I would, therefore, strongly recommend that some modus vivendi should be arrived at, so that we may present an unbroken front.

Wedderburn wrote also to Dadabhai (October 27):

I must not conceal from you that your accepting the Presidentship of the Indian "Home Rule League" has caused considerable perturbation to friends in this country. You and I agree so completely on material matters, that we have only to consider the question of tactics and I send you herewith copy of two letters I have addressed to Mrs. Besant.

Such protests were, however, of no avail. The unbending uprightness, which had marked every phase of his public and private life, was proof against all entreaties that Dadabhai should renounce the Presidentship. Abandoning all hope of inducing him to change his mind, Wacha wrote:

> I feel that it is impossible to convince you when you are of another mind, in ignorance of facts. My respect for you is great, and in view of that respect I hold my tongue. All that I will venture to say is this, that by allowing your name to be associated with the League as its President you are in reality assisting those who by indirect and tortuous means are trying to wreck the Congress which you and other founders have built up with such care, wisdom and foresight during the last thirty years.

The veteran's rejoinder, clinching the issue, revealed the working of his mind. Although often deceived, the erstwhile Professor of Mathematics insisted till the last day of his life that every theory of suspicion should be demonstrated like a theorem in geometry, before he could act on it. In this particular case he saw no reason to discountenance a movement, full of promise for the country's good, merely because his friends suspected that its promoters would work in a manner prejudicial to the Congress.

He, therefore, told Wacha (November 14):

> Sir W. Wedderburn in his letter to you of 18th October (and of which you have kindly sent me a copy) says, "The situation needs the greatest care and discretion and it is essential that all well-wishers of India—and the Empire—should work together, putting aside all personal differences....". Sir W. W. next asks you to send to him by early mail a concise memorandum of the view of affairs taken by our Congress friends (and at present Mrs. Besant also stands out as one of Congress's best friends).

I have no doubt you are sending such memorandum.... The other day when Wadya and you kindly saw me upon this subject we had agreed that we had better make the best of our position and that if you could at any time make out a clear case of harm done to the Congress by the League, I could easily resign.... So far Mrs. Besant has openly kept on saying that she would do nothing to injure the Congress and we have to keep her to her word. Sir W. W. particularly advises us in his letter to you "the situation needs the greatest care and discretion."

Anxious as Mrs. Besant was to launch the League with the goodwill of the Congress, she decided to go slow. It was arranged that the question should be discussed, about the time of the Congress Session in December, at a conference of the leading members of the Congress and of the All India Muslim League.

A Conference was held accordingly, but it could not come to a definite understanding. Even during the year 1916 the scheme did not materialise. This delay saved Dadabhai from a very embarrassing situation. Before the League was duly constituted in the following year, his day of political activity was over. The quiet eventide of rest had come to him at last.

A Year of Worry and Glory

Arduous as is the task of a Member of Parliament at all times, in Dadabhai's case its responsibilities were exceptionally onerous. He had to discharge his duties to his British constituency, as well as to India. Confronted by tried and hardheaded statesmen, what could a single representative of a distant dependency of Britain achieve ? No one expected that he would take the House by storm, but the invincible optimist had strong hopes of extorting a hearing, on behalf of India, day after day, until he could make the Indian question a familiar one and get the House to agree to at least a few measures of reform for which he had been crying in the wilderness for more than thirty years.

His was not the voice which at once took the ear. But rhetoric is not the lever with which the House is moved. Mastery of facts, courage of conviction, earnestness of purpose—these were the levers with which he hoped to move it. A stupendous effort had to be made; for that he was fully prepared, but what about funds? A delicate question; there is, however, no reason to gloss over facts. Rather it is necessary to refer to them briefly so as to indicate against what odds he had to struggle.

Soon after the election, Malabari, who knew what financial difficulties Dadabhai had to contend with, wrote (July 20):

Mr. Mehta from Calcutta wrote to ask if we could raise a fund for you. I asked him to wait till you were consulted. If a call is not well responded to, it would be bad. Dinsha is enthusiastic over your letters and wishes he were by your side. "Then I would die!" he concludes!

As a matter of fact, when he was in the thick of the protracted electoral campaign, Dadabhai had written to Malabari (February 8, 1889) that he had been anticipating a collapse and that the very thought of it had been disturbing his mind and checking free and bold action. That at the last moment he should have to abandon the struggle was, indeed, an appalling thought. Had he remained in Bombay, he might have accumulated money for his children, but he had given up all income—a pecuniary sacrifice greater than that of any other politician of the day, not to mention the separation from his family and the impossibility of rearing his children as he would have liked. The fall in exchange was a further handicap—one-fifth of the limited resources placed at his disposal by a few Indian Princes and personal friends was lost in it. What his needs were he mentioned specifically in another letter to Malabari (January 31, 1890).

Rs. 25,000 is not a great mistake. It only means £1,600. Fram has already spent £800, and will require as much more before he has done. . . . H. H. Rao's money I can partly use towards supplementing my house expenses, as a portion of it would be really for work done. But I cannot take much out of it, as I shall require all I can get for my present purpose and for which I am asking. With the exception of taking as much as would enable supplementing for the everyday house wants and the comfort of die children, I shall need all. In a matter like the one in which I am now involved I cannot depend upon future hopes. You see how soon friends lapse into indifference, as you say is the case at present. Lose or win, I am bound to fight this battle to the end.

After the election the financial problem had become more acute. The calls on a Member's purse are greater than those on a candidate's. How was he to meet those demands when he had not even the means for his own maintenance in England during his membership of the House? It was not known how long he would sit in the House or how soon he would have to plunge into another electoral struggle. If the general election came on suddenly, where was he to find the funds for it ? When such was the predicament in which he found himself, a highly sensational report appeared in the English newspapers. It was announced that since his election to the Imperial Legislature, Dadabhai had received thirteen telegrams from different Maharajas of India with gifts of money varying from £500 to £5>ooo, making in all £28,000. Nay, more. The "Maharaja of Hyderabad" (a designation as fictitious as the report) had sent to Dadabhai an additional sum of .£10,000 to enable him to establish a permanent memorial of some kind—a monument, a public library, or some philanthropic institution in his constituency! Hostile papers made capital out of this canard. The Echo charged Dadabhai with purse pride in the display of riches, and the Globe speculated as to the reason why those Eastern potentates should thus rejoice in the election of one who was not of their blood nor of their religion. Was it an outburst of gratitude or affection, or was it a means of propitiation ?

To check further mischief, Dadabhai contradicted the statements in the following letter sent to the London dailies:

With reference to die statement in your issue of yesterday that I have received telegrams and £38,000 from India, will you kindly allow me to inform your readers that though it is true that I have received many telegrams since my election, I have not received any money from India.

If so much money or even a smaller amount had been poured into the lap of Dadabhai, his friend Malabari would have known it and he would not have sent that letter to Dadabhai, asking him whether a fund should be started to meet his expenses. Funds were, indeed, badly needed. What was received had been well-nigh exhausted, and the sources of supply had dried up for the time being. In reply to Malabari's letter, Dadabhai disclosed his condition, but as regards the proposal to raise funds, he observed (August 10):

I do not like to have any public movement about it. If it can be done quietly ... I should like it. The fall in exchange makes a great hole and with what I have I shall not be able to work with such full effect as I should do. It is not so much for my own personal expenses which I can manage as economically as possible, but there are other expenses of various kinds, printing, subscriptions, etc.... which require a deal of money.

Demands for subscriptions poured in from all directions. Despite his limited means, Dadabhai gave donations, large or small, to a sorts of philanthropic institutions and to individuals in distress.

Captain Penton's petition entailed further unforeseen expenses. The solicitors' charges and disbursements relating to the appeal alone amounted to .£1,670. When the petition was pending, he wrote to Malabari (October 14, 1892):

> About your suggested mode for raising funds for me (from Princes and a few personal friends), all I can say is that I desire quickness.

How pressing and urgent must have been his needs, may be gathered from another letter in the same month (October 28):

> The calls upon me for expense won't wait a day. ... I must have my backbone (my kamar no katho) beyond all doubt. In short, I must have as early as possible my funds in hand for some years.

Then followed a cheerful letter on December 16, stating he had a talk with the Gaikwad who had been very free and kind to him and that it was explained to His Highness that he should remain in the House at least ten years. In another letter (December 22) he said:

> I have written to you about the Gaikwad last mail. He was particularly cordial with me here. Unless Princes come to my aid we cannot expect much from the Seths or the people....

If a lump sum becomes difficult, the next best thing is to have an annual remittance, but it is so uncertain to rely upon and there may be a collapse. The demands on one as a member of the constituency are more exacting than they are when he is only a candidate, both on person and purse. You have always the next election before your face. Our friends do not easily understand the position under which even English candidates and members groan.

Malabari's letters were, however, disappointing. Indifference of friends when approached for financial help is no uncommon thing. One such friend was heard grumbling that Dadabhai was enjoying himself in London. Two other friends, J. N. Tata and F. S. Patel, indignantly refuted the insinuation, and they reported the matter to Malabari just to impress upon him the difficulty of carrying out his scheme to raise subscriptions privately from friends. Dejected as he was by the small amount subscribed in response to private appeals, Malabari wrote under a sense of irritation an article in the Indian Spectator, pleading for public support to Dadabhai in his patriotic work. When Dadabhai saw it, he was completely put out. In anguish he wrote (January 5, 1893):

I have felt much distressed by the article in the Indian Spectator about the public subscriptions for me. I was sorry to read that the subject was dragged into public controversy and that in a manner derogatory to me. . . . Kindly prevent any controversy upon the subject.

In a letter that followed (January 12), Dadabhai dwelt on the same subject:

Do not be disturbed by any failure in getting sufficient funds.... We have gradually to lead on people to a sense of the necessity of making sacrifices for the sake of their country. We cannot expect them to do this at once, and it is our duty the more to bear with them, to lead them on with tact and discretion....

To start a rupee fund or any fund openly will result in failure and even in mischief. That unfortunate article . . . has, as I was fearing, done some mischief. In self-defence Malabari replied (January 28):

It grieves me to read of your grief over my para, in reference to the subscription. It is a strange thing—this political life of yours. All our friends were indignant at the smallness of the fund —I give voice to their indignation which I share. Thereupon the good people turned upon me.... I note your distress and will be careful in future. But excuse my saying that the para, was a general criticism, referring to Fawcett, Bradlaugh, and yourself, and that it reflected the general public opinion of Bombay.

My object was not so much to insist on your claims as to show how much we have yet to learn in the way of political organisation. My second object was to indirectly disprove those who have said in England that you had been helped to thousands.

By the time this letter was in the hands of Dadabhai, he had written to Malabari on February 24:

> Yes, I have now drawn my last balance of my resources. How long it will last I cannot say. Unless more aid comes, of course my only alternative will be to return. I do not despair though. I shall do what I can.

Then followed an account showing how he was "enjoying himself":

> I am here at about 12 O'clock noon and go back home at i or 2 O'clock next morning, all the time working and listening in the House to understand how to vote on every question, and correspondence. It is full twelve hours hard work. I am not able to employ a private secretary to relieve me.

To such straits was the M.P., who was taken by his constituency to be a very rich man, reduced. In the nick of time, however, help came from Baroda. As the first instalment was received a cheque for £1,000. There were prospects, too, of substantial help coming from Gondal, Bhavnagar, and other Indian States, and it did come.

There is no need to go into details. The anxiety regarding the pending petition against his election was also removed by its withdrawal on December 14. Dadabhai now braced himself up for Parliamentary work. To distinguish oneself in the great Imperial Assembly is no simple matter even for tried British politicians. What hope was there for Dadabhai to shine in the midst of that constellation of stars of exceptional brilliance ? His splendour might at least have been dimmed, if he had not altogether disappeared from view.

The Indian luminary, however, lost nothing in brilliance. There was one special circumstance in his favour. Even with the support of the Irish Nationalists the Gladstonian Administration had a majority of only forty in the representative chamber. Consequently, every small group, every unit, was an asset of very great value to the Government of the day. The first Indian M.P. had therefore a better opportunity to find his way in the House and to create a favourable impression than would have been the case if he had been merely a unit in a large majority. Thanks, moreover, to the courtesy of members of all parties, the encouragement of the Premier, the solicitude of old friends like Samuel Smith, Wedderburn, and Caine, and the goodwill and assistance of Lord Kimberley, the Secretary of State for India, and of his Deputy, George Russell, he moved about in the House as if he had been long used to its procedure.

Dadabhai took the earliest opportunity to make his maiden speech during the debate 'on the Address. It was but a personal note, expressing the joy of his countrymen at his election as a member of the House, coupled with an appeal on their behalf for fair consideration of Indian questions. The House listened with deep attention to the Indian member who, for the first time in English history, stood before them to state his views openly and freely.

He stood there in the name of India to thank British riders that they had made it possible for an Indian to stand before this House with the conviction that whenever he had any grievance to bring forward, supported by just and proper reasons, he would always find a large number of other members ready to support him and to concede the justice for which he asked.... The moral force of which the right honourable Member for Midlothian spoke was the golden thread by which India was held by the British power; as long as India was satisfied with the justice and honour of Britain so long would the Indian Empire endure.

Close upon that modest speech followed many embarrassing questions and many intrepid arguments. The Indian member invariably occupied over a page of the Order book of the House of Commons with notices of motions calling for detailed information and returns concerning the agricultural wealth of

India and other matters concerning that country. Well might some member have called for a return from the India Office, showing the special staff needed, and its cost, for satisfying the curiosity of the member for Central Finsbury.

The growing divergence of value between gold and silver was then engaging the attention of the financiers of the world. An International Conference convened at Brussels had proved abortive. Despite the powerful advocacy of the bimetallists of the day to abandon or modify the gold standard, several Powers, including Britain, were against making any fundamental change in their monetary system. The fall in die value of the rupee had, however, hit India very hard and any arbitrary attempt to fix the ratio was likely to hit her harder still.

Dadabhai had been expounding the problem in the columns of The Times and other journals since 1886. He had published also a leaflet entitled Indian Exchanges and Bimetallism, containing his contributions, together with those of his critics. One of the letters to The Times, which attached great value to his views on this subject, was written on board S.S. Malwa, dated Suez, December 23, 1886, when he was on his way to India to preside over the Congress session for that year. It was a brief but emphatic repudiation of all the arguments in favour of bimetallism.

As he was now in a position to raise a debate on the question on the floor of the House, Dadabhai put the question whether the Secretary of State would, before sanctioning any alteration in the system of currency in India, submit the question for the consideration of the House. To this the obvious reply was that the evidence on the question could not be laid before Parliament consistently with the public interests, until the decision arrived at had been announced.

Dadabhai, however, got an opportunity, within a fortnight, to place his views before the House. On February 28 a resolution was brought forward urging Her Majesty's Government to use their utmost influence to procure the reassembly of the Monetary Conference and to impress upon the representatives of the British Government the immediate necessity of finding some effective remedy, in concert with other nations, for the evils resulting from the divergence in the value of the two precious metals. The proposal was equivalent to sending the British Government on a fool's errand at the bidding of bimetallists who had not the courage to suggest bimetallism as the panacea for the financial ills of the world. Dadabhai opposed the motion in a powerful speech ending with a warning couched in the following emphatic terms:

There was a commercial disturbance, coming from demonetisation in Germany, or the excessive production of silver in America, just as storms arise in the physical world. The United States undertook the absurd feat of trying to stop it and keep up the price of silver, and the result was that the more it was stemmed the greater force it acquired.... They must allow laws, commercial, physical, moral, or political, to be governed by nature.

If they tried to stop the storm, the result would be far more disastrous. He was of opinion that England must stick to the sound scientific principle of currency that she had adopted. Nor should she allow the currency of India to be tampered with.

On March 28 Sir Seymour King rose to call attention to the grave and injurious consequences likely to ensue in the Civil and Military Services of the Indian Government from its failure to provide compensation for the reduction of their salaries by the diminution of the value of the rupee. He moved that a Select Committee be appointed to enquire into the matter. It was stated that the Viceroy had already expressed himself before a deputation in favour of granting compensation to the officers concerned. Dadabhai was indignant. "It never occurred to the proposer or to the Viceroy," lie said, "that there was another side to the picture. What was the position of the people of India themselves from the fall in exchange 5 There was not a word of pity or sympathy with regard to those from whose pockets whatever was demanded had to be paid! Truly, the heaviest of all yokes, as remarked by Macaulay, was the yoke of the stranger. So long as this House does not understand that the yoke as it at present exists practically in India is the heaviest of all yokes India has no future, Indians no hope (Loud cries of Oh! Oh!).

You may say "Oh! Oh!" but you have never been, fortunately—and I Lope and pray you may never be—in the condition in which India is placed in your hands.

Then he gave a harrowing picture of the poverty of India, citing his favourite authorities. From that question to the drain of India's wealth was the next logical step. "You ought to have some heart and some justice," he observed feelingly, "to consider from what source this money has to be made up." What was the use of a committee e The Viceroy had made up his mind.

"There has hardly been an instance," he boldly asserted, "in which a Commission has sat on such a matter as this and decided in a manner that can be called impartial and unbiassed. . . . The whole thing is a foregone conclusion. . . . Do not put additional taxation on these poor people."

Dadabhai then moved an amendment to the effect that if a fixed rate of exchange were determined upon, such rate and the actual market rate of exchange should not become an additional burden on the Indian tax-payer. But for a few occasional cries of "Oh! Oh!" and "Question" the House listened admiringly to those home-thrusts. Dadabhai was cheered over and over again as he established one point after another. Even the Undersecretary of State, George Russell, although he had to support the original motion, was most sympathetic. "I go all lengths with him (Dadabhai)," he said, "in wishing to protect the pockets of Indian tax-payers. . . . But if the proposal was carried, the cost must fall somewhere."

The motion was lost. The battle of the rupee ratio was not yet over—in fact, it is being fought even today as fiercely as before. Dadabhai had a good deal more to say and to write on the subject, and it would be convenient to turn awhile from the arena of the House of Commons to that of the Indian Exchange so as to have an uninterrupted glimpse of the position taken up by him in the matter.

The Indian Currency Committee of 1893 overruled the proposals made by the Government of India for stopping the free coinage of silver with a view to the introduction of the Gold Standard. So far their recommendations were in unison with the evidence given by Dadabhai before the Committee. It, however, suggested modifications of the Government proposals which left to the authorities the discretion to take steps, if and when necessary, to close the mints to the free-mintage of silver accompanied by an announcement that, though closed to the public, they would be used by Government for the coinage of rupees in exchange for gold at a ratio to be then fixed, say, 1s. 4d. per rupee.

A representative of Commerce interviewed Dadabhai in connection with this report, and Dadabhai's criticism of the report was published in Commerce (July 5, 1893). The mints were closed and the value of the rupee was divorced from the value of the metal contained in it. By withholding new issues of currency the Government succeeded, after some initial mistakes, in raising the gold value of the rupee to 1s. 4d., at which the rupee ratio was definitely fixed on the recommendation of another Committee appointed in 1898. Before that Committee made its report Dadabhai contributed another letter to Commerce (May 11) requesting the editor to republish the report of the interview of 1893, as the views therein expressed by him had, he maintained, turned out to be true. It was said that by closing the mints India was saved 4d. on every rupee remitted for Home charges; but that, contended Dadabhai, was pure moonshine.

What Government has done is that the Government has introduced a fraudulent rupee, and compelled the tax-payer or the rayat to pay his tax in this rupee—i.e. to pay in a "rupee" that is worth 1s. 4d. instead of what he was in the ordinary course liable for, viz. a rupee of is. In other words, what Government has done is that it has forced the poor rayat to pay one-third more taxation in a fraudulent way than he was liable for, or compelled the poor rayat to part with one-third more of his produce to provide Government with a higher valued coin. . . . The tax-payer is forced to part with the full amount of the produce to buy the £19,000,000, and by the jugglery of using die "rupee" of a higher value, dust is thrown in the eyes of the people that saving is made by them, as if what is said to have been saved had rained from the sky! ... It is the British Anglo-Indian, merchant, trader, official, and non-official, and capitalist to whom the matters are made easy.

Why does not Government perform the following miracles Pass a law that the "rupee" of India must be equal to a sovereign of gold, and that the rayat must pay his assessment in such "rupee"?

...Now the cry is raised to have a Gold Standard. It means that all the little silver that is in British India, as well as the large quantity in Native States, must be deprived of a large portion of its present value, by throwing a large quantity on the market, and to bring a large quantity of gold at a still higher proportion of value, by the large additional demand created. All this loss in cheap silver and dearer gold to be squeezed out of the poor, wretched, famished rayat of India! Who will pay all this price of conversion from silver to gold currency ? Will the British traders, capitalists, officials and non-officials, at "whose cry and clamour this has to be done for their benefit, pay a single farthing towards this conversion, beyond the infinitesimal share they pay of the taxation, and that by exploiting the country to their great profit with the land and labour of the Indians, who come in simply to slave as hewers of wood and drawers of water, to be taxed and "bled" ... for the benefit of the British people, with famine and plague as their only lot? There was a time in the sixties when I had myself joined in pressing for a Gold Standard, when the burden of the conversion would not have been great as it would be at present. The crude, selfish, legislation of the past few years in matter of currency has been awful. As far as the Home charges are concerned, it will be of no benefit or matter to the Indian.

He will have to find or provide produce worth £19,000,000 sterling gold, whether the currency is gold or silver. It will be nice and easy for the officials and the non-officials who have to make remittances, and they will have no bother of fall or fluctuation of exchanges. Were it not for the tribute "cruel, crushing tribute" as Sir George Wingate calls it, to be paid by India, the fall in silver or in exchange would not have been of any consequence, just as in other silver-using, free, self-governing countries.

Trade would have adjusted itself according to the exchange. In another letter published in India (May 27), he complained that there was not a single man on the Committee who had shown at any time that he had studied or dealt with Indian questions from the standpoint of the poor Indian tax-payer, with the exception of David Barbour, who, however, was a judge in his own case, being himself the father of the legislation under contemplation. He submitted two statements to the Committee.

In the first he declared that the closing of the mints was an illegal, dishonourable, and despotic act. The authorities had bungled—what was the remedy ? "Retrace the false step of 1893," he said. "The opening of the mints to the unrestricted closing of silver will correct all the mischievous results that have flowed from the closing of the mints." Further, the true remedy .lay in reduction of expenditure and readjustment of establishments.

The second statement dealt with the evidence given before the Committee, drawing a distinction and emphasising a lamentable contrast between two Indias—the prosperous India of the British and the penurious India of the Indians, and dilating once more on the cruel and crushing tribute extorted from India, A conference of all the Indians resident in England was then held in St. Martin's Town Hall, London, on June 2. From the Chair Dadabhai submitted a resolution as follows:

That fall or rise in exchange does not in itself matter in true international trade, which adjusts itself automatically to the requirements of exchange; that closing the mints or introducing the Gold Standard does not and cannot save a single farthing to the Indian tax-payers in their remittances for "Home Charges"; that closing the mints and thereby raising the true rupee of about 11d. of gold to a false rupee of 16d. of gold is a cruel act of exacting 45 per cent more taxation from the Indian tax-payers, and at the same time of increasing the salaries of officials, and other payments in India by Government to the same extent; that the introduction of a gold standard will simply add more to the existing grievous burdens of the tax-payers to the extent of the cost of the alteration; that the real cause of the terrible evils of poverty, famine, plague, false currency, etc. is what Lord Salisbury calls the "bleeding" of India (or as he says "India must be bled"), and the "bleeding" is further increased by the fall in exchange or rise in gold; that until this most deplorable "bleeding" of India is stopped there is little chance, if any, of saving India and the British Empire from serious disorders or destruction....

During the last forty years the theories of political economy and public finance have undergone many modifications and qualifications, but most of the principles stressed and views expressed by Dadabhai hold good to this day. Although his opposition to the change from a silver to a gold standard would seem to have been ill-founded in the light of subsequent experience, the conception that in the long run a rise or fall in exchange is of no fundamental importance, inasmuch as ultimately commodities are exchanged against commodities, needed emphasis in Dadabhai's days, as it does even today. So also was it necessary to stress the difficulties of abandoning the silver standard and the cost involved, but his unmitigated opposition to the introduction of a gold standard appears today to have been misconceived. Time has muffled the sporadic outcries of the silver interests. The adoption of the gold exchange standard, it is now recognised, has turned out to be an advantage to India. She was thereby linked up to the progressive group of gold standard countries and saved from being the dumping-ground of the white metal which was discarded by country after country. Such a contingency could not, however, have been anticipated by those who lived in the days of Dadabhai. Nor was it realised in his days, as it has come to be recognised only recently, that the word "drain" has been one of the most heavily worked words in Indian Economics.

To revert to the House of Commons, Dadabhai tabled a Bill to provide that the first examination for appointments to the Civil Services of India should be held simultaneously in India and the United Kingdom. Such a Bill was not called for, as it was in the power of the Secretary of State for India to allow the examination. Moreover, with the Home Rule Bill and other questions of social legislation before the House, the Bill had not the slightest chance that year. Dadabhai knew that, but his object was merely to raise a debate. With great foresight he arranged for a resolution to the same effect being tabled by Herbert Paul simultaneously with the Bill.

Nothing was left to chance. The consummate canvasser had called on members individually and succeeded in impressing upon not a few the reason and justice of the demand. The chances of the Ballot brought Paul the privilege of opening a discussion on the question and moving his resolution on June 2. It was seconded by Dadabhai and supported by Wedderburn. All the arguments in favour of the proposal, with which the reader is now familiar, were successfully put before the House by Dadabhai.

Once more he drew a distinction between the declared policy of the rulers and the pernicious operation of the system of government. "Be just and fear not" was the policy of the people and the Parliament of England: whereas the policy of the Anglo-Indian system was "Fear and be unjust." It was for Parliament then to determine whether the declarations made in the name of God and before the world should be acted upon or not.

After a memorable debate the motion was agreed to. It was the proudest moment in Dadabhai's career; all India rejoiced with him. It was, in fact, his victory, for though the resolution was moved by Paul, it was inspired by him, and the support it secured was almost entirely the result of his active lobbying. It was also India's victory—a victory of right over might, of justice over aggression.

A resolution is, however, one thing; executive action another. At best the vote was a snatch one. It had caught Government napping. Not anticipating defeat, they had not rallied their forces for the private members' night. It seemed, therefore, probable that the resolution would remain inoperative. The Lords, moreover, had set their face against it. Dadabhai called upon all his friends, particularly Banerjee, Malabari, and Wacha, to meet that challenge. In a letter to Banerjee (June 16), he suggested a powerful agitation all over India as a counterblast to the opposition in England:

Petitions innumerable should pour into the Commons, approving of their action and praying for practical effect. The whole Conservative party and the Government are against. "We have the Irish and a portion of the Radicals with us. This is a supreme moment. Success on this occasion is of vast importance to our cause. Write to every part of India, rouse it up.... Such a good fortune may not again occur to us for some time. All the moral forces and exertions of the past 40 years from 1853 when the first political associations were formed in India have come to fruition. It will be our own fault if we lose this fruit now.

In his letter to Malabari he observed: "India on this supreme occasion must help herself. She cannot send too many petitions." About this time Dadabhai received a letter from his son-in-law, Fram Dadina, complaining bitterly of the injustice done to Indians in the Educational Service.

Even at the schools (he said) they are introducing raw men from England, superseding tried masters of fifteen and twenty years' experience. Our position is so desperate that it is difficult to keep control. Yet I think in stating our case these men have to be approached as the greatest benefactors that the world had produced. Such incidents confirmed Dadabhai more and more in his contention that Indianisation of the Services was the very foundation of all reform.

Home Rule is scarcely the word (said Dadabhai to a representative of Pearson's Weekly); we don't want anything in the least like what the Irish want. Our movement at present is only to obtain for Indians admission to the Legislative Councils as elected representatives and a fair share in the Civil Services.

Come, Mr. Naoroji (said he), do you mean to say that the end and object of all political agitation in India is to get a handful of young men into the Civil Service! How many would it affect?

Not one in five millions, I suppose.

Ah no (replied Dadabhai), it means a great deal more than you recognise. It is the very foundation of prosperity and adversity. The resolution of the House was not binding on the Government of India. It rested with the Secretary of State in Council whether to instruct the authorities in India to give effect to it or not. Lord Kimberley was, however, good enough to write to Dadabhai that although he was personally opposed to the suggested reform, he would not allow his personal opinion to stand in the way and that lie had, therefore, forwarded the resolution to the Government of India. This left a ray of hope that powerful agitation in support of the reform might soften the official opposition.

Till the end of the year Dadabhai continued his exhortations for extraordinary effort in India to raise a hue and cry for implementing the resolution of the Imperial Parliament. "Muhammadans must come out strongly everywhere," he wrote in one of the letters. In cooperation with Wedderburn and Caine he also set about forming a small party in the House of Commons pledged to give attention to Indian affairs. Wedderburn, always helpful as a colleague, and Caine, another unfailing friend of India, invited a few members to dinner on July 27, and an Indian

Parliamentary Committee was formed with Wedderburn as Chairman, and Mr. Herbert Roberts (now Lord Clwyd) as Secretary. The basis of the Committee was a shrewd suggestion made by R. T. Reid, M.P. (subsequently Lord Loreburn), in a letter addressed to Hume in 1885.

I would recommend you to secure two or three men, as influential as you can, in as many constituencies as you can, and get them to write to the candidate, exacting no pledge as to the course of policy but a simple pledge to give attention to Indian affairs, and publish the correspondence in local papers. Every candidate in the three kingdoms would pledge himself to so easy an obligation. One in ten would keep the pledge and thus give a nucleus of listeners in an Indian debate. The publication of the correspondence would make them afraid wholly to neglect business they had so publicly pledged to consider.

In the opinion of the Anglo-Indian Press simultaneous examinations for the Civil Service meant Babu raj, and the prospect of being governed by the Bengali Babu was a regular nightmare to the European community. "Experienced Anglo-Indians assure us," solemnly averred St. James's Gazette (June 12), "that the change proposed by Mr. Paul might lead to consequences almost as disastrous as the Mutiny. In India the Pioneer could not brook the country-wide agitation in favour of the reform.

Having got hold of a letter written by Dadabhai to the provincial secretaries of the Congress Committee, in which it was suggested that a clear and pronounced expression of public opinion should be communicated to the English Press so as to help the cause, it declared that the whole agitation was artificial and was merely "the work of Congress wire-pullers obeying Mr. Naoroji's detailed instructions." The Shimla correspondent of The Times flashed the news of the sensational exposure of the agitation to that journal:

I have done (retorted Dadabhai, August 9) what is done every day in this country by the powerful and influential The Times and the whole Press, by every organisation of every important movement, by the leaders of all parties, and, in short, by all the machinery that is employed in this country for every important movement. That the enthusiasm of India on the passing of this resolution is thoroughly genuine and spontaneous there cannot be the remotest doubt. The subject was taken up by the Indian Press and by the people generally, immediately on the arrival of the news by telegram and three weeks before my letter reached India. . . . Sir, India is following the good lessons which England has taught her—to agitate constitutionally and persistently for any just cause, and that we are determined to continue to do.

There being a general desire in India that Dadabhai should be invited to his motherland and given a rousing reception, the Lahore Committee of the Congress invited him to accept die office of President of the next Congress session, and he arranged for absence of a few weeks from his new scene of activities, little dreaming that his path homeward would be darkened by a dire domestic calamity.

Just as he was returning from his hospital work in Cuteh Mandvi, on the morning of October 7, Dadabhai's son Adi died of heart failure in the prime of life, leaving his wife with seven children ranging in age from I to 12. His fifth daughter, Khorshed, was born after his death. Deep sympathy was expressed by Dadabhai's friends in England and India. Amongst heaps of letters of condolence received by him from all parts of the world, there was one from Malabari, which, brief as it was, struck a touching note of solace:

I know you have enough of faith and fortitude to bear up against this grievous loss. Remember, all India is your son. Nothing could have been more prostrating than this calamity to a loving father like Dadabhai, but he bore the loss with remarkable fortitude and did not allow his private grief to intrude upon his public utterances or even upon his private correspondence. He attended to the Parliamentary work regularly, as if nothing had happened, and wrote to friends in India as before, giving his views and advice on the problems of the day.

It was not merely for India that Dadabhai had worked during that memorable year. He had rendered signal service to his electors individually and to his constituency generally. Proposals came to him almost every day from the Central Finsbury United Liberal and Radical Association and from the local authorities and individuals of the Division, asking their representative to raise questions in the House, or to use his good offices for some improvement or some relief. With his usual assiduity and alacrity Dadabhai attended to the mall. When, therefore, the constituency heard of his impending departure for India, the Council of the Liberal and Radical Association passed a resolution (September 28) wishing him Godspeed and according him their "hearty approval and thanks" for his persistent efforts in favour of popular rights and also for "his continuous attendances at the House of Commons during the session of unprecedented labour."

A member for a constituency has to do many things for it besides watching its interests in the House of Commons. He has to attend not only political meetings called by his own political party, but also those numerous social and charitable functions which are allied to no party. Besides warmly interesting himself in various charitable undertakings, Dadabhai took lively interest in the work of several friendly and temperance societies in Knsbury.

He was an Oddfellow, a Forester, a Druid, and a Good Templar, and was at his best when presiding over a Band of Hope Society and addressing the little children, whose hearts he knew so well how to touch. He had also many engagements with the London Municipal Reform League and various Trades Unions, Trade Societies, and Working Men's Clubs, which had supported him heartily at the election. To the Women's Liberal Federation, the National Union of Women's Suffrage Societies, the Women's Franchise League, and other organisations for the advancement of women he was a pillar of strength. They all came to him for subscriptions, advice, and cooperation in their activities.

The Member for India was in constant demand for addressing meetings of various organisations and clubs in his constituency, political and non-political; and he took delight in acceding to such requests so far as possible. Even the London Chamber of Commerce and the Institute of Bankers and other commercial bodies throughout England invited him to speak on economic and financial questions. All this made Dadabhai feel more and more conscious that he was but an instrument by which India had been enabled to make her voice heard in and outside the House of Commons and that his conduct and attitude as the first Indian

Member of Parliament should be such as to pave the way for other Indians to the Imperial Assembly.

On November 10 Dadabhai called on Lord Elgin, the Viceroy-designate of India, with a view to enlisting his sympathy in connection with the Indian problems awaiting solution. "I was the talker all the time," he wrote to Malabari, "upon my various views, and he a listener, and now and then he put me pertinent questions."

Owing to his bereavement, the public celebrations arranged for giving him a hearty sendoff to India had to be abandoned. Nevertheless, on the night of November 17, some fifty Indians had assembled on the platform of Charing Cross Station to bid him Godspeed.

Hero's Home-coming

Dadabhai's home-coming was marked by unparalleled enthusiasm and rejoicing throughout the country. His elevation to the highest Assembly in the British Empire marked an epoch in the political evolution of the Indian people. That historic event, coupled with his early victory in getting the House of Commons to endorse his demand for holding in India and England simultaneous examinations for the Civil Service, appeared to have advanced the political education and raised the political aspirations of India more than years of activities of all the national organisations put together. His triumph meant the triumph of the people, and their feelings of joy, and their sentiment of unity and solidarity thus awakened, were exquisitely reflected in the popular demonstrations held in his honour. The mail boat carrying Dadabhai was timed to reach Bombay harbour by midnight on December 2. The whole city was astir before daybreak. Crowds of people began to converge towards the place of landing. By 7 a.m. the Apollo Bunder was packed with a dense mass of people. The pier was decorated with flags and flowers and multicoloured bunting. In front of the structure facing the harbour was a motto in letters of gold, "Welcome Mr. Dadabhai Naoroji, M.P."; its companion motto on the other side being "God Save our Queen-Empress and the British Empire." Hundreds of flags and banners were carried by members of numerous deputations sent by various organisations from various parts of the Province. The roads leading to the Bunder were gay with flags and festoons, and there were mottoes, put up on coloured cloth bearing Dadabhai's portrait, thanking the Finsbury electors and welcoming "the bravest, noblest, and best son of India." On one of these banners was inscribed the benediction, "God bless thee, our selfless man and stainless gentleman," and on another the prayer, "India wants 100 like ye for her salvation."

There was not a road leading to the Bunder which was not thronged by hundreds and hundreds of citizens; and everywhere along the route were seen groups of women and children waiting to have a glimpse of the simple man of whose heroic exploits they had heard such fascinating stories. Here, there, everywhere were schoolgirls and schoolboys, with garlands in their hands, ready to greet the man revered as the Rishi (Saint) of India. The steamer was, however, behind scheduled time. She was not even signalled in the morning. The Reception Committee of citizens, after a hurried consultation, decided that the landing should take place at four o'clock in the afternoon.

The disappointed folk made their way home, but they turned out once more, long before the appointed hour, and came hack to the pier along the route fixed by the Committee. At 4 p.m. the steam-launch conveying Dadabhai and the members of the deputation arrived at the pier. He was dressed in his national costume—black coat and turban and red silk trousers. At the first glimpse the crowd made such a rush towards him that he could not meet even his two daughters and grandchildren, who were eagerly waiting for him in the pavilion. He had to be literally pushed by Pherozeshah Mehta, Chairman of the Reception Committee, into the carriage that was kept waiting near the pavilion.

In that imposing conveyance, drawn by four gray horses, Mehta and Javerilal Yajnik took their seats with the distinguished visitor.

A procession of carriages followed him, and his progress from the pier to his house in Khetwady brought to memory the scenes of triumph of the victorious commanders made famous in history.

From windows, from balconies, even from housetops, thousands of dusky faces peered down on the moving throng below, and until the conquering hero reached his home the sky was rent every minute with cheers and hurrahs. Almost every family and every institution brought their quota of flowers and poured them into the carriage in which he kept standing all along the route, bowing to the people.

At 6 p.m. the procession arrived at Dadabhai's house where he was received by his family, including his daughters and grandchildren who had hastened there from the Bunder. Among the friends who went with him into his house was his friend and colleague Seymour Keay, M.P., who had been a fellow-passenger with him on board the steamer.

It was, indeed, a welcome that even royalty might have envied. The first to congratulate Dadabhai on such a magnificent reception was the Governor of Bombay, Lord Harris. That gracious act of the highest citizen of Bombay made a happy people more full of joy. Two members of the Council, the Honourable Messrs. H. M. Birdwood and A. C. Trevor, and the Chief Justice, Sir Charles Serjeant, called on him later.

Members of numerous deputations from Puna, Satara, Belgaum, Sholapur, Surat, Broach, Naosari and other parts of the Bombay Presidency then met Dadabhai at the rooms of the Bombay Presidency Association, where he was requested by Wacha to relate to them his experience regarding his struggles to gain admission to the House of Commons. After referring to his first unsuccessful contest, which had enabled him to advertise himself loudly in the centre of the Metropolis, Dadabhai told the audience how on a vacancy occurring at Central Finsbury, he had jumped in at once. He had met with many disappointments, but his last trump card was India, which did not fail to excite interest. Referring to Captain Penton's petition, Dadabhai said it was easy to make indictments, but difficult to prove them.

Ultimately, like wise and sensible men they came to terms. He had been received in the House very cordially, and had obtained support even from Conservative members.

"And was not the late Prime Minister discomfited by your presence?" asked Dinsha Wacha.

"No" replied the high-minded man, carefully refraining from uttering a single word against the statesman whose ill-conditioned tongue had brought ridicule on himself. He merely remarked that the words used by Lord Salisbury had made him popular all over the United Kingdom. He was invited everywhere, and wherever there was a placard announcing his presence, there was sure to be a large and successful meeting.

On December 18 numerous addresses were presented to the popular hero at the Town Hall of Bombay by various organisations and deputations, the first being that of the Bombay Presidency Association, In thanking them all for the welcome extended to him at the Gate of India, beyond all the dreams of his dreams, he told them that such events as his election were a triumph and proof of the beneficent side of the British rule. He deeply felt his responsibility. He was hardly yet at the threshold of his work for India.

Dadabhai was then invited to unveil the portrait of Sir Dinshaw Petit, the retiring President of the Bombay Presidency Association. It was at his instance that this mill magnate had accepted the Presidentship of the Association and plunged into politics. With the greatest gratification, therefore, Dadabhai unveiled the portrait and complimented Sir Dinshaw on the catholicity of his benevolence.

On December 20 the President-elect of the Congress, accompanied by Wacha, Honorary Secretary, left Bombay for Lahore by the Ahmedabad mail. The wave of enthusiasm that had swept over the country swelled during this journey. Whatever the hour of arrival of the train at each station, day or night, midnight or dawn, men, women, and children in crowds came forward with the customary floral tribute for the darshan (sight) of the Grand Old Man.

At Baroda, where he had been given a loving sendoff as ex-Dewan, nineteen years ago, he was welcomed by the Dewan and the Nagarsheth of the day, and an address, enclosed in a casket, and a shawl were presented to him. A Hindu youth enlivened the proceedings by offering to the Indian Gladstone a silk-woven portrait of the Grand Old Man of England.

At Ahmedabad, in reply to the municipal address, he recalled with gratitude the shelter and help given to the ancestors of the Parsi community who had made Gujarat their home after their exodus from their fatherland. At Delhi, after the presentation of the municipal address, a procession was formed and Dadabhai was taken to his hotel through streets lined by people, who gave him an ovation, the like of which the people of that historic city had not witnessed before. At Amritsar the political Rishi of India was invested by the officiating priest of the Golden Temple with a robe of honour, according to the Sikh ritual—a signal honour for a Parsi.

At Lahore, which in those days was rarely stirred to enthusiasm on political issues, the Punjabis, including the Muhammadans, were intensely jubilant. As Dadabhai's carriage could only move at a snail's pace through the narrow and crowded streets, it took the procession no less than five hours to go from Lahore station to the Congress camp. On both sides of the road there was one unbroken mass of citizens. Almost every quarter of an hour his carriage, drawn by overjoyed students, with drums beating, bands playing, and banners flying, had to be stopped and cleared of bouquets, garlands, and loose flowers with which it was covered.

The address presented by the Reception Committee of the Congress referred in eulogistic terms to Dadabhai's study and mastery of Indian problems and of his advocacy of the cause of India: "The greatest gift the Parses have bestowed on India," it added, "is your own good self."

Then followed an address from the Muhammadans and another from the citizens of Lahore. The students of the capital of the Punjab, too, presented an address, stating that his historic victory had taught the younger generation what an Indian, despite all handicaps, could dare and do. In reply to all the addresses, Dadabhai said that his first and most earnest advice to them was that they should be loyal to the British Crown. The British people were always willing to do justice to Indians. Of that his election as a Member of Parliament was an indubitable proof. After exhorting them to rise above sectional feelings, he said:

> I am a Hindu, a Musalman, a Parsi, but above all the Indian My greatest happiness has been this, that all

> Hindus, Musalmans and Parses have expressed their joy at my return. . . . India Has a great future before it. I bless India. I bless you.
>
> "He had a welcome," wrote William Hunter in The Times, "such as has only on one occasion been rivalled even by a Viceregal ovation. His reception at Lahore has perhaps not been surpassed since the days of Ranjit Singh."

In the midst of such unbounded public enthusiasm and jubilations, however, Dadabhai's heart was sore. Terribly cut up as he was by the loss of his only son, who had cheered him in his patriotic struggle, he grieved for his sorrow-stricken widow even more. Meeting her for the first time after her bereavement, he was overwhelmed with grief. What about her future ? He gave her all the encouragement he could to remain in Cutch with the children, instead of returning to Bombay. Her implicit faith in his judgement and her own courage and patience enabled her to return to Cutch and accept the post of tutor to the heir apparent to the throne, which the Maharaja of Cutch had kindly offered to her. Thus was the connection of the family with the Cutch Durbar, which had commenced years before, when Dadabhai had helped it in its dispute with the Political Agent of Cutch, continued for many more years.

In his presidential address, Dadabhai exhorted the Punjabis not to play into the hands of those who were inciting them to oppose the holding of simultaneous examinations for posts in the Civil Service.

I have always understood and believed (he said) that manliness was associated with love of justice, generosity, and intellect... And I cannot understand how one could or should deny to you and other manly races of India the same characteristics of human nature. Yet we are gravely told that on the contrary the mainliness of these races of India is associated with meanness, unpatriotic selfishness, and inferiority of intellect, and that, therefore, like the dog in the manger, you and the other warrior races will be mean enough to oppose die resolution about Simultaneous Examinations, and unpatriotic and selfish enough to prevent the general progress of all India. Can offence and insult to a people, and that people admitted to be a manly people, go any further ?

He maintained that the efforts of the people of India had succeeded in creating not only an interest in Indian affairs among lie people of the United Kingdom, but also a desire to promote; he true welfare of India. There was, however, need for further agitation. "We must keep our courage and never say die."

Dadabhai then referred to the efforts made by Lal Mohan Ghose to enter Parliament, and observed:

> We owe a debt of gratitude to Deptford and also to Holborn, which gave me the first lift. . . . My mind also turns to those good friends of India—Bright, Fawcett, Bradlaugh and others—who pioneered for us, prepared for the coming of this result, and helped us when we were helpless.

Speaking of the reception given to him in the House of Commons, he said:

> It was everything that could be desired. The welcome was general from all sides, as the interest in Indian affairs has been much increasing, and there is a desire to do justice to India. Mr. Gladstone on two occasions not only expressed his satisfaction to me at finding an Indian in the House, but expressed also a strong wish to see several more. The attendance on Indian questions has been good, and what is still better, the interest in Indian debates has been earnest, and with a desire to understand and judge rightly.

Grateful as the Indian member was to his British colleagues, he was bound to express his special thanks to the Irish Labour and Radical members. Two days before his departure from England be had received this message:

> Don't forget to tell your colleagues at the Congress that every one of Ireland's Home Rule Members in Parliament is at your back in the cause of the Indian people.

The crucial question was: "What is to be our future work" Dadabhai pointed out how much remained to be accomplished in connection with the question of reforming the Councils. The real living representative voice of the people was not to be heard at the Legislative Councils. There should also be, he said, direct representation from India in the Imperial Parliament. All their imperial questions and relations between India and the United Kingdom, and their appeals, could be settled in Parliament alone. There should, therefore, be some reasonable direct representation from India in the House of Commons. "Under present circumstances," he continued, "we have a right to have direct representation. I hope the time is not very distant when we may successfully appeal to Parliament to grant us the true status of British political citizenship."

Then followed all the oft-repeated statements and arguments regarding the impoverishment of India, the costly services, the military expenditure and the burden of taxation. The Duke of Argyll characterised the charges as an unjust and illegal tribute to England, but mark, said Dadabhai, the words of Lord Cross:

> "I am certain that in the course of a few years the Indian people will force us to do them justice."

This is just the feature (said Dadabhai), to beforced to do justice, which I always deplore. We desire that all necessary reforms and acts of justice should be spontaneous on the part of Britain, in good grace and in good time as gifts claiming our gratitude, and not to wait till it was forced, with loss of grace from the giver and the loss of gratitude from the receiver.

The return journey from Lahore to Bombay via Agra, Allahabad, Bhusawal, Jalgaon, Khandwa, Manmad, and Nasik was another triumphal procession. It was the same story over again—enthusiasm of the people at white heat, deafening cheers, addresses and floral tributes galore, plentiful sprinkling of rosewater, bands playing, flags flying, all testifying to the cosmopolitan population's appreciation of and gratitude for the patriotic work done by the greatest Indian of the day, and demonstrating beyond doubt that national unity, even in a country divided by caste and creed, was not a dream.

On June 12 Dadabhai received the Bombay Municipal Corporation's address, eulogising his services to the City in every line of public activity. After several other functions in his honour he took his departure for England on January 22, by the mail steamer Satluj. A demonstration of the college students of the city having been organised in his honour, he drove up, on his way to the Bunder, to the porch of the Elphinstone College. Amidst scenes of lively enthusiasm an address was presented to the first Indian Professor of the College, who had returned to them, bowed with the weight of three score years and eight, as the acknowledged political teacher and modeller of the nation and the inspirer of its hopes and aspirations. "In our younger days," he said in reply, "we are said to be the hope and promise of our land. Now it rests upon you to fulfil that hope and promise in the future."

A large number of students then attempted to unyoke the horses from Dadabhai's carriage. The writer of this memoir was one of them. The scene is still vivid in his mind, and he has a lively recollection, too, of the cracks of the whip of the Parsi coachman, which kept the students at bay. Failing in that attempt, some of them walked in front of and some behind the carriage to the Apollo Bunder. Then a deputation, headed by the famous Parsi chronicler, Mr. R. B. Paymaster, proceeded on board the Satluj to give him a sendoff worthy of the revered guru whose life work it had been to teach, prepare, and organise myriads of disciples, old and young, to rise to the status of a free nation.

Historic Debates

"The Chairman and several members of the Central Finsbury United Liberal and Radical Association met me at the Station and gave me a 'good reception." Wrote Dadabhai to Malabari on his return to London. Thus auspiciously begun, the year 1894 ended in memorable work in the House of Commons.

The victory of 1893 in the battle of the Services had been nullified by the guerilla warfare carried on by the Government of India. "The House of Commons," said a distinguished judge, "had the power to do anything except to make man woman"; but in this case the bureaucracy in India had proved too powerful for the House. The victory of 1894, however, led to the fruition of

Dadabhai's strenuous efforts for the appointment of a Royal Commission to enquire into the question of Indian expenditure. It was his lifelong contention that a full and independent Parliamentary enquiry should be instituted not only into the condition and wants of the people of India, not only into the financial condition of the country, but also into the general system of government.

In the course of the Indian Budget debate Samuel Smith moved a resolution demanding such an enquiry. It led to a luminous discussion on Indian affairs such as the House had rarely listened to before. The terms of the motion enabled members on both sides to travel over a very wide area. Despite great conflict of opinion the debate was conducted with good temper. All the members who took part in it, namely A. Scoble, George Chesney, Seymour Keay, Richard Temple, William Wedderburn, and H. H. Fowler, spoke with full and personal knowledge of the intricacies and difficulties of the problem; they gave expression to divergent opinions on many points, according to their own angle of vision, but they were all actuated by one and the same motive, namely, to discharge honourably the sacred trust that had devolved upon the British nation. As to the wisest method of discharging the trust, it was impossible to expect them to see eye to eye, but they were all agreed that the supreme consideration should be the benefit of the people of India.

In opening the debate, Samuel Smith made it clear that he did not move the Resolution in any spirit of antagonism to the British Government. He could give the same assurance on behalf of those who supported it. Their desire was not to attack British rule, but to improve it. The main complaint of the Indian people was that the British system of government was too expensive for a poor country. He held that they were right. Having been associated with Dadabhai in the study of the question for nearly forty years, and having revisited India a little while ago, he produced facts and figures to establish the impoverishment of the country. The abyss that swallowed up the resources of the country was its growing military expenditure. The Indian people, said Smith, had no Parliament of their own; they made their mute appeal to the Mother of Parliaments. He begged the House not to reject it.

Dadabhai rose to second the Resolution. It was clear he was asking the House for a large draft upon its indulgence. His colleagues, however, listened good-humouredly to his speech, overlaid though it was, as usual, with all the quotations, facts, arguments, and appeals with which they had been made familiar by his treatises on the subject. He pointed out that the main features in the administration of the eighteenth century were "gross corruption and oppression by the Europeans," and that in the nineteenth century the "heavy weight of the European services" had reduced the country to a state of abject poverty.

Some weeks ago the right Hon. Gendeman the member for Midlothian wrote a letter to Sir John Cowan in which he stated that the past 60 years had been years of emancipation.... The Irish, the Jews, the slaves, all received emancipation in that wave of humanity which passed over this country ... in the very year in which the right Hon. Gentleman began his political career, the people of India also had their emancipation at the hands of the Liberal Party. It was the Liberal Party that passed the Act of 1833 and made the magnificent promises, explained both by Macaulay and Lansdowne. I would ask the right Hon. Gentleman to say whether, after the Liberal Party having given this emancipation at the commencement of his political career, he would, at the end of it, while giving emancipation to 3,000,000 of Irishmen, only further enslave the 300,000,000 of India?

The decision relating to the simultaneous examinations means riveting back upon them every chain broken by the act of emancipation. The right Hon. Gentleman in 1893, in connection with the Irish question, after alluding to the arguments of fear and force, said: "I hope we shall never again have occasion to fall back upon that miserable argument. It is better to do justice from terror than not to do it at all; but we are in a condition neither of terror nor apprehension, but in a calm and thankful state.

We ask the House to accept this Bill, and I make that appeal on the grounds of honour and of duty." Might I, then, appeal in these days when every man in India is thoroughly loyal, when there is loyalty in every class of the people of India, and ask is it not time for England to do justice to India on the same grounds of "honour and duty"?

George Chesney thought India's case was similar to that of people who were compelled to call in the aid of a doctor or a lawyer. It would, of course, be better for a man if he could cure himself in sickness, or if he could conduct his own lawsuit. But nobody would contend that because the man found it difficult to pay for the services of his doctor or lawyer, he should not be called upon to do so. The question was whether India had paid too much. He believed that the benefits which she had derived from the assistance of England, were far in advance of any pecuniary liability she had to bear.

Seymour Keay, who followed the official apologist, pointed out that those who had been singing the praises of the Government of India had missed the cardinal point of the Resolution under discussion—namely, that however excellent the government of India might be, the condition of the people of India was such that they could not discharge the enormous expenditure connected with it. It was not a question of the value of the government, but a question as to whether such a government could be sustained by the people.

The Secretary of State for India was not opposed to an enquiry, but what, he asked, was "a full and independent Parliamentary enquiry"? He believed all Parliamentary enquiries were independent. Perhaps the mover meant impartial. Or did he mean to restrict the class of members to be put on the Committee ? The proposal was to enquire into the condition and wants of the Indian people and their ability to bear the existing burdens, the nature of the revenue system, and the possibility of reductions in the expenditure; also the financial relations between India and the United Kingdom, and the system of government in India generally. That was a tall order. The Chancellor of the Exchequer was not prepared, in the previous year, to refer the British Constitution to a Select Committee. It was not to be expected that the House would now sanction referring the Constitution of the Government of India to a Committee. After all, any question relating to the Imperial policy with reference to India must be a question for the responsible Government of the day—no House of Commons would allow any Government to shelter itself behind the report of a Committee in dealing with such a question. The Secretary for

India admitted that it would be wise from time to time to have an enquiry as to how the revenues of India were spent. He suggested, however, that the motion might be withdrawn; in that case he would undertake, on the part of the Government, that at the commencement of the following session they would propose the appointment of a Select Committee to enquire into that question. Samuel Smith accepted the suggestion, holding himself and his supporters free to ask for an extension of the scope of the enquiry so as to enable the Committee to deal with the tax-paying capacity of the people of India.

Before a commission was appointed, Dadabhai raised another debate on the question to bring within the purview of the enquiry the question of apportionment of certain expenditure between England and India. On the Address in reply to the speech from the throne he moved, on February 12, 1895, an amendment to add the following words to the Address:

And we humbly pray that Your Majesty will be graciously pleased to direct Your Majesty's Ministers, to so adjust the financial relations between the United Kingdom and British India, with regard to all the expenditure incurred in the employment of Europeans in the British-Indian services, civil and military, in this country and in India, that some fair and adequate portion of such expenditure should be borne by the British Exchequer in proportion to the pecuniary and political benefits accruing to the United Kingdom from Your Gracious Majesty's sway over India; and that the British Treasury should sustain a fair and equitable portion of all expenditure incurred on all military and political operations beyond the boundaries of India in which both Indian and British interests are jointly concerned. He was not asking for charity. All he asked for, he averred, was that India should be justly treated. India fully appreciated the blessing of law and order under the British regime, but some law and order were absolutely essential to the existence of Europeans in that country as well as to the maintenance of the British rule.

The next question was: What was India's benefit and what was Britain's?

India has to pay for European services in both countries two hundred millions of rupees annually...Hundreds and thousands of millions of money are consumed and carried away in that way, and it places a monopoly of everything in British capital. We cannot compete with it, and the result is that you have not only the benefit of the officials receiving that money, but, under their patronage, of providing British traders, merchants, farmers, shipowners, planters, capitalists, and others. You have naturally a monopoly of all that has to be done, and the profits are all the profits of the British; we work for the British and for British profits, and the Indians are in a way worse off than the Southern slaves, for die reason that those slaves were taken care of and housed and fed by their masters. Further, they did not work on their own property, but the Indians do work on their own property, and give the profits of their work to the capitalists of European countries. The benefits received by the Indian are insignificant when compared with Britain's benefits.

Once more he put in a powerful plea for a policy of righteousness.

You may create an Empire by brute force, but you will never maintain it except by moral force founded on justice and righteousness ... if I asked that even the whole expenditure in regard to Europeans should be defrayed by the British exchequer, I would be amply justified.

It was one of his most impressive speeches in the House. His colleagues might or might not accept his statements or his views, but none could question the fairness of his demand for an enquiry. The Secretary of State pointed out that the issues raised in the amendment pertained to matters of Imperial policy and were not questions for a Select Committee; but he was not against an enquiry into the question whether an unfair share of home charges was placed on the Indian Exchequer. The mode in which that enquiry should be conducted had not yet been decided.

Reasons had been urged upon him to show that a Parliamentary enquiry was not the best mode. Accidents happened to Parliaments. They lasted a certain number of sessions; they might come suddenly to an end. Accidents, too, happened to members; members of one Parliament might not be members of the next. It had, therefore, been urged upon him whether it would not be desirable to have a small, but thoroughly efficient and impartial, Royal Commission to enquire into the question. Not only on behalf of his colleagues in the Government but also on behalf of his colleagues at the India Office and the Indian Government, he warmly assured the House that it was their desire not to oppress India, not to bleed India, not to injure India, but to go on in the career of progress that had characterised the rule of India by Great Britain.

Dadabhai then withdrew his amendment and sat down triumphant. He succeeded because he had mastered the subject and had facts to support his contention and because the House was convinced of his earnestness.

A proof of the desire of the Government not to injure India was a Bill for imposing duties on the import of cotton manufacture into India. The representatives of the vested interests, however, resorted to a manoeuvre to smother the measure. On February 21, 1895, Sir Henry James asked leave to move the adjournment of the House in order to discuss that "definite matter of urgent public importance."

Dadabhai rose indignantly to protest. Did he wish to see the Empire in India endangered, were he a rebel at heart, he said, he should have welcomed that motion. Such motions would increase the feelings of dissatisfaction and irritation among the Indian people which, if continued, would assuredly bring about disintegration.

I appeal to the Unionists to vote against this motion or they will drive the first nail in the coffin of British rule in India. . . . Remember, whatever you are, you are still like a stepmother. Children may submit to any amount of oppression from their own mother, but from their stepmother they will always demand the strictest justice.

Could he appeal to the Home Rulers ? If they meant Home Rule, they meant that it must rest entirely on the integrity of the Empire, but never was a motion brought before the House more separatist than the one under consideration:

> The passing of this motion would be the passing of a motion of disunion. Perhaps you may not feel the effect for some time, but I impress upon this great assembly that though a revolution may not take place tomorrow, it is the accumulation of many years, of

> many disappointments, many inattentions, that at last produces a revolution. Do not forget 1857. I, for one, desire from the bottom of my heart that the British rule and connection may last for a very long time.

About this time Russia was bent upon building up a vast Asiatic Empire. The Russian bogey was a nightmare to Britain. A fresh rumour of Russian invasion then formed a central topic of discussion in English newspapers. Dadabhai took the opportunity to give his views on the subject in an article entitled "The Fear of A Russian Invasion," which was published in the September number of India. Calling attention to the most important element in the problem, namely the attitude of the people of British India and of the Native States, he observed:

> If the system of the present despotism, drain and distrust are continued, sooner or later, perhaps sooner, if Indian human nature is like all other human nature, great trouble will ensue, whether Russia can invade or not. Invasion by Russia sinks into insignificance compared with the troubles that the British Indian system itself is storing up. I have been crying in the wilderness for a long time. ... If the internal problem is satisfactorily solved, we may quite contentedly leave Russia to her own devices....

Let there be a contented, not a distressed, British India and Englishmen may snap their fingers at any external danger.

How were the Indian authorities promoting contentment in India? Let Dadabhai put this question in his own stirring words, addressed to the Indian Expenditure Commission:

> Is it productive of loyalty and goodwill to tell the Indians, "you will be kept down with the iron heel upon your neck of European services—Military and Civil—in order to maintain our power over you, to defend ourselves against Russian invasion, and thereby maintain our position in Europe, to increase our territory in the East, and to violate all our most solemn pledges?

And all this at your cost, and mostly with your blood, just as the Empire itself has been built up. We have the power and for our benefit; and you put your Parliament and your Proclamation into your pocket."

"Are the Indian people dissatisfied with our rule?" asked a representative of Great Thoughts in the course of an interview with Dadabhai, shortly after the debate in the Commons (August 8,1895):

> Dissatisfaction is growing every day (replied Dadabhai), and he would be a bold man who asserted that it would not one day lead to some terrible disaster.

The country has since been often on the verge of disaster which, however, thanks to the Congress policy of non-violence, has so far been averted.

I prophesy (said Dadabhai, in reply to another question) that this constant violation of pledges, this persistent opposition to Indian interests and the deterioration and impoverishment of the country by an evil administration, must lead, sooner or later, to a rebellion. I hope I may prove a false prophet, but in the interests of the British Empire I say that forces are gathering, vast and powerful, which will succeed in shattering the British Indian Empire, if the present evil and destructive system of administration be not thoroughly reformed. . . . The Indian authorities are doing everything in their power to tempt Russia to invade India, both by their policy of dissatisfying the Indian people with their rule, and by making an easy road for Russia through the mountains of Afghanistan at our expense.

What then do you consider would be a wise policy to pursue with regard to India ?

To satisfy her with the justice of British rule (replied Dadabhai), to be honest and honourable in all our solemn pledges and thus to make Indians feel that to fight for the British rule is to fight for their own hearths and homes and property. With Indian subjects of such a temper you could defy half a dozen Russias.

In another interview given to G. W. Tooley, and published in The Humanitarian (June 1895), Dadabhai gave expression in more emphatic terms to his apprehensions of a revolt in India. Whether your past system was a righteous one for India may be a matter of argument, but face to face with an awakened population such as India now has, and will have more and more every year, the present system of government is an absurd and dangerous anachronism.. Russia shows you what will happen in India unless Indians are given more interest in the government. There will be secret societies. Do not misunderstand me (said he earnestly), there is immense gratitude in India to England. The present generation feels the benefit it has derived from education. . .. But succeeding generations will not feel that. They will start where men in India today leave off. They will have no personal memory of old India.

However improved the conditions in which they find themselves, they will accept them as a matter of course. They will demand more, and if they do not get it, they will rebel. No account of the work done by Dadabhai in the House of Commons would be complete without a reference to the part he took in the debates in the House concerning the opium trade.

Early in his career as a business man he had expressed his abhorrence of trades pandering to the lowest forms of sensual indulgence and had informed his partners that he would not touch the profits derived from the firm's dealings in opium and wines and spirits. He had also told Lord Harrington in his memorable correspondence with him that the opium trade was an instance of the demoralisation of the British Government itself. In 1886 he found several members of the House of Commons and other British citizens waging a war on opium, and he readily plunged himself into the contest. The Rev. Goodeve Mabbs, Secretary to the India and China League, called on him to seek his active cooperation in organising a concerted attack on the policy of Government. As he was then engaged in his first electoral campaign, it was considered desirable to suspend active efforts.

Soon after the election, however, he threw himself heartily into the movement. The object of the League was not confined merely to the suppression of the opium trade. It aimed at creating a powerful public opinion on Indian questions of a moral character themselves, or which were related thereto, and to carry on an agitation in that behalf. The practical measures principally promoted comprised, besides withdrawal from the opium trade, Indian Financial Reform and "native participation" in the Indian Government. In 1888 another organisation was formed, called the Society for the Suppression of the Opium Trade, with offices at Broadway Chambers, Westminster. Appealing to the great heart of England, it called all true Christians to a holy war.

How Britain came to be responsible for the evil may be briefly told. In several parts of the Indian Empire Government had a monopoly in the growth, manufacture and sale of opium. They licensed every poppy plant that was grown, subsidised the cultivator, bought the crop at a fixed price and manufactured the drug expressly for the Chinese market; sold it by auction at Calcutta and pocketed the profits. Public sentiment revolted against such a traffic, but Government pleaded their inability to do without the opium revenue and their apologists refused to admit that opium taken in moderation had any deleterious effect.

The Christian missionaries, who were unhappy eyewitnesses of the dire distress, disease and degradation directly attributable to the policy pursued by Government in this matter, were very bitter in their complaints to their friends in England. One of them burst out in indignation:

Bishop Heber sweetly sang

> Waft, waft, ye winds, His story
> And you, ye waters, roll
> Till, like a sea of glory,
> It spreads from pole to pole.
>
> But in the very deed we are saying
> Waft, waft, ye winds, the opium
> Prepared in England's name,
> To bring us golden millions,
> Whatever may be the shame.

These crusaders won a partial victory on the floor of the House of Commons on April 10, 1891. On that day a resolution was passed, affirming that the system by which Indian opium revenue was raised was morally indefensible and expressing the opinion that the Government of India should "cease to grant licenses for the cultivation of the poppy and sale of opium in British India, except to supply the legitimate demand for medicinal purposes," and that they should at the same time take measures to arrest the transit through British territory of opium cultivated in Indian States. The opium question was thus raised to a position it had never before occupied.

Dadabhai was pleased with the progress made, but it seems he was greatly disappointed that the real grievance of India for which his heart was aching and bleeding was lost sight of by the leaders of the anti-opium party. On October 31,1892, Joseph Alexander, Secretary to the Society for the Suppression of the Opium Trade, sent him a draft memorial to the Secretary of State for India, making China, not India, the prominent subject on this occasion, and asked him to join the deputation which was appointed to present it.

Dadabhai pleaded his inability to participate in the proceedings and wrote in reply:

As the Indian National Congress has not spoken yet, the views I express are only my own. You know already that I am in full sympathy with the moral object of the Society, and I have made some sacrifice for it. You also know that according to my view the Society unfortunately does not realise the real source of the disease and of all our other woes. Its members do not seem to have ever asked themselves the question why India is so poor as not to be able to pay for her own wants of government and why she must depend either upon poisoning another people, or upon the charity of the English people, or upon further grinding taxation beyond what she is already subject to, even to the oppressive taxation of a very absolute necessity of life like salt.

Then followed his lament over the millions drained away from the poor country, and his prayer that the British public would "look a little deeper into the Indian problem." When the question was once more raised in the House of Commons by Alfred Webb in June 1903, Dadabhai took the same line of argument. He had been studying the question, he told the House, for years and had edited a pamphlet against the opium traffic forty years before. While he maintained that that traffic was a curse both for England and India, he wished to point out that it was a mere fringe of the great question of Indian administration under the system then prevailing. Why should not the Commission, that was proposed to be appointed, go into the whole question?

This debate was memorable for the lucid exposition of the case by Gladstone. Speaking on behalf of the Government, he had the candour to admit that it happened not infrequently in human affairs that those who ought, from their position, to know the most and the best, yet from prejudice and prepossession knew the least and the worst. While, therefore, he refrained from supporting the viewpoint of the authorities on the spot and was prepared to refer the matter to a Commission for enquiry, he took the opportunity of explaining that Government had ceased forcing the trade upon China. They had left the matter to China herself except that the opium which they allowed to be exported and for which they derived a large revenue was sent to that country to be received by China, if she chose to receive it.

The Commission that was appointed made its report in 1895. The anti-opium party was not satisfied with its findings. It complained bitterly that having appointed the Commission, Government had proceeded to "dry-nurse" it. The witnesses were directed; the anti-opium party was not allowed to bring up a single witness. There was further agitation. A public meeting was organised to strengthen the hands of Joseph Pease, the hero of several struggles in the past, in launching another battle. Dadabhai was one of the soldiers in that fight. There was another debate in the House on May 29, 1895, hut the defeat of the Government on the question of the supply of cordite, its resignation and the subsequent dissolution of the House on July 8th, put an end to Dadabhai's activities in that direction.

Drink was another curse which Dadabhai hoped to see eradicated during his lifetime, and it seems best to give here a brief account of his activities for the suppression of that evil. In his two lifelong colleagues in politics, Caine and Samuel Smith, he found two ardent champions of the temperance movement in England. When Caine was in Bombay in the year 1888, he called a conference of representative Indians where a strong desire was expressed that an organisation should be formed in Great Britain, to act in conjunction with branch associations in India, with a view to saving India from the growth of the drinking habit amongst the people. The Anglo-Indian Temperance Association was inaugurated accordingly, with Samuel Smith as President. Dadabhai was a zealous member from its inception and a member of the Executive Committee for several years.

The cooperation of the National Temperance Association of Great Britain was secured, and public opinion was stirred in both countries. A wave of temperance enthusiasm then swept over India such as is witnessed today under the regime of Congress ministries pledged to the policy of prohibition. Branch Committees were formed in all the principal cities of India and a network of Temperance Societies was established throughout the country.

Lectures were organised and suitable literature distributed in every Province; deputations from England were sent to India with a view to the encouragement of the workers and the extension of the movement. It was Dadabhai's contention that Indians were not a drinking people and that the religion of large numbers of them had prohibited the use of intoxicating liquors.

All that was needed was to prevent wines and spirits going to India, but while giving India Western civilization, the British Government had introduced in that country, which was by religion and life abstinent, what Caine called "the most Western of all institutions," the excise system, and with it the liquor-shop.

Almost all the distilleries in India belonged to Government. They let out liquor-shops by public auction to the highest bidder who undertook to sell the largest number of gallons of liquor from the distilleries.

The Association got a resolution carried in the House of Commons (April 1889), calling upon the Government to introduce drastic reforms in the Indian Excise administration. In their annual statements exhibiting the moral and material progress of India, Government took credit for having restricted the use of illicit intoxicants. But did it affect the sobriety of the people?

In that romantic publication itself was to be seen from year to year evidence of considerable increase in the excise revenue, which was due not merely to improved excise administration but also to the increased consumption of "licit liquor."

The moral evil of the yearly growing consumption of liquor, the harvest of crime, destitution, disease and death, was apparent to many; but its economic evil was not so readily realised. Addressing one of the Temperance Lodges, on April 8, 1891, Dadabhai pointed out that the Drink Bill of the English nation amounted to about £130,000,000.

Now (said he) if so much money were simply thrown away into the sea, it will be but a small evil. But the evil is doubled and multiplied. So much material, the gift of nature and labour, fit for the food of man, is converted into so much not only ton-nourishing but destructive material. While, therefore, on the one hand the people are deprived of food with all this money, they are on the other hand demoralised by the drink that takes the place of the destroyed food. This want of food, then, not only diminishes so much production and power of labour, but makes the labourer worse than useless, inflicting poverty, starvation and misery upon him and his family and causing crime. I do not know how the misery and suffering of the general deterioration of the whole race can be valued by any amount of money.

...A few figures speak more eloquently than a volume of words. I take the total cost of drink to be about £130,000,000. This means that about the same amount would have supplied the whole people of the United Kingdom all the year round with all the bread (70,000,000), butter and cheese (£35,000,000) and milk (£30,000,000), or the same amount would have supplied all the people all the year round the whole house rent (£70,000,000) and all the woollen and cotton and linen goods (66,000,000).

Fancy all this good not only not obtained, but on the contrary evil to that amount inflicted upon the people and, thereby, the power of reproducing all that wealth more or less destroyed. But worst of all—there is general deterioration of the nation and the diminution of the average length of human life.

In his opinion, the position taken up by the Association, namely the Veto, was the only right course to adopt. Wherever a good majority of the people desired to get rid of the evil, they should have the power of stopping it. It was simply the right application of the democratic principle that the good of the people at large, and not the indulgence or supposed pleasure of a few, should decide the condition of a community.

Dadabhai continued:

> The Liberal programme has definitely accepted the "Veto"— stick hard to it! Now is the time to make a supreme effort Send the Liberal Government in and hold it fast to die fulfilment of its pledge, and the oldest of us will live to see the accomplishment of the "Veto," and the destruction of the evil as far as human means can accomplish it!

In pursuance of a resolution passed at the Annual Meeting of the Association, presumably at the instance of Dadabhai, a considerable number of Indians resident in London, mostly students, met at Westminster Town Hall, to inaugurate an "Indian Brotherhood of Total Abstainers." Samuel Smith presided and blessed the movement. He believed, with Dadabhai, that one of the most hopeful and effective ways of grappling with the drink evil was to make the rising generation detest it and regard it as its duty and life's purpose to destroy it. The Indian Brotherhood was formally inaugurated and Dadabhai was elected President.

The elements of English society to which the promoters of the organisation belonged (he observed) were often despised as faddists and fanatics; yet it was mainly to the efforts of that section of the community that all the great moral and social reforms of the country were due; to wit, the abolition of slavery, the emancipation of the Jews, the removal of Roman Catholic Disabilities, and many other similar movements. The founding of this Brotherhood is a little seed sown for the emancipation of India, and as such he was proud to be connected with it. Another promising feature about it is that Hindus and Muhammadans were able to meet together and to take concerted action upon the great question which affected all communities alike.

The Brotherhood does not appear to have promoted the cause of abstinence to any appreciable extent. It was not, however, to be expected that a floating population of students could achieve much in that direction. Dadabhai was content to see young students interested in the temperance movement and carrying with them to India a sense of abhorrence of the drink habit. Ever optimistic, he looked forward to the day when all India would vote for prohibition. Speaking on the resolution moved by him at the meeting of the Anglo-Indian Temperance Association, held on April 17, 1905, regarding the action of Government in withdrawing the Bengal Excise Bill, and referring it back to local officers, he observed:

They had 300 branches of the Association in India, and this meant that people of all classes, creeds, and of every position from the top to the bottom, were learning the great lesson of associating together, becoming like brothers to each other, working for one great cause. . . . These 300 societies would grow into 3,000 and many more, and the 300,000,000 of human beings in India were being prepared for a higher and more civilized condition of life. This association was starting not only the cause of breaking down drinking in India, but the equally good cause of raising the people to a higher position of thought and of union which would be of the greatest use to them.

Unseated

Long expected announcement of the appointment of a Royal Commission was made towards the end of May 1895.

By a Royal Warrant, dated May 24, Commissioners were appointed, with Lord Welby as Chairman, to enquire into the administration and management of the Military and Civil Expenditure incurred under the authority of the Secretary of State for India in Council or of the Government of India, and the apportionment of charges between the Governments of the United Kingdom and India for purposes in which both were interested. Dadabhai was invited to join the Commission. He was the only Indian member, but there were two British members as good as if not better than Indians—Wedderburn and Caine.

A seat on the Royal Commission meant arduous work, particularly for Dadabhai, who had been agitating for years for the appointment of such a Commission. At the first session of the Indian National Congress he had moved a resolution asking for an enquiry into the working of the Indian administration through a Royal Commission. After ten years the request was granted.

It was up to him to make out a strong case for reform. He had to convince the hard-headed statesmen constituting the Commission that all that he had been urging against the foreign rulers was not mere talk, that every statement made by him was based on facts and figures and that what he had urged and wished to bring home to his colleagues was supported by the evidence of capable witnesses. He had also to equip himself with complete data to cross-examine hostile witnesses, particularly the official block. He had, moreover, to make up his mind and ask his friends in India to make up their mind and to state to the Commission in clear and definite terms what it was that India wanted as a practical and efficacious remedy of all the ills of which she had been complaining. Even for a giant like him the task seemed overwhelming. Had he the time to cope adequately with it ?

The dissolution of Parliament on the heels of the Commission's appointment should have left him free for the work.

But Dadabhai would not thus allow himself to be excluded from the House. He had now greater claims on the suffrages of Central Finsbury than ever before; and he was adopted as the candidate for the constituency at a meeting of the United Liberal and Radical Association, held on March 14. Heartily approving of the admirable manner in which he had performed his duties in the House of Commons, the meeting pledged itself to use its best exertions for his election.

The chances of success for a Liberal were, however, very poor. During the term of office of the Liberal Parliament, important questions seriously affecting various powerful interests had come to the front. Death duties, Land questions, and a trend towards progressive Labour legislation had roused the ire of landlords, capitalists, monopolists, and other monied interests.

The question of Local Option had antagonised the publicans, who worked like one man to save themselves from the threatened ruin of their business. The question of Disestablishment and Disendowment had frightened the Church interests, and the question of abolition of the House of Lords had enraged the aristocratic element in the country. To quote Dadabhai's own words in a letter to Wacha, "the parson, the peer, the publican and property were fighting a life-and-death struggle against the coming doom."

Slender though the chances of success against such a combination force were, Dadabhai threw himself heart and soul into the struggle. In his address to the Electors he pointed out how he had fulfilled his promise that he would devote all his time to Parliamentary duties and that the local wants and interests of his constituency would have his special attention. In 1892 there was only one division in Parliament, and he had voted in it. In 1893-94 the Session was divided into two parts. In the first part there were 310 divisions, in 304 of which Dadabhai had voted.

During the second part of the Session he was absent for some months owing to his visit to India, but in 1894 he had voted in 231 divisions out of 246. In 1895 there were 139 divisions and he had voted in 118. Few members could claim such a record of regular attendance. When he had to miss a meeting, he was always paired so that not a single vote had been actually lost by the constituency. Dadabhai claimed that he was closely attentive to Committee work also and that the local wants and interests of Clerkenwell had always had his prompt, earnest, and careful attention. He then stressed the good work accomplished by the Liberal and Radical Party during the three years, but although a good deal of progressive legislation had been put through, much of the great Newcastle Programme still remained to be carried out.

It followed that all Liberal and Radical electors should exercise their sovereign power and send back the Liberal Party to carry through the great work entrusted to them in 1892. A few of the items of the important work which lay before them he enumerated as under:

For Irish Home Rule, the Liberal Party are bound by every duty of honour, and even by self-interest. It will be one of those glorious landmarks of civilization in British history with which it is replete during the present century. The Welsh Disestablishment; Home Rule for London in all its various important requirements; the restriction of the Veto of the House of Lords, if not its Abolition; Taxation of Land Values for National and Municipal Purposes (a Bill for the latter purpose had been twice introduced by him); Division of Rates between Owners and Occupiers; Payment of Members; Perfect and Easy Registration of Electors by Responsible Public Registration Officers; One Man One Vote; Residential Adult Suffrage; Eight Hours; and Direct Popular Veto of the Liquor Traffic.

Enthusiastic meetings were held in support of Dadabhai's candidature and powerful appeals made by local Liberal leaders to support their "present faithful, devoted member." One of the leaflets ran as follows:

Who stood by the Poor Costers in Farringdon Road? Why, the Radical Clubs and Trade Unions. Then Costers, Vote for Radical and Trade Union causes and D. Naoroji.

Similarly, the Irish National League backed the Indian Gladstone, so that in spite of the storm that was blowing over Liberalism, Dadabhai's prospects did not seem quite gloomy. On the eve of the election wrote Martin Wood: "I hear hopeful reports of your prospects; go ahead."

Dadabhai was, nevertheless, caught in the storm. The wave of reaction which submerged William Harcourt in Derby and John Morley in Newcastle was equally destructive in Central Finsbury. While Dadabhai was busy in the House of Commons, his opponent, the Hon.W. F. B. Massey Mainwaring, had been assiduously pushing his claims to the seat. Besides ample leisure and unlimited resources, he had two powerful allies in the Church and the liquor interest, and he won the seat by a majority of 805 votes, the figures being 3,588 against 2,783.

Whilst a distinguished Indian patriot was thus unseated, another Indian, M. M. Bhownaggree, who had no pretensions to a mastery of Indian problems or to patriotic service, but whom, according to general belief, the Unionist Party had put forward as a counterpoise to Dadabhai, was returned for Bethnal Green.

He defeated the Liberal candidate, G. Howell, by 160 votes. His political creed differed from Dadabhai's so radically that his election gave rise in India to serious apprehensions. Indeed, Bhownaggree's attitude was then spoken of in Congress circles as Anglo-Indianism run mad. Although he was not so abjectly pliant as he was often represented to be, soon after he entered the House he was named "Bow-and-Agree" and "Bow-the-Knee." It might have been a matter of some consolation for India if instead of one so distrusted, another Indian, W. C. Banerjee, who had been attempting to wrest Barrow-in-Furness from the Unionists, had been elected. But while the Liberals were routed in almost every contested election, the famous Bengali lawyer was also among the wounded.

India heard of Dadabhai's exclusion from the House of Commons with deep regret. He, however, took his defeat calmly. It did not make his courage flag for a moment. In a letter to Sir George Birdwood (July 25), he said:

> The wave against the Liberals has been irresistible. However, I am not depressed or discouraged. ... In the well-nigh fifty years of my public life I had my successes and reverses, and the present defeat cannot affect me more than any did before.

The high-toned message which he sent to his fellow-countrymen shows that his failure simply made him face the world with redoubled energy.

In such a general wreck of the Liberal Party, I have suffered as one of them. But the only policy upon which I have acted through life—the policy of "Go on with patience and perseverance" whether successful or unsuccessful in any good cause—is the one upon which I shall act now as ever before. As long as I have the health and opportunity of serving my country I shall continue to do so. This is the last work of my life, and I intend to go on with it. I mean, therefore, to try to get into the House of Commons again, as it is there that the battle of the grievances and necessary reform of India and the stability of the British Empire have to be fought. The good of India is the good of the British Empire. Vast and powerful forces are working and growing in India. If the statesmen of the day do not direct them to the promotion of the interests of the Empire, producing satisfaction and prosperity among the people, they cannot and should not expect that these forces will not go against the British rule and end in some disaster. My humble efforts have always been, and will continue to be, directed to avert this calamity as far as an individual's efforts can go.

The moral he drew from the result of the election is of profound significance to the student of socialism and class warfare.

In 1688 (said he in a letter to Wacha) the Aristocracy usurped the place of monarchy, leaving the people in the cold as ever. The evolution of two centuries has at last transferred the sovereign power to the people. A portion of the masses do not seem to have realised their sovereign power and they have made themselves the instrument of their own suicide . . . and the disaster of the present election is the defeat and suicide of the working men by a section of their own ranks who have succumbed to influences which have always mastered them, which have always kept them under heels and which have always used every legislative and administrative means to keep them demoralised and subjected. Their defeat itself will help in wakening them up to a clearer sense of their powers . . . and the present catastrophe is really the defeat and discomfiture of the masses by the classes.

Wacha enquired, whether it was true that Dadabhai had refused to accept a sum of Rs. 5,000, offered to him by J. N. Tata towards his election expenses. Dadabhai replied that he had thankfully declined the offer. "I may say" he added, "that the expenses will be more—Rs. 15,000."

To Malabari also he wrote:

> I am alright about finances. This election cost just as much as usual. It is not merely the cost of the election, but it is the running expense all along which tells heavily.

The reason why he could afford to refuse financial assistance is stated specifically in a letter to Narendranath Sen (October 20):

> I thank you for the earnest way in which you have recommended to other people to support me with funds for the next election. But ... I do not need any money help. I cannot tell you how that is—beyond that there is some silent patriot in India who appreciates the future result of my work and with full knowledge of my position and expenditure has supplied me with all I needed before and would need for some time to come.

> Had I not found such a friend of India, I should not have been able to do what I have done, however little or much it may be, and what I may hereafter be able to do.
>
> What I need is not money. It is an awakening of earnest patriotism among the people at large—an understanding of their degraded position and poverty—and a continuous loud cry and agitation for remedy till the British public is convinced of this awakening and that the Indian people mean business.

That silent patriot who supplied all his needs for the future was, it appears from other correspondence, though his name is not specifically mentioned, His Highness Maharaja Shri Bhagvat Singhji, the Thakore Saheb of Gondal, who was his lifelong friend and admirer.

During the time Dadabhai sat in the House and, subsequently, during the days he was sitting on the Royal Commission on Indian Expenditure, there was a desire generally expressed in India and England that he should be knighted. In a letter to Fram Dadina (August 12, 1897), Dadabhai deprecated the idea and stated that those who were moving in the matter could not understand how embarrassing it would be to him.

It is best to pause here to notice Dadabhai's firm efforts to discourage such attempts in subsequent years. The Shah of Iran also wished to decorate Dadabhai. The news was conveyed to him by Bhownaggree. Dadabhai wrote in reply:

> With reference to the intimation about His Majesty the Shah's intention of manifesting his goodwill towards our community of which we had such exceedingly gratifying assurance from His Majesty—by bestowing upon me a decoration, I fully and deeply appreciate the great compliment which I should feel in receiving it. But as the prevailing sentiment in my mind at present is not to have any personal decoration, I think it will be as well for me to keep to this sentiment. I repeat that I feel the compliment and honour most deeply and gratefully.

After his retirement from active public life, the proposal was often revived. Dadabhai would not, however, agree to his name being submitted for any decoration. His lifelong friend Wedderburn was no stranger to his emphatic views on the subject, but even he was seized, in the year 1911, with a feverish desire to see Dadabhai knighted, not because Dadabhai needed such a recognition, but because Wedderburn thought that an honour to him would mean an honour to the Constitutional Party in India.

Lord Sydenham, the Governor of Bombay, was only too willing, but would Dadabhai consent? Wedderburn wrote to Gokhale.

Soundings were taken, as would appear from Wedderburn's own letter to Gokhale (October 19, 1911):

I am glad that you agree with me as to the public benefit, both to the Government and the Constitutional Party, from an honour conferred on Mr. Dadabhai. I thought we were in a fair way to accomplish it, but now there is a bolt from the blue. I learn privately that Mr. Dadabhai has intimated his unwillingness to accept any honour. This is quite a natural feeling, looking to the independence of his character and entire absence of self-seeking, but in the public interest I think we should ask him to overcome his reluctance. I always knew that he had no wish for recognition, rather that it was distasteful to him, but looking to the great public benefit from an honour to him as the father of the Constitutional Party and a believer in the ultimate justice of the British people in India, I thought he would acquiesce. It would, as an act of statesmanship, rank with Lord Hardinge's reception of the Congress Deputation.

Dadabhai, however, adhered to his decision, and the spectre of knighthood, which had disturbed his peace of mind from time to time, was at last laid at rest!

Indian Expenditure Commission

We have already recorded several difficult tasks essayed and accomplished by Dadabhai, but his prolonged and vehement struggle for instituting an enquiry into the financial administration of India, his arduous work on the Royal Commission appointed for the purpose, and his efforts to get others to convince the Commission of the need for reform, beat all records. He could never have done justice to his work on the Commission had he been simultaneously saddled with Parliamentary duties. The loss of his seat in the House of Commons was, therefore, a blessing in disguise; it set him free to concentrate all his time and energy on that all-important work for the better government of India.

Before the dissolution of Parliament and before the Commission was constituted, he had written to Wacha (January 31, 1895):

Do you think you can get leave and come here for six months to work here for preparing material for the Select Committee in conjunction with Morgan Brown (Secretary to the British Committee of the Congress) and for lecturing about, as the British Committee may direct?

Wacha could not then embark on that mission. Now, however, relieved of Parliamentary duties, Dadabhai was free to draw up a case himself. He merely wanted friends in India to send separate statements supporting the case.

Lord Welby was a capable and considerate Chairman. The other members of the Commission were all seasoned statesmen, devoid of anti-Indian bias. Nevertheless, from the commencement Dadabhai feared (and his apprehensions came true) that with Wedderburn and Caine he was in a minority of three. At the very first meeting there was a sharp cleavage of opinion as to the scope of the subject-matter referred to the Commission. It was suggested by some of his colleagues that the apportionment clause had for its object only the settlement of the disputes between the India Office on the one hand and the War Office and the Admiralty on the other. Against thus restricting the enquiry Dadabhai entered an emphatic protest. In the course of the debate in the House of Commons, on his amendment to the Address, he had made it clear that he was praying for an adjustment of the financial relations between the United Kingdom and British India with regard to all the expenditure incurred in England and in India. Moreover, the Secretary of State for India had stated that Government were quite willing that such an enquiry should take place. In the terms of reference to the Commission there were no restrictions, nor was there any reference to the particular matters in dispute between the India Office and other departments of the Imperial Government. Yet the majority attempted to whittle down the enquiry.

"The beginning does not augur well," wrote Dadabhai to Wacha on May 26. In the next letter (June 6), he stated:

All such Royal Commissions have a great disadvantage that however honest, sincere, and independent any particular member may be, it is difficult for him to see things from an Indian's point of view or put himself in the Indian's place.

Officialdom seemed to be bent upon thwarting him, as it had thwarted his efforts to get redress in the matter of the Civil Service examination. He too must be ready for a counterattack.

Hence the following request, in a further letter to Wacha, for the supply of munition (July 25):

If you can possibly send me some specific instances in which the Government officials approach persons to get evidence on their side—send them.

In the midst of this preliminary work for the great enquiry the Civil Service question was not shelved. Nay, it formed part of the enquiry itself. Dadabhai was determined to raise the issue once more in connection with the investigation. At the same time pressure was to be brought continuously on the authorities in England to give effect to the Resolution of the House of Commons. He kept on exhorting friends to overwhelm the authorities with monster petitions. For instance, in a letter to Raja P. Mohan Mukerjee, it was urged:

All India and Bengal especially must unceasingly make efforts to demand and obtain justice. We must have thousands of petitions to the House with hundreds of thousands of signatures, continuous agitation in India—meetings all over the country—and the British people and Parliament must see that India is earnest and dissatisfied and will not cease agitating till the reform is made—and then we may be sure that it will be made and justice will be done to us.

Similar letters were sent to several prominent Indian politicians and circular letters to all the Congress Committees and other organisations in India:

Though I am out of Parliament at present, do not on any account slacken your efforts to go on sending petitions from all parts of your district on simultaneous examinations. They will be duly presented and when the time comes for action they would be exceedingly useful...

Dadabhai then began writing a series of notes expanding the case for India as argued by him in the House of Commons. The first note was placed in the hands of Lord Welby on October 17.

In it he expounded the scope of the enquiry, quoting chapter and verse to show that the intention was to ascertain whether the existing system of the administration and management of expenditure, both in England and in India, secured sufficiency and efficiency of services, and all other satisfactory results "at an economical and affordable cost"; whether there was any peculiar inherent defect, or what Bright called "fundamental error," in that system; and whether there was any necessity or otherwise of every item of expenditure. Then he quoted the authority of the Duke of Devonshire (Lord Harrington in 1883) to show that India was insufficiently governed. A country insufficiently governed could not be efficiently governed. As regards cost, so great an authority as William Hunter had stated that India could not afford to pay for the increasing amount of administrative labour at the English rates, which were the highest in the world, and that she could only afford to pay for it at her own rates, which were, perhaps, the lowest in the world. The inherent drawback in the prevailing system was the evil inseparable from the governance of a remote foreign dominion. To ascertain the necessity or otherwise of the expenditure, every item of it in both countries had to be considered.

The second part of the reference to the Commission related to the apportionment of the charges between the Governments of the United Kingdom and of India for purposes in which both were interested. Dadabhai desired that all the purposes in which both the countries were interested should be first ascertained, that every item of expenditure incurred for such purpose should be examined and that it might then be determined how far each of the countries was interested therein. The next thing to do, lie suggested, would be to ascertain the comparative capacity of each country, so as to fix the right apportionment. Then followed a long dissertation on the extreme poverty of India, the alarming expenditure and the crushing burden of taxation. No less an authority than Gladstone had admitted, as far back as 1870, that India was a country "too much burdened/' and, in 1893, that her expenditure, especially the military expenditure, was "alarming."

"From the beginning of the British connection with India up to the present day" complained Dadabhai, "India has been made to pay for every possible kind of expenditure for the acquisition and maintenance of British rule, and Britain has never contributed her fair share (except a small portion on few rare occasions such as the Afghan War) for all the great benefits it has always derived from all such expenditure from the revenues of India."

On a perusal of this formidable note, Caine wrote to Dadabhai:

> I concur in all your views... . We shall, I am afraid, be headed off at every turn with the ridiculous "policy" restriction. If it is stretched too tightly, as I fear it will be, it is quite possible we three may have to leave the Commission in a body as a protest.

Thus from the commencement the pro-India trio appear to have anticipated trouble. Already they had lost all hope of converting the majority to their views, and the following extract from Dadabhai's letter to Wacha (November 7) shows that he had even visualised a minority report:

A supreme effort is to be made now in this Commission. We may not get another opportunity of the kind for a generation. Whether the Commission accepts your representation in part or full, or not at all, will be of no consequence. ... It will be an antidote to any mischief of the report of the Commission and will enable us to make our own Minority Report with effect.

The great necessity is that we must be supplied with complete proof of each point in the letter or any other points you may think proper to take up. . . . From what has transpired it seems that an effort is made to show that the administration in all departments as it exists at present is all that can be desired.

Then followed instructions to Wacha that he should draw up a memorandum of what it was proposed to establish and send it to the principal centres for filling up the details and for the adoption of such a representation in each Province either by a recognised organisation or at a public meeting.

No administration or management of expenditure (he added) can ever be satisfactory unless those that supply the means have their will in and management of it. In other words, the Budget must be completely debatable, as in this country, in a Legislative Council in which the Indians themselves are fairly represented.

Similar instructions were given to Surendranath Banerjee, Veera Raghavachariar, Pandit Madan Mohan Malaviya, Motilal Ghose, and numerous other Congress workers.

The very next day he wrote to Wacha:

> In addition to what I have written to you in yesterday's letter I want to say that I particularly desire to have every information of facts and figures and cases to support my propositions about the insufficiency and inefficiency of the services and the inconvenience, trouble and expense caused thereby to the people.

Then came a suggestion from Caine that the British Committee of the Congress should ask the Congress to select two witnesses to give evidence before the Commission. Dadabhai asked Wacha to send a precis of the evidence for the information of the Commission with the names of the witnesses so as to reach him before January 20,1896. The names of Pherozeshah Mehta, Surendranath Banerjee and Ghose were suggested. Dadabhai wanted Wacha as a third witness, if he was not one of the two selected. Dr. K. N. Bahadurji was then in England—one of the few medical men of the day who took part in politics, with nationalist tendencies.

He was nominated a witness by various medical organisations in India to give evidence on the questions affecting the Indian Medical Service. Wacha was prepared to give evidence; and his name was submitted by Wedderburn.

There was another eminent Indian whom Dadabhai longed to see pitted against the official hierarchy—Mahadev Govind Ranade, the distinguished jurist, economist, and social and political reformer, highly esteemed for independence, impartiality and sobriety of views. Would he go?

Dear Ranade (wrote Dadabhai imploringly, June 18,1896), you have an opportunity now to do the greatest service you can to our poor country that you will have in your lifetime. Come and support me in your own able way. ... If this want of honour, honesty and righteousness of the British Indian authorities—and the terrible misery as its result—be made clear to the British public by such authority as of you three (Mehta, Wacha and Ranade) supporting me—what may not happen to our good?...

You are distinctly admitted as in the position of an independent non-official—with the authority of die impartiality and independence of your life. Your position being thus admitted, you have nothing to shrink from in giving an emphatic and clear view of the deplorable condition of India.

It seems Ranade was prepared to make the necessary sacrifice to serve his country, but the Government of India did not favour the idea of a High Court judge being asked to give evidence before the Commission. They suggested that the Bombay Presidency Association might be asked to select a witness, and it appointed Wacha. With Wacha went Gopal Krishna Gokhale as the representative of the Deccan Sabha. The other Indian witnesses were Surendranath Banerjee from Bengal and G. Subrahmania Aiyar from Madras. But before they crossed the seas Dadabhai had put in several notes for the edification of his colleagues.

In the second note, submitted in December 1895, Dadabhai submitted that it was necessary for the Commission to know the results of the administration and management of the Indian expenditure as reflected in the moral and material condition of India. With that end in view, he forwarded the correspondence he had with the India Office regarding statistics showing the poverty of the Indian masses. The third note furnished statistics required by Act of 1858, but not fully supplied by the Government of India. After submitting elaborate tables concerning production and distribution and after citing eminent authorities, Dadabhai maintained that he had shown that one of the results of the prevailing system was the extreme poverty of the mass of the people of British India, "suicidal to British name and rule, and destructive and degrading to the people of British India."

An analysis of the terms of reference as regards apportionment of charges was the subject-matter of the fourth note submitted on February 15, 1896. He put a moderately just apportionment of charge in this way:

India and England should pay all salaries which are to be paid to their own people, within their own limits, respectively, i.e. England should pay for all Englishmen employed in England and India should pay for all Indians employed in India; and as to those in one country who are employed in the other country, i.e. Englishmen employed in India, and Indians employed in

England—let there be some fair and reasonable apportionment between the two countries—taking, as much as possible, into consideration their respective benefits and capacity of means. As to pensions, a reasonable salary being paid during service in India, no pensions to follow; so that, when Europeans retire from India, there should be no charge on England for pensions, the employees having made their own arrangements for their future from their salaries. By this arrangement India will not only pay all that it would pay for a government by itself, supposing the English were not there, but also a share in the cost in India for what England regards as absolutely necessary for her own purpose of maintaining her Empire in India.

As regards the navy, Dadabhai maintained that "on no ground whatever of justice could India be fairly charged any share for it, except so far as it fell within the principle of actual service in Indian harbours."

Let India have complete share in the whole Imperial system and then talk of asking her to contribute to Imperial expenses.

Then will be the time to consider any such question as it is being considered in relations with Ireland, which enjoys short of Home Rule, which is vital to it, free and full share in the whole Imperial gain and glory—in the navy, army, and civil Services of the Empire. Let all arrangements exist in India as they exist here for entrance into all the Imperial Services here and elsewhere and it will be time and justice to talk of India's share in Imperial responsibilities.

Another important question the Commission had to consider was that of expenses incurred outside the limits of India. Every war carried on beyond the frontiers of 1858 was distinctly and mainly for Britain's Imperial and European purposes. It was solely to keep her own power in India; still India did not want to ignore indirect and incidental benefit of protection enjoyed by her and would be willing to pay a fair share according to her means.

> "What was it," asked Dadabhai, "if not shabby, to throw the expenses of Prince Nasrulla's (Shah of Iran) visit upon the Indian people?"

Then there was the mutiny of 1857. The causes were the mistakes and mismanagement of the British peoples' own authorities; the people of India had not only no share in it, but were actually ready at the call of the authorities to rise and support them. The British supremacy was triumphantly maintained, but what was the reward for the people ? The whole payment to the last farthing of the cost was inflicted upon the people. Let Lord Nortlibrook say how shabbily they were treated:

> "The whole of the ordinary expenses in the Abyssinian expedition were paid by India, the argument used being that India would have to pay her troops in the ordinary way and that she ought not to seek to make a profit out of the affair. But how did the Home Government treat the Indian Government when troops were sent out during the Mutiny? Did they say, We don't want to make any profit out of this ?' Not a bit of it. Every single man sent out was paid for by India during the whole time, though only temporary use was made of them, including the cost of their drilling and training as recruits until they were sent out."

Since then you have in a marked way been treating the people with distrust, and inflicting upon them, unnecessarily and selfishly, a larger and more expensive army to be paid for as wholly as the army of the Mutiny, viz., including the cost, or a portion of the cost, of their drilling and training as recruits until they are sent out, though all the troops are in this country, and they form an integral part of the British Army. And the whole expenditure of the frontier wars, including Chitral, is imposed upon the Indian people, though avowedly incurred for Imperial and European purposes, excepting that for very shame, a fourth of the cost of the last Afghan war was paid from the British Exchequer, thanks to Mr. Fawcett At Glasgow, on November 14, 1895, Mr. Balfour said: "You all remember that the British Army—and in the British Army I include those Native soldiers, fellow subjects of ours who on that day did great work for the Empire of which they are all citizens."

This is the romance. Had Mr. Balfour spoken the reality, he would have said, "include those native soldiers, the drudges of ours, who on that day did great work for the Empire of which they are kept-down subjects." For does not Mr. Balfour know, that far from being treated as "fellow subjects" and "citizens of the Empire," the Indians have not only to shed their blood for the Empire, but even to pay every farthing of the cost of those wars for "our Empire" and "our European position," that however much these Indians may be brave and shed their blood for Imperial purposes, or be made to pay "cruel and crushing tribute," they are not allowed any vote in die Imperial Parliament nor a vote in the Indian Legislative Councils on their own financial expenditure, that their employment in the officering of the army beyond a few inferior positions of Subedar Major or Jamadar Major, etc. is not at all allowed, that they are distrusted and disarmed—are not allowed to become volunteers, that every possible obstacle is thrown and "subterfuge" resorted to, against the advancement of the Indians in the higher positions of all the Civil Service, and that the simple justice of allowing Indians an equality to be simultaneously examined in their own country, for Indian services, decided by Act and resolution of Parliament, and solemnly pledged by the great Proclamation, is resisted by every device and subterfuge possible unworthy of the English character.

Is it not a mockery and an insult to call the Indians "fellow subjects and citizens of the Empire" when in reality they are treated as under-heel subjects?

After this scathing indictment it was a relief to Dadabhai to relate, in his fifth note, an episode in the British Indian Administration which reflected credit upon all concerned, namely, the maintenance of an Indian dynasty on the throne of Mysore.

This being once settled (said Dadabhai), though against all previous opposition, and necessitating the withdrawal of almost all Europeans from the Services, all the authorities and officials concerned, to their honour and praise, instead of putting any obstacle in the way, or trying to frustrate the above intentions, discharged their trust most loyally, and with every earnestness and care and solicitude to carry the work to success. The Blue Books on Mysore from the despatch of 16th April, 1867, to the installation of the late Maharaja in 1881, present a bright chapter in the history of British India, both in the justice, righteousness and statesmanship of the decision, and the loyalty and extreme care of every detail in carrying out that decision with success and satisfactory results.

That the financial prosperity of the State was secured not by resort to new taxation in any form or shape was a fact which Dadabhai commended for special consideration to the administrators of British India.

In the very nature of things the present system of administration and management of Indian expenditure in British India cannot ever produce such results, even though a Gladstone undertook the work. Such is the result of good administration in a native state at the very beginning. What splendid prospect is in store for the future if, as heretofore, it is allowed to develop itself to the level of the British system with its own native services, and not drained as poor British India is. ... The obvious conclusion was that the only natural and satisfactory relations between an alien's supremacy and the people of India could be established on that basis alone. The natural system had all the elements of consolidation of British power, of loyalty and stability, and of prosperity of both countries, whereas under the system prevailing in British India all human instincts were tending against the alien rulers and must inevitably end in disintegration, rebellion and disaster. No grapes from thistles!

The sixth note asked the Commission to bear in mind that all the loans made to India formed part of the imports and were already paid for and included in that part of the exports which was equal to the total imports. "The foreign capitalists," he added, "not only make profits with their own capital, but they draw even their capital from the taxation of the poor people themselves."

Then followed a statement (November 3,1897) on the admission of Indians to the covenanted Civil Service in India. In it Dadabhai traced the whole history of the question down to the Resolution of Parliament in 1893.

A Conservative (Sir Stafford Northcote) proposed, and a Liberal (Duke of Argyll) passed the Act of 1870 to do some justice. A Conservative (Lord Cranbrook) insisted upon carrying it out. A Liberal (Lord Kimberley) began to undermine it, and another Conservative (Lord Cross) gave it the deathblow—though, to the humiliation of the House of Commons, the Act remains on the Statute Book. "What faith can the Indians have on any Act of Parliament? Today something gíven, tomorrow snatched away; Acts and Resolutions of Parliament and Proclamations notwithstanding.

Once more Parliament did justice and passed the Resolution, in 1893, for simultaneous examinations, to share the same grievous fate as all its former enactments. And the Indian Executive thus stands proclaimed the supreme power over the heads of all—Parliament, People, and Sovereign. ... In connection with India generally, the Englishman (with some noble exceptions) deteriorates from a lover of liberty to a lover of despotism, without the slightest regard as to how the Indians are affected and bled. He suddenly becomes a superior, infallible being, and demands that what he does is right, and should never be questioned. (Mr. Gladstone truly called the "argument and law of force" as the law and argument of the present Anglo-Indian rule.) "Our boys" is his interest. The "boys" of others may go to the dogs, perish or be degraded for what he cares.

Dadabhai then submitted the correspondence which he had carried on with the War Office and the Admiralty, respectively, on the admission of Indians to Commissions in the British Army and to Commissions in the Royal Navy. The gist of the argument in this correspondence was that by excluding Indians from Commissions in the British Army and Navy the authorities had laid down a rule inconsistent with the Act of 1833 and the Proclamation of 1858. His ninth and final note furnished a table showing expenditure on wars beyond the Indian frontiers and containing, so to say, the official confession of the cost of the Forward Policy to the people of India.

Dadabhai was not content with merely placing his statements before the Commission. They might or might not be taken into account in compiling the report. If, however, he appeared before the Commission as a witness and urged the issues raised by him in those notes, the Commission would, he thought, be compelled to deal with those issues. In that hope he subjected himself voluntarily to the fire of cross-examination as a witness.

There were several passages-at-arms between the Chairman and the witness. To cite one instance.

The Chairman asked: "What is it that you want? Do you wish to sweep away the whole English scheme ?"

> "Yes, as it is" was Dadabhai's reply.
>
> "I want to know whether you wish to get rid of it bodily?"
>
> "There you misunderstand me."
>
> "What proportion would you keep?"
>
> "There is no proportion there. You must serve the double purpose both of maintaining the supremacy in a very remarkable and a very efficient manner and at die same time the people must feel that they are governed by themselves."
>
> "I merely wish to ask you whether you propose to retain any part of Civil Service—the European Service?"
>
> "Only the highest portion such as the Viceroy, the Governors, the Commander-in-Chief. Let us have the whole Civil Service, leaving alone the high level of die Europeans as the controlling power."

"Then you would have the Viceroy, etc.?"

"These certainly."

"No Englishmen beneath them?"

"I do not see any necessity for others."

"And by degrees you would evict them all?"

"We may go gradually higher up."

"But the history of India is that the people have been continually slaughtering each other?"

"What have you done here ? What is the history of Europe? We do not want to go back, because we have learnt as you have learnt."

"Is your recipe for reviving the prosperity of India to let loose the Pindaris?"

"Not necessarily. Those days are gone. . . ."

"Do you remember what Sir Madhava Rao, Prime Minister of Baroda, said to Lord Roberts on the subject of India for the Indians?"

"What did he say?"

"He said it would be like loosing the bars of the cages of the Zoological Gardens and letting out the animals, that very soon they would all be dead except the tiger—the tiger was, I believe, the war-like people of Northern India".

"Is this the result of 150 years of British rule that we are not civilized enough to observe law and order."

It was, on the whole, a brilliant performance. The severity of the cross-examination gave him the opportunity of driving home all his points and, incidentally, impressing his colleagues with his grasp of the facts and figures bearing on the issues involved.

Since the year 1896, many a change has taken place in the financial administration and management of India and in the machinery of government. It is, therefore, scarcely necessary to go into the details of the evidence placed before the Commission or of its recommendations. A few points of conflict between the majority and minority may, however, be noted. The majority held that the growth of expenditure had outstripped the normal growth of the tax revenue by Rs. 5,555,000, but that if the increased cost of exchange, amounting to Rs. 13,800,000 included in the expenditure, were eliminated, the normal growth of the tax revenue was more than sufficient to meet the largely increased demands of military and other services. On the question of apportionment of charge, the majority report recommended that the United Kingdom should contribute 50,000 towards the yearly charge of the office of the Secretary of State, one-half of the military charges of the fortress of Aden and of the charges of the Legation and Consulates in Iran. It also formulated principles which should guide, although they might not govern, the payment for Indian troops employed out of India, e.g. that India had no direct and substantial interest in the employment of forces in Europe, in Africa, west of the Cape of Good Hope, and in Asia, east of China; that she might have a modified interest in questions affecting the East Coast of Africa as far as Zanzibar, and the African Islands in the Indian Ocean except Madagascar, but that she had a direct and substantial interest in questions affecting Iran and Afghanistan and the coasts and islands of Arabia and of the Persian Gulf and port of Central Asia adjacent to the borders of India or Afghanistan.

Dadabhai, Wedderburn, and Caine were not satisfied; they submitted a separate report. The question to be considered was whether the Government of India, with all its machinery, had or had not promoted the general prosperity of the people in its charge and whether India was better or worse off by being a province of the British Crown. The scope of the enquiry was, however, so restricted as to ignore the broad lines which it should have followed. Important factors had been omitted from the calculations as, for example, the additional heavy burden imposed upon the tax-payers by enhancements of land assessment, by changes in Abkary regulations and by the closing of the mints.

In dealing with the dispute between the India Office on the one hand, and the War Office and the Admiralty on the other, the Commission appeared to have assumed that the India Government represented the India of the Indians, as though India were an independent country, having its own resources at its own command, and able to negotiate for its own conditions and terms!

Arguments and conclusions based upon such an assumption must necessarily be fallacious.

Instead of supporting the majority's proposal for the appointment of a Comptroller and Auditor-General, the minority report recommended the annual appointment of a Select Committee of the House of Commons to enquire into and report upon the financial condition of India. In order to give the Indian tax-payer an opportunity of making his voice heard, it recommended that the non-official members of the Viceroy's Council should have the right to move amendments and divide the Council upon the provisions of the Budget. It also recommended that a sufficient number of representative Indians should be nominated to the Council of the Secretary of State. It further proposed that there should be at least one Indian in the Executive Council of the Viceroy.

The question of the Services was once more put forward with all the wealth of detail which Dadabhai had at the tip of his fingers. The Congress of 1898 had passed a special resolution to the effect that the Constitution of the Higher Civil Medical Service of India was anomalous, indefensible in principle, injurious in its working, and unnecessarily costly. The time had arrived when in the interests of the public, of medical education, and of the advancement of medical service and of scientific work in the country, also in the cause of economic administration, the Civil Medical Service should be reorganised and wholly detached from the military service. Dr. Bahadurji had supported this demand in his evidence, and the minority report recommended the proposal as deserving of consideration.

As regards allocation of cost, it appeared to the minority from certain speeches made by Lord Curzon and Lord Kimberley that the main instruments by which British rule in India was maintained were a strong European military force, a European Civil Service, and a contented Indian population. Without those combined factors the conditions necessary to British rule could not be produced. The maintenance of those instruments of British rule being clearly an Imperial interest, the Imperial Exchequer should bear a proper share of the expense involved.

What was a proper share ? The minority were of opinion that Britain should pay for all British employed upon Indian work in Britain, that India should pay for all Indians employed in India, and that as regards British employed in India and Indians employed in Britain, the expenses should be shared equally. To make the British share still more moderate, the cost of all European Agency on behalf of India, wherever employed, might be divided half and half between India and the Imperial Exchequer.

Wars carried on beyond the Indian frontier were an indivisible part of the great Imperial question. It followed that the whole cost, ordinary and extraordinary, of such wars should primarily be borne by the Imperial Exchequer, India contributing in proportion to the benefit accruing to her for the protection of her frontier or other circumstances arising out of the war. The only case in which, perhaps, an exception might be made was that of defending the Suez Canal if actually threatened. India might in that case be called upon for a contribution, provided, however, that other British Colonies and dependencies in Australia and the Far East also paid their share.

There was no note of despondency in Dadabhai's letters to his friends concerning the Commission's report. He felt that his labours had not been thrown away. Such as it was, the report had taken cognizance of some of the inequities against which India had to contend.

> "It is enough for the present," observed Dadabhai in a letter to Hormusji Wadya (May 27), "that this is the first occasion on which Indian views had free expression and we owe that to Lord Welby. It is in itself not a little gain."

In thus being content with ever so small an advance and looking even on that as a gain worth having, the Grand Old Man of India was acting in consonance with the maxim of Marcus Aurelius and following in the footsteps of the Grand Old Man of England. An important domestic occurrence of the period was the wedding of Dadabhai's second daughter. She insisted that her father should be present to give her away. He pleaded inability to leave England, as the work of the Commission demanded all his time and attention. She, no less dogged than her father in her resolutions, put off the event sine die! At last came from her "everloving father" a pressing appeal (November 5, 1896), which made Dr. Maki Dadabhai Naoroji relent and consent to become Mrs. H. M. Dadina.

Nothing can delight me more than to be present at your wedding. But I am helpless. I have undertaken a duty which, I have no doubt you will agree with me, I must perform. This is nearly the last work of my life, and its fruition as far as it can go. Unless you wish me to throw away the whole work of my life, it is impossible for me to stir. . . . The manner in which the people of India received me and for which we all were so glad shows what I owe to them. To the difficulty of my work Mr. Bhownaggree has become a great addition. No, dear, give up the idea of my presence. As it is not quite certain that I can go in the winter of 1897, it is useless, my dear child, to wait.

Another letter of the period to "Dears All" (July 2, 1897) throws a sidelight on the state of Indian womanhood even after fifty years of progress in female education:

I had no idea that the bicycle was for Maki. I do not know whether she would like to ride in Bombay or whether people would like to see her ride, or whether any good number of Parsi ladies are riding at present. Considering the profession she is to follow, it would perhaps not be desirable for her to create any prejudice against herself at present.

British Rule Lacking British Principles

Even whilst he was deeply engrossed in the work of the Royal Commission, Dadabhai was mainly instrumental in organising a vigorous platform campaign in England on behalf of India. For more than forty years he had cherished hopes for a change in the official outlook. For four decades he and his friends, British and Indian, had made unceasing efforts to bring to the notice of the British people the grievances of India and the defects in the system of administration of the country. They had received the sympathy and encouragement of numerous individuals and large audiences throughout the country, but they had failed to create any appreciable impression on those who held the reins of office, whether they were Conservatives or Liberals. The psalmist's allotted span of life was exceeded; the end might come any day; yet he could scarcely see a ray of hope for his motherland. Was he to give up the struggle? On the contrary, he was determined that the last days of his life should be devoted to a more extensive and more intensive campaign throughout the United Kingdom, demanding for India British rule on British principles.

His letters during the period breathed the same spirit of staunch determination to continue the fight. To J. N. Tata he wrote on May 27, 1897: "Nothing can be accomplished without perseverance and doggedness. Because the Government has resisted it (the proposal for simultaneous examinations), there was the greater necessity to fight out the matter with greater and more energetic persistence and noise. . . . Because Government will not grant, therefore give up, is not the policy which will get anything for us." Similarly, in a letter to Prithivi Chandra Raj, he wrote on October 29: "We have to do much pioneering work.

We cannot expect fruit at once. ... It will be absurd to shrink now." In another letter to G. Subrahmania Aiyar (September 4), he said: "Keep up, as you say, the spirit of the people do not be cowed down. That's the only way to deal with Englishmen.'

Bubonic plague broke out in Bombay in 1896; it was spreading throughout India in 1897. To the chronic disease of poverty and the periodic tragedy of famine was thus added another calamity. Oppressed by the thought of such misfortunes and misery of his country, Dadabhai came to ascribe them to the drain of her resources. In his letters to friends in India he observed: "How could it be otherwise, under the present system of rule of 'bleeding' India in crores and crores every year?"

It was the year of the Diamond Jubilee of Queen Victoria's reign. In his letter to the Queen (February 5), he could not help striking a jarring note:

The most striking consequences of the utter violation of Her Majesty's most sacred pledges and of Acts and Resolutions of Parliament are the extreme impoverishment of the people of British

India and the infliction upon them of all the scourges of the world war, pestilence, and famine. May I hope to look forward to a beneficial change in the present great occasion of Her Majesty's reigns To James Gordon Bennett, proprietor of the New York Herald, he wrote (February 18):

I feel much puzzled that while so much sympathy has been aroused about the perishing millions of my poor countrymen in India, your paper, so foremost in humane work, has not opened a subscription in the United States.

Prince Ranjit singh of Jamnagar, who had made a name for himself on the cricket field of England, was then busy arousing sympathy for the suffering people of India. To him Dadabhai addressed the following words of advice (March 4):

You have to distinguish the appeal for the relief of the present calamity from the necessity of preventing such calamities in the future, and if you can in some way impress upon your hearers their great duty to see that this is looked into, you will do a service both to England and to India. You will also be able to impress upon them that during the last fifteen years since the last great famine this country has added to its wealth from India four or five hundred millions sterling and that from that great abundance England is bound to give in abundance. Even one per cent will mean four or five millions. . . . There are people who do not, and cannot, come to relief works—women, children, old and infirm, and, more pitiful still, the respectable who would on no account seek relief and would prefer to starve and die—here private charity is most needed.

Dinsha Wacha and Gokhale arrived in London in April 1897 and stayed with Dadabhai at Cambridge Lodge, Southfields. Surendranath Banerjee and Subrahmania Aiyar, the other two Indians deputed to give evidence before the Royal Commission, were also in England at the time. Taking advantage of the presence of these practised speakers, Dadabhai and his colleagues organised a "platform campaign" throughout the United Kingdom, to bring effectively to the notice of the British public the actual condition of India and the wrongs of the Indian population which cried aloud for redress. Dadabhai was one of the prominent speakers at lectures delivered at South Lambeth, Sunderland, Clapham,

Edinburgh, Hastings, Lewisham, and other places. Public meetings were also held in Yorkshire and Gloucester and the Baling Division. The time of the year was not favourable; nevertheless the speakers drew large audiences.

The campaign for the year 1897 culminated in a Resolution passed at a conference of Indians resident in the United Kingdom, held under the auspices of the London Indian Society, on December 28, at Montagu Mansions. The resolution was moved by Dadabhai from the chair. In spite of its portentous length, it seems necessary to quote at least some paragraphs to show what emotions were then swaying the mind of the veteran mover:

That of all the evils and terrible misery that India has been suffering for a century and a half, and of which the latest developments are the most deplorable, Famine and Plague, arising from ever-increasing poverty, the stupid and suicidal Frontier War and its savagery of the wholesale destruction of villages, unworthy of any people, but far more so of English civilization, the unwise and suicidal prosecutions for sedition, the absurd and ignorant cry of the disloyalty of the educated Indians, and for the curtailment of the liberty of the Indian Press, the despotism—like that of the imprisonment of the Natus—and the general insufficiency and inefficiency of the Administration; of all these and many other minor evils the main cause is the unrighteous and un-British system of government which produces an unceasing and ever-increasing bleeding of die country, and which is maintained by a political hypocrisy and continuous subterfuges, unworthy of the British honour and name, and entirely in opposition to the wishes of the British people, and utterly in violation of Acts and Resolutions of Parliament and of the most solemn and repeated pledges of the British nation and Sovereign.

That unless the present unrighteous and un-British system of government is thoroughly reformed into a righteous and truly British system, destruction to India and disaster to the British Empire must be the inevitable result.

That Indians desire, as their highest patriotism and best interests, the continuance of British rule, and, as British subjects, they demand that such British rule must be based on British principles and British institutions, on British citizenship and not on existing despotic, un-British and selfish principles, of which the present disaster and misery are the natural and bitter fruit.

That, as a necessary immediate instalment of justice, a large portion, if not the whole, of the famine and plague expenditure, and the whole cost of the present unwise Frontier War must be met from the British exchequer, remembering that England drains from India some thirty or forty millions every year.

Lastly, that die Frontier War and Forward Policy must cease and that the whole frontier question be carefully reconsidered so as to render all Afghanistan a powerful and impregnable barrier of an independence-loving and war-like people against any foreign invasion of India.

He had been told, said Dadabhai, that the resolution was couched in very strong language. It was not, however, his language; it was the language of some of the most eminent British statesmen. To take the word "subterfuge," for instance; it was the word of a Viceroy, Lord Lytton, and also of the then Prime Minister, Lord Salisbury, who had distinctly stated that the whole conduct of the authorities—and Dadabhai was speaking of the authorities only—had been a political hypocrisy. Lord Northbrook having urged that the Cabinet and the Government of India were bound to act in consonance with the Royal Proclamations, Lord Salisbury had said: "What is the use of talking in this manner 2 It is all political hypocrisy!" In a private minute, Lord Lytton had stated that the Government had been deceiving the people, that there had been deliberate and transparent subterfuge in not carrying out the Act of 1833 and that they had been doing it intentionally and knowingly. "There is no morality in war," was one of the blunt sayings of Napoleon. Dadabhai could not have been unaware of it, but despite half a century's bitter experience in the school of politics he could not reconcile himself to the fact that the same sweeping negative was as true of the eternal contest between the rulers and the subjects the world over, particularly where the rulers were alien.

As regards the policy of choking up the natural safety valves for the indignation of the educated classes, Dadabhai said:

Gagging the Press is simply suicidal. There never was a greater mistake than to prosecute Mr. Tilak and those poor editors who were, perhaps, not known beyond their villages. This was a new departure from the principles on which British government was conducted. Now you are introducing the Russian system under which a man can be arrested and imprisoned and sent away without trial and without reason being given.

On the day after the lecture Hyndman wrote to Dadabhai:

> Let me offer you my sincere congratulations on your resolution and speech at the Indian Conference. . . . There can be no doubt whatever that the blundering in India has now brought matters to a crisis and that the Government must begin to look facts in the face. That there is great alarm at what we may call by courtesy "head" quarters there can be no question—but fear is a very bad counsellor, and it is deeply to be regretted that our principal statesmen deliberately refused to act, or even to think, years ago.

About this time, it caused some uneasiness to Dadabhai's friends to find him seeking the support of Socialists in his crusade.

The Hindu Patriot considered it a dangerous policy. Dadabhai, on the contrary, considered it a good fortune to have such allies:

> Do not be prejudiced (he said, April 8) that it is the Socialists who are helping us. If you know thoroughly the enormous and various difficulties we have to move Englishmen in the Indian cause... you will realise the value of the help we are getting from the Socialists, and that is mostly because Mr. Hyndman is at their head....When he first wrote his article on the "Bankruptcy of India" he had not dreamt of socialism ... it is an unexpected good fortune that the Indian cause has been taken up by a powerful and advancing organisation to whom the future largely belongs. We have not got the means of creating such an organisation; no existing organisation yet helps us. This democratic organisation is the only one . . . that has taken in hand our cause.

While, however, he fully appreciated the value of Hyndman's whole-hearted support, Dadabhai stoutly rejected his persistent advice and appeals for a change in the method of agitation. Hyndman believed in making a vigorous stir. Year after year he grew more impatient and more bitter in his condemnation of the spineless agitation of Indians.

At the house I was staying at with my wife at Tunbridge Wells (he wrote to Dadabhai in one of several undated letters) I met two young Indian barristers, Mr. Tyabjee and another, who both know you. I told them I thought a great opportunity was being allowed to slip by in not getting up a plain-spoken memorial to the India Office on the subject of this Famine in India. ... I also said that I think it a mistake to ask for charity instead of demanding justice. It cuts the ground from under the feet of those who, like myself, are doing all that is possible to help India. Nothing will be done unless some serious agitation is set on foot. I knew Lord George Hamilton intimately in old days. He is merely a smart tool of his own and other aristocratic families working for the Imperial right to extort wealth. He will do nothing unless he is frightened of the consequences of his supineness. Another word I must say. I cannot help feeling contempt for the Indians here and in India who, instead of seriously taking up their own cause in a serious way, leave all the work to be done by a man of yours (sic), and pass such a silly resolution of congratulation to the Queen as was passed at the Indian National Congress the other day. Congratulations for what? For having ruined India for two or three generations to come ? It is pitiful. Men in high positions have said to me, "Where is the evidence of discontent, Mr. Hyndman ? Where is the cry for justice from the people of India themselves ? If the people are so poor and oppressed, as you say they are, surely we should hear a little more of it than we do hear!" What answer can I make to such a challenge? There is no answer. For outside of yourself what is any native of India doing ? Even the paper India itself is a poor, clique-edited, badly written sheet which doesn't interest even me. It is time to be up and stirring, if any good is to be done.

I will help, and so will our organisation and Justice, as much as possible; ha "Providence helps those who help themselves."

Even Martin Wood's powerful advocacy of India's cause gave little satisfaction to the irate Socialist.

I have got a letter from Mr. Martin Wood (he wrote, February 1, 1897). He doesn't understand my method of getting up an agitation at all. He is an excellent person, but he is more likely to provoke tears and sleep than excitement on any subject.

In another letter he told Dadabhai that it was absolutely necessary that they should put their heads together so as to decide how to make a vigorous stir. They met, not once but often, and the discussions must have been most exciting. Dadabhai has not left behind any note about the interview, but his letter to Hyndman, written after the conversations, gives us an idea of the fundamental difference of opinion between them.

With reference to my visit to you on the 16th instant, I have carefully considered the matter again and I remain of the same view as I then expressed to you that after reading your article in Justice I cannot any more work with you and the S.D.F. on Indian matters. My desire and aim has been not to encourage rebellion but to prevent it and to make the British connection with India a benefit and blessing to both countries, which it can certainly be, but which unfortunately has not been the case to India, owing to an evil and unrighteous system of government being persisted in by the executive authorities, in spite of the wishes of the sovereign, the people and the Parliament of this country to govern righteously.

A letter to Motilal Ghose (July 23) also makes Dadabhai's position clear:

> I, of course, cannot join him (Hyndman) on the line that India may rebel.... Our stand is confidence in the British people, to persistently but constitutionally agitate till we inform the British public of the evils of the present system of government and get it reformed on righteous lines. They take a view of the British rule and express it which I cannot prevent. But whatever view they take or express, one thing is clear that their motive, as they say, is the good of India and England, their own country, which Mr. Hyndman considers as identical.

Hyndman did not press his views any more for a while, but he reverted to the charge early in the following year.

What do you judicious people gain (he asked, February 19) by your moderation ? What does your journal India gain by its dullness that can be felt? To the naked eye, and even to the microscope, nothing! They just kick you and pass sedition acts over you, and lie about you, even more than they do with us.

We, at least, have the satisfaction of chasing them, deriding them, making them look ridiculous, and driving them into furious anger. Moreover, we are getting ready for the inevitable crash which is coming—not in India alone. Suave, moderate gentlemen don't get much attention when "the band begins to play," so they might at least be heard now—but they aren't.

Dadabhai, however, wrote in reply (February 22):

> All that you say is true, but Indians cannot do yet what you say. You should realise their position in every respect.... India represents Indians, not Englishmen, and India can only speak as Indians should.... The Government are now openly taking up a Russian attitude, and we are helpless. The mass of the people yet do not understand the position. John Bull does not understand the bark. He only understands the bite, and we cannot do this.

Despite this difference of opinion as to the methods of agitation, their personal relations were as cordial as ever. Dadabhai had the gratification to join in the movement for a complimentary dinner to Hyndman in recognition of his public services on behalf of the people for twenty-five years. At the dinner, given on May 11, 1898, Dadabhai responded to the toast, "International Solidarity and Progress.'

To the wrongs of India one more was added by the prosecutions instituted against journalists for sedition. It was part of the policy of repression pursued by the authorities as a counterblast to Indian unrest. Dadabhai regarded the prosecutions as a "political blunder." "They are doing the very thing they desire to prevent,' said he in a letter to Wacha (September 30). "Fear will lead to such acts which in turn produce the very effects feared. It is a sad thing for India, the weakening of British connection at British hands."

Later, he unburdened his mind at some length in another letter to Wacha (April 28, 1898):

> The Natu case is very unfortunate for Government themselves. It is the greatest blow they have given to British power and prestige. The idea of the insecurity of liberty will now never leave the Indian mind. A generation of reparation and good behaviour would hardly repair the mischief. It has hurled the British power down the hill half a century. Russia's name loses its terrors.

Well, it is a pity. Is retribution coming so soon, I wonder! The reports of the excesses committed during the Frontier War also caused much anguish. This savage warfare on the frontier on the part of the British destroying all villages (he wrote feelingly to another friend, December 9, 1897) is a great disgrace to the civilization of Britain, and it is the destruction of one of the finest races of the world for thousands of years. It is a great crime against humanity. The British love independence, but is it not strange that they destroy others for loving independence like them?

Another incident, known as the "Apology Incident" in the career of Gokhale, cast a gloom over the Congress circles. When he was in England in connection with the work of the Welby Commission, Gokhale, who had yet to grow in political stature and wisdom, received letters describing the ravages of the plague then raging in Puna and the high-handed action of European soldiers appointed to inspect private houses. One of the epistles conveyed to him the report then current among the Puna people that two women had been violated by some soldiers and that one of the victims had thereupon committed suicide. He related the story to a small Committee of members of the House of Commons, to whom lie had been introduced by Wedderburn; he also gave an interview on the subject to a representative of the Manchester Guardian. The Bombay Government cabled to say that the report was a "malevolent invention."

There were no proofs to substantiate the story. Not only Gokhale but also his friends, Dadabhai and Wedderburn particularly, had to look small. Returning to India, Gokhale called upon his informants to come forward with evidence. They had nothing to urge in corroboration of the report. It was all hearsay. He refused to divulge their names and took on himself the responsibility of circulating the unfounded story. The only honourable course open to him in the circumstances was to tender an unqualified apology to those whom he had defamed. It was a bitter pill to swallow. The apology he tendered was, however, full and complete.

Now came castigation from unexpected quarters. Gokhale's colleagues and the Indian public generally felt humiliated by what seemed to them to be an abject apology. Even his friends in England were puzzled as to the need for the withdrawal of his statements in the manner in which he had retracted them.

Gokhale's explanation was given to Dadabhai in his letter of August 6:

I have written to Sir William explaining the circumstances under which withdrawal of the allegations became the only honourable course open to me.... Briefly, the situation was this.

Before my arrival here, the government had ceased to be British government and had assumed the role of Russian government. Arrests and deportations on the charge of disloyalty had spread such profound panic in Puna that any kind of substantiation was out of the question. Government, moreover, had decided not to hold a public enquiry into the complaints by a Commission.

Retraction, therefore, was the only course left open to me. In the step I have taken I have bowed to circumstances and have acted in accordance with the best advice available. I know my action has done much harm to the cause which is so dear to the hearts of us all and which I meant to serve all the while.

Dadabhai sent him a soothing reply, asking him to dispel the thought of retirement from public life, but offering at the same time a few words of advice:

> You are young, you have a long, earnest, and by no means easy work before you. "Never say die." Do your duty perseveringly. You are excitable and I shall

> be consoled even for your present troubles if you can now, after the present painful experience, learn to be cool and calm and to consider a matter before acting. The cause you have to work for is beset with difficulties. But do not despair.

How kind of you (said Gokhale in reply, September 16) to write as you have done! I was prepared for a much more severe reproof, and you have written in such gentle and encouraging terms! All I can say is that all my energies will now be devoted to making amends for what has happened.

All the while, Dadabhai was in communication with Congress leaders, particularly with R, N. Mudholkar, to make the session of 1897 a success—and such a great success it was that he felt proud of Mudholkar.

You and your Province have good reason to be pleased and proud... You have managed all with great tact and with your head on your shoulders. You have now shown what Indians can do. You know how solicitous I was that you should show on this occasion that Indians can stand on their own legs, and you all should have greater pride that you have helped yourself without the extraneous prop of an M.P. from here or any Englishman.

To the Secretary of the Mahajan Sabha of Madras also he preached the gospel of self-help (July 29):

> We must now show that we can help ourselves and do not need to lean upon others. We must give up the idea of having Englishmen as our Presidents. We must have Indians as Presidents. . . .We must seek our promising young men and, though they may not be much known, the very fact of becoming a President adds one to the list of men of position and influence.

Throughout that era of repression, Dadabhai was visualising a titanic struggle between the people and Government. In a letter to Wacha (March 3, 1898), he said:

> We are thrown back many years; the authorities are openly throwing aside their mask and hypocrisy of benevolence, and the people, on the other hand, are

beginning to feel that something is wrong, and a fierce struggle is in prospect. Let us meet it as it comes, with coolness.

The annual dinner of the London Indian Society was held on November 1,1898. In proposing the toast to the Empress and the Royal Family, Dadabhai said: "While expressing our attachment to the Queen, we cannot help feeling that her noble proclamations for the welfare of her Indian people have been interpreted by her Ministers in exactly the opposite light to that in which we view them."

We still believe (he added) that die British people have a conscience. We look to them for justice, and I hope the time will come, although I may not have the good fortune to live to see it, when all things will be changed and Her Majesty's best wishes realised.

In proposing the toast of India and the Indian National Congress, Professor A. F. Murison said:

Sir W. Hunter was not regarded as a feather-headed man, even by The Times, and yet he had declared his belief that the general programme of the Congress would actually reach accomplishment by the end of the century. As the blood of the martyrs was the seed of the Church, so the vituperation of officialism and the lackeys of officialism contributed to the impulse of the Congress movement.

Dr. Sarat Mullick ventured to dip into the future and to assert that the time would come when the President of the Indian National Congress would be consulted by the Governor-General and an Indian himself would hold the high and important position of Governor-General.

While carrying on this agitation, Dadabhai earnestly believed that he was fighting not merely in the interests of poor India but also in the interests of the British Empire. "Injustice will bring the mightiest on earth to ruin"—the slogan for which he was indebted to Lord Salisbury—were no mere empty words.

Those words, he apprehended, spelt the Nemesis of the British Empire, and he was never weary of warning British friends of the danger inherent in the policy pursued by their countrymen in

India. It was the same feeling of apprehension that made him write to George Freeman (February, 1898):

Really the prospect for the British Empire does not look very bright if the present infatuation for keeping other nationalities under heel is persisted in. It is the most effectual way in which they are digging their own grave. At present in India they are going from bad to worse and wiping off whatever merit there was in the British name by Russianising the system by repressing freedom of speech and the liberty of the subject.

Writing to the same friend, six months later (August 25), bout the growing sea-power of England, to which Freeman had offered, Dadabhai pointed out that when Asia would be connected with Europe by railways, such power would not be of much avail.

England's only strength (he added), if she is wise enough to see it, against all Europe, is in the contentment, prosperity, and desire of India herself to keep up England's connection. England can then command a resource of strength that can defy all Europe.

...India is England's greatest strength and its greatest weakness, as she would have it.

Once more, while writing to this friend, he sounded a learning (November 24):

> I am afraid the race question will become in time a burning one. The backward races in other parts of the world seem destined to have a bad time. The European greed will be too much for them. But the Indian question will be a terrible matter for England, if she does not look out. Once India is fully roused, and in these days of rapid development of political and moral forces this may come much sooner than we can expect, it will be impossible for England to hold her own firmly.

Stirring the British Public

During the month of November 1898, Dadabhai went campaigning in Lancashire. It was part of a country-wide campaign planned by the veteran crusader. Special attention was paid to Lancashire, as much harm had been done to India in the interests of Lancashire trade, and as Dadabhai believed that much real good could be done, both to Lancashire and India, if the Lancashire people realised what the real condition of India was and what could really promote the cotton trade between England and India. The first lecture of the series was given under the auspices of the East Manchester Liberal Association, in Chorlton Town Hall, on November 14. "Are you aware," asked Dadabhai, "that the drain of wealth from India acts as 'protection' of Indian industry ? It is a well-known economic law that a tribute—and forced payments to another country have the economic effects of a tribute—not only takes from the tributary nation the amount paid but also raises against them the price of all foreign goods."

Dadabhai then addressed several meetings successively at Castleton, Chorley, Atherton, and Enutsford. W. A. Chambers, Romesh Dutt, and Bipin Chandra Pal, all excellent orators, took part in the propaganda. The British Committee of the Congress was also active. W. S. Caine gave a lecture on the Indian National Congress. Everywhere the apostles of Indian reform were hailed with delight. Dadabhai told the audiences that his firm had been in Lancashire for over twenty-five years and that, therefore, he could claim to know something of Lancashire and the ideas of its inhabitants. John Bright had advised his countrymen that there were only two ways in which Britain could get good out of India for themselves—one of these was by plunder, and the other by trade. British people, said Dadabhai, would prefer the second alternative. For that, however, India must be rich, whereas the value of the whole produce of the people was not more than Rs. 20 per head per annum. What could be expected from such a people as regards trade?

The argument went home to the business men present. The grievances of India, which were brought to their notice, evoked sympathy for her people, and the proposed reforms seemed to them to be just and reasonable. "If," said a Manchester merchant, in proposing a vote of thanks to Dadabhai, "we could have some more addresses like that of Mr. Naoroji, there would be no excuse left for the ignorance about India which now prevails." Almost all the chairmen and speakers at subsequent meetings expressed the same sentiment. The question before them was: how to enable

Indians, who were their wards, to develop their lives and policy in the best way for themselves?

Dadabhai then called attention to the treatment meted out to Indians in South Africa. A public meeting was held, on November 22, in the Friends' Meeting House, Manchester, under the auspices of the Manchester Society for the Protection of Native Races. The Rev. J. S. Moffat moved: "That this meeting welcomes the formation of the Manchester District Society for the Protection of Native Races, and pledges itself to do everything in its power to further the objects of the Society."

In seconding the resolution, Dadabhai spoke of the hardships of the British Indian subjects who had gone to South Africa. Then he asked them to look into the conduct of things in India. The civilization of that country, he reminded them, was "a thousand years old." Its people were advanced in arts and sciences when people in England were running about the woods without clothes.

The disabilities which hampered the Outlanders in the Transvaal were rife in India.

Another series of meetings in Lancashire was then arranged for Dadabhai. Between 12th and 15th December Dadabhai addressed large meetings at Stretford, Oldham, Failsworth, and Rossendale. The burden of the song was the same. Lancashire complained that India did not take more of her goods. The total exports to India from Great Britain and Ireland did not exceed 1s. 6d. per head of the population of India. . . . "Make it possible for the 250 or 300 millions of India to take £1 per head of British products, and it would be out of the power of England to supply the demand!"

A good many other meetings were thus addressed in all parts of England.

During the year 1900 there was another famine in India, the worst experienced during twenty-five years. Dadabhai was again actively at work. He delivered an address at Edmonton, April 29. There was, he said, a chronic state of famine in India. Even in years of average prosperity and average crops, scores of millions had to live on starvation diet. They could not expect to draw blood from a man day after day and yet expect him to remain healthy.

A gratifying feature, however, in connection with the famine was the attention paid by publicists to the question of the annual drain of the wealth of the country.

In June and July he had a crowded programme of meetings all over the country. British friends also took part in this programme. On June 28 Mrs. Charles Mallett gave an address on the Indian Famine, with Dadabhai in the chair. Dadabhai then addressed a garden meeting at Anerley and a meeting of the Metropolitan Radical Federation at Plumstead Radical Club. In his old constituency, Finsbury, he delivered an address to the Lighthouse P.S.A. Society.

Meetings were also held in aid of the Famine Relief Fund. At one of the meetings held at the United Methodist Church, Walthamstow, taking as the text the words of Lord Salisbury, "as India must be bled," Dadabhai affirmed that, despite her grievances, India had been loyal to the British Crown. At the same time he sounded a warning: "Do not expect that that loyalty cannot fail."

This was no empty threat. India at the end of the century was not the India of 1852 when Dadabhai had made his first political speech. Everybody knew that there was grave unrest in India, but Dadabhai knew much more. He had heard from Hyndman that the authorities had been anticipating serious trouble and were at last awakening to the gravity of the situation.

How long do you think (asked Hyndman, January 22, 1900) the present system in India will last? From what I can hear, there is a growing feeling among the dominant classes that we are on the verge of a serious crisis. Three days later, he confirmed the report:

The impression that there is a growing opinion as to die probability of a serious crisis in India, partly economic, partly revolutionary, comes to me from Anglo-Indian Officials and their letters home as well as from conversations reported to me, in which the new Governor of Bombay took part. The main fear is of some sort of rising. I have seen two letters from men now in India, and high up too, to their relations here which breathe spirit of distrust, not to say alarm, through their pages. In particular, one man writing to his daughter declaims against the imprudence of the Government in inviting the troops now locked up in Ladysmith from India at all. He says that the general feeling among Europeans is one of coming trouble.

Very few, even in India, appreciated what Hyndman was doing almost daily for their country, but he too, like Dadabhai, continued his labours with singleness of purpose.

With the single exception of yourself (he wrote, March 29) I never receive a word of acknowledgment from anybody. Yet, again, with the exception of you, I have done more for India than any man living. However, that doesn't matter. Humans are pigs anyhow, in India as in England. But I object to starving pigs, so I go on all the same.

Then he commenced harping once more on his favourite theme. Yes, I saw your memorial in India. I consider it much too humble in tone. After all, though politeness is well, after compliments and so forth, you are a representative of 250,000,000 of people—a great position and one which in my judgement calls for even haughty language on your behalf. One of the commonest charges brought against India is that its natives are "servile." You are very far from that. But die tone of your memorial jars on me, I must say. I remember being with my old and honoured friend—Giuseppe Mazzini, the great Italian—one day in his poor rooms in the Fulham Road. We were talking in the easiest and pleasantest way. To us was shown in an emissary from King Victor Emmanuel. You should have seen the old man straighten up and have heard him talk. It was one power talking to, and almost down to, another. And, what is more, the emissary treated the old man with a deference that I don't believe, great nobleman as he was, he would have shown to the Czar of Russia or the Queen of England. It was the consciousness of his own capacity and the force behind him which gave Mazzini that standing. The time has gone for imploring, if ever it existed. You have the right to speak out and you will gain more by it.

Had this advice anything to do with the change in the tone and temper of Dadabhai's agitation in England during the succeeding years ? Once more Hyndman had a fling at India.

I look through India weekly. But how dull, how desperately dull and uninteresting! Do pick up some able young man and give him charge.

In his opinion, Wedderburn, too, was frightfully dull. It is very unfortunate (he observed, April 7) that Sir W. W. is such a bad and unimpressive speaker. Most of the people on our side unluckily lack the power to put things in a clear, vigorous and interesting way.

In the same letter he stated:

> Thank you for your letter. We have to cheer up each other. I am going on and I think, at last, we are making way slowly.

The efforts made by the enemy to silence us are the best possible evidence that we are producing some effect. This letter also gives an indication of the daily effort of Hyndman to help India:

I have sent my article, with a short addendum on the debate in the House of Commons, to Die Neue Zeit. I have posted also a letter to the Manchester Guardian.

Here is another letter (July 23), showing how intensely anxious he was to get a move on. Undoubtedly, August would never do for meetings, but we have then to begin our arrangements for October. We must all work in our own way. If I have succeeded—and I have succeeded—in rousing the attention of a considerable part of the English people to the mischief of our rule in India, this has been done and similar things have been done in all ages, not by mild examinations of truth but by vigorous attacks and the use of strong language. I can quite understand that nice gentlemanly mediocrities who, like the Walrus, "greatly sympathise,' don't approve of and would gladly boycott me. But I know very well what I am doing and these half-baked personages will have to reckon with me on home as well as Indian and foreign affairs before long. I am glad you think there is a movement where above all there ought to be movement. You deserve to live long to see some portion at least of the change for which you have worked so hard and so long.

Thus did his irrepressible friend go on stirring Dadabhai from day to day to self-assertion. One more letter (July 24), and we shall have done with the Hyndman correspondence of this period.

You are, indeed, thankful for small mercies! As against the £250,000 the Government, instead of giving a grant-in-aid, are inflaming the drain by yet another loan. Even so they will draw £11,000,000 this year. At this rate it will take another century or more to drive the thick end of the wedge. Your only hope is a general shock or overturn. But the men who are pretending to work in favour of India today—and the greater part of it is pretence—would be as sorry to see such a break-up of the infamous capitalist system as Lord George Hamilton or Sir Henry Fowler. The Government is not in the least afraid of moderate remonstrances nor care for the recommendations of Royal Commissions—*ex. gr.*: the Royal Commission on Housing the Poor, 1880.

On October 13, 1900, Dr. Mullick gave a reception at Hotel Tudor in honour of Dadabhai. The special object was to afford a number of young Indians interested in the National Movement an opportunity to meet and greet the Grand Old Man who was, day after day, getting more and more anxious about the struggle that lay ahead, the struggle which called for many new recruits to relieve the members of the old guard. There was a very interesting assemblage of Indians and British friends of India. Romesh Dutt, Digby, and several British friends recalled some of the main lines of the patriotic work which Dadabhai had pursued with commendable courage and steadfastness and with notable success.

Digby's comparison of Dadabhai with John Bright deserves special notice:

The only English statesman with whom lie (Dadabhai) could be at all compared was John Bright, with whom he had many characteristics in common. Bright started a political career, holding certain definite views, and at the end of a long life he found that practically the whole people of the country had accepted them. Where he began, there he finished. So too with Mr. Naoroji. What he advocated years and years ago he was still advocating, and there was constant proof that at last his views were gaining acceptance. . . . Mr. Naoroji had done that for Indian politics which steam-power had accomplished for traction purposes; he had opened up entirely new lines of thought and action; he had demonstrated the only way in which India could once more become a great and prosperous nation.

Dadabhai was delighted to have the opportunity of appealing to the youth of India to come forward and to relieve old men who had all their lives been working on behalf of India. In undertaking that task, they would, he assured them, enjoy many advantages which the older men did not possess.

We had to work (said he) in the face of the darkest ignorance of Indian matters, but now we have accomplished the labours of the pioneers; and now that light has penetrated the darkness, we hold that the time has come when the burden should be shifted on to your shoulders. .. . What is the task before you? You have to expose the real secret of the poverty of India. I have, time after time, dealt with reasons and excuses given for that poverty, such as land taxation and decadence of native industries. But these, after all, are only red herrings drawn across the path.

As long as the bleeding goes on, there can be no hope for India.

There would be difficulties in their way, he added, but they should not despair. The English Press had taken up the Indian problem with all seriousness; before long it would become one of the great domestic questions before England. In the Royal Commission's report there was an acknowledgment of injustice to India. Thus a beginning had been made; the British conscience had been aroused, and the outlook was far more hopeful than it had ever been before. "Go doggedly forward!" said the veteran soldier to the would-be recruits. "Learn a lesson from John Bull himself."

Dadabhai had robust faith in the youth of India—rather unusual for grey heads controlling national organisations. His heart went out in admiration for the young men who were determined to offer resistance to the long-tolerated hauteur and high-handedness of the bureaucracy. When even his own lieutenants such as Mehta, Wacha and Banerjee were getting impatient of what appeared to be extremist views and rebellious attitude of young Indians in certain quarters, their hoary-headed mentor wanted more and more young men to come forward and hold aloft the torch of freedom. Certain Anglo-Indian newspapers had, a year before, criticised young India in scathing terms. Referring to their outbursts, Dadabhai remarked, in a letter to Romesh Dutt.

As to the cry of the Anglo-Indians about young men, it is always their dodge. . . . We shall have to do our work with young men if Indians are to speak here at all, and youth is not to be despised. It is die enthusiasm of youth, with some direction, that has always carried important changes in the world and will always do so. It is these youths to whom the future belongs.

We are now passing away; recruits must be prepared to take our place. Despising them as mere youths is a great mistake. Let us guide them.

Six months later, writing to Chambers, whom he had invited to address Indian youths resident in England, he wrote (October 5):

Several of these young men are rather touchy and it will require all your usual tact to handle them in giving them any advice.... You may take this opportunity of impressing upon them that, as residents in this country, they have a great duty and responsibility towards their country. Any well-directed effort here will always be far more effective, as this is the fountainhead where the chief work lies. It is exceedingly necessary that a strong Indian association or society should exist here; that is to say, that the Indian Society should consist of all the residents as members and that it should be well supported financially. Every Indian resident here can certainly spare a guinea a year for the sake of his country.

The time had come to organise the activities of ardent youths devoted to the cause of the motherland. Missionaries were needed everywhere to serve India and propagate the gospel of freedom. This idea was put forward in a concrete form to Gokhale in a letter written a few years later, when Dadabhai saw the youth of the country responding cheerfully, in ever-increasing numbers, to the call.

For the purpose of inspiring the people with the desire for understanding the duties and rights of British citizens (said he, October 1905), each province should furnish a band of young, well-educated men to become the missionaries of this work and to devote themselves under suitable organisation to do it.

Side by side with the work to be done in India there must be vigorous propaganda in England. We cannot accomplish our object by working only in India or only in England. They are two halves and by their combination only can die whole work be done. . . . The tide is with us. The English people and Press are beginning to understand the wrongs of India. Asia is waking up.

The Isles of the East are becoming like the Isles of die West, and we may fairly expect that our Emancipation is not far off. My only word is—never despair.

A notable manifesto was issued over the signatures of Wedderburn, Hume, and Dadabhai on October 19, 1900, addressed to the President-designate of the Congress at Lahore. It passed under review fifteen years of Congress work and marked a new stage in the history of that organisation. It was a critical stage—a parting of the ways. Whether the constitutional movement should develop into its full usefulness, by drawing together die rulers and the ruled and by promoting the welfare of both India and England, or whether the efforts that had been made should end in disappointment and reaction, would depend, said the illustrious trio, upon the attitude and action of the Indian people. "We, who were among its originators," they observed, "have now well-nigh completed our work as pioneers; we have given the lead to the younger men and must look to them to take up in larger measure the burden of the work."

The Congress had tried to remove the tendency to underground discontent and secret conspiracy, which was a danger necessarily attending an administration conducted by foreigners on autocratic lines. The official attitude towards the organisation was, however, one of disapproval and suspicion. Despite all obstacles the Congress had accomplished its object to obtain solidarity of public opinion. It held the field as a national representative assembly. However vehemently it might have been first assailed, the Congress views on questions affecting India, such as the forward policy beyond the North-Western Frontier, the plague regulations, the famine grant and the financial relations of England and India, had prevailed. The Royal Commission had unanimously found the charges placed upon India to be unfair to the extent of a quarter of a million sterling per annum.

Accepting the finding, Government had conceded to India a small measure of financial justice.

It was the old, old story of the shield—silver on one side and gold on the other. Much work remained to be done to present both the sides to all concerned. India was lying prostrate from accumulated misfortunes. All available forces had to be brought together in order to raise her up and lead her again into paths of prosperity. The first step in that direction was to ascertain, by searching enquiry, the causes of her downfall and to devise remedies suited to her peculiar economic condition. The work in England was great and difficult; the workers were few and were overtaxed both as to physical endurance and financial resources.

That was why Wedderburn was driven to retire from Parliament to economise his resources for direct work on behalf of India.

The times were critical. By hard, earnest work and united purpose, the Congress might constitute itself a valued adviser to the Government of India and an influence in England tending to strengthen the Empire. On the other hand, if the necessary sacrifice and self-denial were not exercised, if the constitutional effort were allowed to lapse from want of courage and constancy, the work of years would be thrown away and a danger would arise that the physical sufferings of the masses might lead to counsels of despair. "Against such a conclusion," declared the three stalwarts, "we, who have given our best years to the service of India, will, to the last, use our best efforts in the interests alike of India and England."

The little Somerset town of Shepton Mallet was honoured, on November 7, by a visit paid by Dadabhai at the invitation of Mr. and Mrs. Chambers, parents of W. A. Chambers, to whose championship of the cause of Indians Dadabhai paid a warm tribute. He was sometimes taxed, said he, with not speaking enough about the good England had done for India, but he could not pay England a higher compliment than that he should be desirous that her connection with India should continue for a long time. So far as the rule in India was good rule, and something like British rule, they were grateful for it; but their misfortune was that un-British rule was far in excess of the good British rule.

"The White Man's burden," as Kipling called it, meant to Indians a very different thing from what it did to the white men. To the Indian it meant that the burden was the white man upon the Indian's shoulders. The Indian was willing to take his fair share of the burden, but was it fair to put upon his shoulders the whole charge of what was to him a foreign service inimical to his interests and perhaps even injurious to him e This was only a prelude to other speeches in the same key.

"The Indian Famine: Its causes and remedy," was the subject set down for discussion at the weekly meeting (November 24) of the St. John's Literary and Debating Society, Kennington. The principal speaker was Dadabhai. The remedy was to be found, said he, in two words—honour and justice. There was not die slightest necessity that India should suffer in order that England might gain. If only the right policy were adopted, India could be made again prosperous and, at the same time, England would reap ten times the benefit she had had from the connection.

On December 5, at the Mildmay Radical Club at Stoke Newington, Dadabhai delivered a lecture on Indian subjects after an exhibition of vocal music by a number of young ladies, members of the Mildmay Singing Class. "If present conditions continued," he averred, "if Indians were treated as slaves, an explosion must come. Let Indian subjects be treated in the same way as British subjects—that is all I ask."

On the first day of the first year of the twentieth century die Commonwealth of Australian Colonies was inaugurated. It was an event of vast importance to the British Empire; to Dadabhai, as an Indian, it afforded food for reflection. Why was it that a very small part of the British Empire, with a population of less than five millions, had been progressing during the last century by leaps and bounds until it had become one of the most flourishing portions of the earth, while the great Empire of India, which had been connected with the British nation more or less for two hundred years, and which had been controlled by most highly paid administrators, was in a most disastrous condition and was reduced to the state of the poorest country in the civilized world?

Thanks to the lesson which the United States had taught England, when they gained their independence, the British Colonies had since been treated justly and righteously. Similar treatment had not, however, been meted out to India. The declaration of policy had been as good as could be desired. But the principles laid down in the Proclamations were violated and disregarded. There had been bleeding instead of nourishing, and British helotry had been substituted for British citizenship.

Dadabhai unburdened his mind on that depressing topic at a lecture he gave on "India" on January 14, 1901, at the Penge and Beckenham Liberal and Radical Club. He had no desire to dwell on the past; he preferred rather to look forward. Would the new century bring a favourable change in policy which would be productive of good results for both England and India? Oncc more he appealed to the British authorities to pursue a righteous policy.

On January 31, Dadabhai delivered another address on the "Condition of India" at Toynbee Hall, Whitechapel, which was followed by several more on Indian famines and their causes.

On March 22 the Castle Street Congregational Chapel was packed to overflowing, when the Castle Street Pleasant Hour Society and the Broad Street P.S.A. assembled to hear Dadabhai on the question of "the Relations of England and India." Dadabhai had then a busy week at Reading. How active he was, despite his 77 years, is shown in the following extract from a letter from Gideon Ashdown (March 1) in the Reading Standard:

He rose at 7 a.m. Sunday (February 17), and at 9.30 addressed die Church St. Adult School for 45 minutes; and afterwards was driven by Dr. Hurry to the Abbey Ruins where Mr. Naoroji was treated by the doctor with twenty minutes interesting description. He indulged in a little rest and after luncheon went to Castle Street at 3 p.m. and addressed upwards of a thousand people, who listened with rapt attention for 50 minutes while the famous Indian orator unsparingly criticised their government of India, showing how they had failed in their duty. He then partook of tea and, as an aid to digestion, proceeded to Bridge Street Assembly Rooms and addressed an enthusiastic body of men and women on education, occupying one hour in speech and answering questions.

At a public meeting held at the North Camberwell Radical Club and Institute, on April 23, Dadabhai delivered another address on the "Condition of India":

It is for you, as electors of your country, you who have the sovereign power in your hands, to see why there has been a loss of thousands of Indians in famines. You have not spent a shilling in the formation of the Empire. The blood that was shed was also Indian blood. You have been regularly draining and bleeding us of millions of money. . . . These millions do not go to make you any better off, they go into the pockets of tie capitalists. Britain claims that Britons shall never be slaves, is it her intention that she should make others slaves? You must insist that your representatives in Parliament do India justice.

The meeting passed a resolution to the effect that the system of government in India was diametrically opposed to the principles initiated in the Act of 1833 and that the faithlessness of the British Government in this matter was the primary cause of the misery and suffering prevailing in India.

Mainly due to Dadabhai's campaign, the twenty-third report of the National Liberal Federation, which was issued about this time, contained more than one reference to India. The introductory paragraph concluded as follows:

The death, suffering and distress which famine and disease have produced in India are again to be deplored, and the closest examination ought to be made to see if any readjustment of the financial system of India could be devised which might mitigate the recurrence of these national disasters.

The platform campaign was extended even to a pulpit. Through the courtesy of the Rev. John Page Hopps, Pastor of the Free Church, Croydon, who lent his pulpit, on Sunday, April 21, Dadabhai gave a sympathetic audience a harrowing picture of the condition of Indians. "Do not believe me as gospel," said he, "study for yourselves!"

At the Westminster Town Hall, on May 24, a conference of Indians resident in the United Kingdom was held to adopt resolutions regarding the amelioration of the condition of the Indian people. Dadabhai presided. Resolutions pointing out the fundamental cause of the extreme poverty of India and the exhaustion of her wealth, similar to those adopted at previous meetings, were passed.

Dadabhai also presided at the ordinary meeting of the London Indian Society, held on June 2. A. Das opened a debate on Indian Trade and indicated the need for Indians developing different trades and industries. About this time, Dadabhai received a prospectus of a joint-stock concern, called "Indian Development Ltd." Thanking the Directors for the copy, he said:

> "I think the correct title for such companies should be 'Indian Exploitation Ltd." In elucidation of his comment he enclosed a few extracts from his letter (October 20, 1898) to the Currency Committee.

"British Democracy and India" was the subject of another discourse at the North Lambeth Liberal Club on July 4. On whose shoulders rested the responsibility for the miserable condition of India ? "It rested," said Dadabhai, "on the shoulders of the British democracy." He appealed to it to exercise its power and make the British Government fulfil the pledges given to India.

On October 20 a debate was raised on an address, delivered by Dadabhai, on British Rule in India, at the Brixton Literary and Discussion Society. On November I, he addressed a public conference, held under the auspices of the Liverpool Peace Society, on "India and Militarism." The policy of imperial expansion involved risk of explosion. On the authority of a Parliamentary return, obtained by Morley, Dadabhai stated that the British had waged no wars beyond the frontiers in pursuance of an Imperial policy dictated solely by the fact that India was the only part of the Empire which had an extensive frontier adjoining the possessions of a great European Power. Colonel Hanna, an Indian officer of experience, had shown that between 1878 and 1896 the "forward policy" cost Rs. 7,141,000,000.

During the period, scores of millions of Indians went all the year round without enough food to eat and millions perished in lean years of famine.

Under the auspices of the Young Scots' Society, Dadabhai gave another lecture on the "Condition of India" in the Oddfellows' Hall, Edinburgh, and yet another on the same subject to the members of the London branch of the Society.

At Galashiels, there was one more lecture, and scores of them at different places for three more years. Everywhere he emphasised the urgency of strengthening the British rule in India by reforming it.

On March 20, 1903, Dadabhai visited Portsmouth and delivered an address on "India" under the auspices of the Portsmouth Ethical Fellowship. Lord Curzon had expressed his surprise that India should have resented British capital going out to India. When Britain poured her wealth into America and China, his Lordship never heard those natives complain, that they were being ruined. When America flooded England, as she was then doing, with resources of her accumulated capital and commercial genius, none "at home" sat down and bewailed their cruel lot at being bled by foreign brains. Dadabhai retorted that Lord Curzon had suppressed the most important factor, so far as India was concerned. The capital that went out to India was not British capital. It was the wealth first plundered from the country, which went back to India for what they called "development," but what he called despoliation of India's resources.

For whose benefit and for what purpose (he asked) is the development, when all that is produced is carried away to this country? Supposing Great Britain had plundered America and China in the way she had plundered India, and from that plunder it had monopolised the country's resources and brought them to Great Britain, would America and China accept the position as benefit? In the case of America, they brought with them their own capital, and it was welcomed, and so would India, if she were allowed to use her own resources for her own benefit.

Then, coming to the question of the drain, he said, "It was a case of bleed, bleed, bleed continuously, and no time at all for the wound to heal".

An important public meeting, convened jointly by the British Committee of the Congress and the London Indian Society, was held at Caxton Hall, Westminster, on July 30, to protest against the proposal to tax the people of India for maintaining a garrison of British troops in South Africa. Dadabhai moved the principal resolution protesting against the proposal and repudiating the plea that such a force should be paid by India as a reserve in the interests of India. No words, he said, were more often used and abused in official literature than the words "Indian interests" and "Indian needs." Every burden imposed upon the Indian people for British interests was hypocritically believed to be for Indian interests, dust being thus thrown in the eyes of the British public and the world. Then he related how India was bled, and asserted: "Far from being required to contribute to the African garrison, we demand in common justice that the British exchequer should contribute to the cost of the European army in India."

An impartial spokesman on behalf of India on this occasion was Lord Welby, who seconded the motion. After full consideration, he observed, the Royal Commission had pointed out in its report that India had rendered important service to England by repeatedly lending her forces. On the other hand, the two-thirds of the British army stationed at home and in the Colonies constituted a reserve on which India might rely in times of emergency. Judging, however, from the past, India had more frequently aided England than England had aided India. The Commission had, therefore, recorded its deliberate and unanimous opinion that, of the two, England profited more by the arrangements for reciprocal assistance. The claim put forward by the British Government that India should contribute to the English garrison in South Africa was, in Lord Welby's opinion, unprecedented, unjust and unwise.

In the midst of this intensive campaign on behalf of India Dadabhai paid close attention to the question of the treatment of Indians in South Africa. That, however, is an episode which will form the subject-matter of a separate chapter. He was also actively engaged in combating two great social scourges, the liquor traffic and the opium traffic. He had, moreover, thrown himself into the turmoil of another electoral struggle with vigour and ardour which youth might envy. That struggle will also be described in another chapter. Such activities, at his age, deepened the feeling of veneration with which his countrymen watched his career. It culminated in the decision to celebrate in India, as well as in England, the anniversary of his birthday as "Dadabhai Day." The first celebration was held on September 4, 1903; thereafter, till the end of his life, Dadabhai Day was celebrated with great enthusiasm.

It has already been shown that out of the amount raised in the year 1869 for a testimonial to Dadabhai, a small amount had been set apart for his portrait. This amount lay with the secretaries for years, and the matter escaped attention. On the death of the last secretary, however, it was discovered that the amount with interest had increased to Rs. 8,000. With the sanction of the High Court this sum was handed over to three new secretaries to give effect to the resolution of the subscribers.

Before an enthusiastic audience, the portrait was unveiled on November 24, 1900, by Ranade, who was then a judge of the High Court. He described Dadabhai as the best product of British education. In learning and industry, especially in industry, he believed, Dadabhai had no equal. "Englishmen," said he, "should feel proud of Dadabhai as a unique figure in Indian history. The era of British conquest was followed by that of consolidation. Then came the era of reconciliation and reconstruction. On what lines was the work of reconstruction to be carried on by the younger generation ? These were laid down in Dadabhai's own words. The people of India should regard the existence and continuance of British dominion in that part of Asia as an unquestionable fact. That was the very foundation, said Ranade, of the whole edifice. But there was another aspect of the problem— "by reason of the conquest and of the consolidation the people of India should be raised to a place of equality among the other nations of the earth."

It might be said, added Ranade, that in the work of reconciliation, Dadabhai's "extreme position" had not been so helpful and so serviceable to the cause of India as they might have expected. But anyone who had studied Dadabhai's writings and his speeches would say that such a calumny as that would never lessen the affection and esteem in which the people held him.

In his writings as well as in his speeches there was not a single sentence or expression, even the most casual, which could be pointed out in support of the allegation that he had created a gulf which did not exist before.

This was the last public function performed by Ranade before death prematurely laid low that intellectual giant of India. Dadabhai sent from England a letter of condolence to Mrs. Ranade through Gokhale. Her reply (February 22, 1901), indicates the feeling of reverential regard in which Dadabhai was held by Ranade.

She knows—what everyone who stood close to Mr. Ranade knew well—that the high example set by you of single-minded devotion to the country's cause had exercised a large influence on Mr. Ranade's mind, and throughout his life he used to speak of you in terms which a pupil in India uses in speaking of a teacher.

Self-government: the Only Remedy

Early in the year 1904 Lord Curzon committed the greatest folly of his life. Forgetting that the wounds inflicted by the tongue are worse than those made by the sword, in the course of his convocation address at the Calcutta University he made an imputation of untruthfulness against India, ancient and modern. A new life was then stirring among the people of India; everywhere her educated sons were recalling her great past and longing to regain the place she once occupied in the civilized world. To have insulted, at that psychological moment, the people of a country that had given to mankind great philosophies, great art and a great literature was, to borrow the words of Dadabhai himself in connection with the partition of Bengal, equivalent to depositing a large store of dynamite under what Lord Curzon himself had aptly called "the pivot of the British Empire."

The whole country arose as one man to protest not only against that insulting speech but also against the general policy of the overbearing Viceroy's administration. Nations are governed by sentiment as much as individuals. The sentiment of the Indian people having been outraged, reason and justice were silenced in the wholesale condemnation of a Viceroyalty distinguished, in the earlier years at least, for great sympathy, sagacity, and statesmanship. Even those who might be called the Tories of India were antagonised by the lofty ruler just as King James II had turned the squires and parsons of his day into rebels. Large and influential meetings were held in Calcutta, Madras, Bombay, Lahore, Allahabad, and other places in India, where citizens who had never before taken any part in politics, citizens who even disliked the agitation carried on by the Congress, stood with the political agitators of the day on a common platform and repudiated most vehemently the aspersions cast upon the character of the people by the representative of the King-Emperor in India. They also condemned in strongest terms the measures adopted during his Viceroyalty.

Dadabhai shared his countrymen's feelings of resentment on this occasion; he rejoiced, at the same time, to find their national spirit thus stirred to its depths. Hitherto he had been crying in the wilderness with a mere handful of colleagues. Now, however, the whole nation was up in arms against the principles and policy under which India was governed. No such event had taken place before in the history of British India. It showed the signs of the times. The seeds he had scattered broadcast were bearing fruit—a New India was rising to view, a New India conscious of her rights and pulsating with fresh ideas of freedom. Reviewing the situation, he thought they were then at the parting of the ways. The future could not be a continuance of the past. The Curzon regime had brought popular unrest to the danger-point. People in India were clamouring for the recall of the Viceroy. Dadabhai does not appear to have encouraged such a demand. As usual, he had no quarrel with individuals. He was out to fight the system which led to misgovernment. He, therefore, asked his countrymen, whilst they were infuriated against Lord Curzon, to go to the root of the matter and to demand an instantaneous change in the system of administration. There were only two alternatives before both the people and the rulers—peaceful evolution of the administration of the country, or explosion.

> "Misrule of India" was the subject of his lecture on March 18, 1904, before the members of the Penge and

> Beckenham Cooperative Society. It was not a wise policy, he told the audience, quoting Lord Harrington, to introduce among Indians European literature, civilization, and progress, and at the same time to tell them that they should never have any chance of taking a share in the administration of their country, except by getting rid of their European rulers. While England was thinking of the expansion of the Empire, he added, "an upheaval and an explosion might, perhaps, take place in that part of it which alone entitled it to the name of Empire."

The demand for self-government followed soon afterwards. Responding to the toast of "The President," at a gathering of the London Indian Society, on June i, Dadabhai asked the question whether Indians were to remain for ever the hewers of wood and drawers of water, to slave and perish. Without pausing for an answer, he declared:

There is only one remedy to the present dishonourable, hypocritical and destructive system—a system that would break up the Empire, if not saved by a peaceful and prompt revolution. That remedy is self-government under British paramountcy. I earnestly press upon the Indian people to claim unceasingly their birthright and pledged right of British citizenship, of self-government.

When this one fundamental remedy will be accomplished, every other evil or defect of the present system . . . would right itself.

On July 8 Dadabhai delivered a lecture under the auspices of the West Croydon Social Union, on the "Condition of India." He presented to the audience two pictures: (i) of the best hearts and intellects of America, demanding without pressure that Congress should declare the independence of the Philippines in good time, and (ii) of nine-tenths of English people, ignorant of what the real relations between England and India were, showing not the slightest desire and making not the slightest effort to understand the real position. He implored them to think of their responsibilities in the matter.

One of the ways of awakening the British public to its duty was to have a sort of permanent paragraph inserted in friendly newspapers calling attention to the grievances of India. Dadabhai drew up the following paragraph, and it appeared in India regularly about this period:

The present system of British rule in India by ever-increasingly plundering and draining away the resources of the people deliberately produces extreme impoverishment and thereby causes famine, plague, and starvation on an ever-increasing scale for some 200,000,000 people. Further, the present system is dishonourably violating the most solemn and Parliamentary pledges and the declared honest policy of the British people.

It is therefore the duty as also the greatest interest of the British people to put an end to the present deplorable and unrighteous system and compel their Government to honestly take steps to introduce as speedily as practicable self-government like that of the Colonies under British paramountcy.

Dadabhai then attended an international gathering of Socialists at Amsterdam. It created a stir in India. He had been lecturing for years under the auspices of varied organisations; his audiences were composed of people belonging to all classes of society; he did not, however, expect much support from the well-to-do classes.

His hopes were centred in the Labour force which was growing every day. It was the working class, he believed, that could and would help India considerably. It was, therefore, extremely desirable that the people of India should win that force to their side. Irrespective of that consideration, however, his innate sympathy with labour drew him to the working classes. Testimony of such sympathy comes from two prominent Members of Parliament. Speaking at a meeting, on November 1904, at North Lambeth, the constituency which Dadabhai was then nursing, Wedderburn observed:

> There was no section of the House with which he (Dadabhai) was more in sympathy and accord than the labour section. If returned, he would, for all practical purposes, be an additional Labour member.

In a letter to Mr. M. R. Masani (February 19, 1929), Secretary, Congress Socialist Party, India, the Right Honourable George Lansbury, M.P., confirms this impression:

> My personal contact with your countryman was entirely political, and I can only say that none of us ever appealed to him in vain for assistance in great public movements organised for the benefit of the masses. He was foremost in his championship of Home Rule for Ireland and for the great measures of social reform which at that time the Radical party was putting forward. I am quite sure that had he been younger and was now living in this country, he would have been one of the foremost men in the Labour Party. I hope one of these days we shall find another such as he standing for Parliament and standing on the broad basis of international Socialism.

A striking proof of his Socialistic tendencies was given by Dadabhai when at a Conference of Democrats, held on July 29, 1905, held under the auspices of the Metropolitan Radical Federation and the National Democratic League at Holborn Town Hall, he moved, as Vice-President of the League, a resolution demanding the establishment of a universal system of old age pensions, based entirely upon citizen rights and free from the taint of pauperism. He was, besides, one of the few politicians in England who had mastered the subject of British industrialism.

Under the title of The Rights of Labour he had formulated and published a scheme for the establishment of Industrial Commissioners' Courts and for the recognition and protection of Labour as a property. If legalised, it would have ensured justice to all wage-earners and perpetual industrial peace.

The International Socialist Congress met at Amsterdam from August 14 to August 20, 1904. Delegates from all parts of the world attended the Congress to discuss the question of Colonial Policy, and. Dadabhai was received there as an honoured guest representing the people of British India. At the sitting held on August 17 the question of India was introduced by a British delegate, S. G. Hobson, on behalf of the "British Section," and with the approval of the Commission on Colonial Policy. The resolution condemning the system of British rule in India, which he moved, had the familiar ring of the resolutions passed at various public meetings under Dadabhai's lead. It referred to the plundering and draining of the resources of the people, which caused extreme impoverishment, and called upon the workers of Great Britain to enforce upon their Government the abandonment of the dishonourable system of administration and the establishment of self-government.

The President, Van Kol, a retired Dutch civil servant, and a member of the Dutch Parliament, then introduced Dadabhai to the assembly. In calling upon him to address the meeting, he asked the audience to rise and stand in silence to mark their respect and commiseration for the suffering millions of India.

His words were the signal for one of the most inspiring manifestations of fellow-feeling. As Dadabhai walked slowly to the centre of the platform, he had a rousing reception. The delegates, about a thousand, leapt to their feet and stood uncovered before him in solemn silence. Then their thoughts turned from the Indian people to the dignified presence of their representative himself, and they gave him a tremendous ovation. It was a most impressive spectacle—the exploited and downtrodden working men and women of Europe expressing their goodwill and extending their hand of fellowship to the suffering millions of India.

So overpowered was Dadabhai by feelings of gratitude that when he spoke his voice trembled a little, but as he proceeded to lay the case for India before the delegates, it rang clear and resonant from one end of the concert-hall to the other. Most of them did not, before translation, understand a word of what he said, but his delicate features, his refined face, his white hair, and his dignified figure impressed them immensely. The delegates who understood English punctuated his speech with applause, but when the speech was translated into German and French, the Continental delegates were even more emphatic in their demonstrations of agreement and approval of the downright and incisive presentation of the case of the afflicted millions on whose behalf he was speaking. They had no idea that an Indian could be so cultured and so captivating as the venerable man who stood before them.

The burden of Dadabhai's song was the drain of India's wealth and the poverty of the people. What hope was there of a remedy? This rests (said Dadabhai) in the hands of the working classes. Working men constitute the immense majority of the people of India, and they appeal to the workmen of the whole world, and ask for their help and sympathy. Let them condemn the wrongs done in India. We constantly denounce barbarities. What does barbarity mean ? Does it not mean that, when a savage knocks down a weaker man and robs him, an act of barbarism has been perpetrated ? The same applies to nations, and this is the way in which the British Government is treating India. This must end.

Imperialism of brute force is barbarism. The Imperialism of civilization is the Imperialism of equal rights, equal duties, and equal freedoms. The remedy is in the hands of the British people.

They must compel their Government to fulfil the promises that had been made to India. The remedy is to give India self-government. She should be treated like the other British colonies.

The resolution was carried without opposition. "That means," said the President, "that this Congress brands Great Britain with the mark of shame for its treatment of India." The report of the Congress was read all over the world, and Dadabhai had the satisfaction that his appeal on behalf of his motherland attracted considerable attention in the United Kingdom. On the other hand, his action in associating himself with the Socialists was severely criticised in the Anglo-Indian Press.

Socialism was then, as it is even now, a red rag to it. But it was not so much his participation in the Congress as his vehement impeachment of British rule that roused the ire of many a journalist. The Times of India remarked that Dadabhai owed it to himself, if he intended to continue political work on behalf of his country, to explain how his name came to be associated with a charge against the British Government of robbing the people, purposely creating famines and carrying on an execrable and dishonourable system of administration. There were still a good many people in India, it added, "whose respect for Dadabhai would lead them to hope that it was open to him to dissociate himself from that outrageous outburst of continental insolence."

Dadabhai was, no doubt, being driven gradually to extremism, at least in his public utterances. Year after year his criticism of the defects of British rule in India increased in acerbity. It was the result, clearly, of dire disappointment. As yet, however, he had not lost his faith in British justice, nor did he waver in his adherence to the Congress policy of constitutional agitation. In a letter written to him, Wedderburn had expressed his concern at the growing impatience of young men who ridiculed the idea of India getting justice at England's hands without a convulsion.

Dadabhai gave in his reply the reason for their impatience and indicated incidentally what made him adhere to his faith.

The new generation is getting impatient. They cannot restrain themselves, as the passing generation does. The older people have had their eyes opened to the high character of British institutions and they became attached to them. They cannot now readily throw aside their first love or attachment. The new generation have no such sentiment.

To the first love, indeed, he remained steadfastly attached till the last day of his life, although, as we have seen, the course of such love "never did run smooth."

During the first week of November, Dadabhai was down with influenza. He could not, therefore, deliver a lecture on India at North Lambeth which had been announced in the papers.

Sir William Wedderburn and Mr. J. M. Parikh, one of the lieutenants of Dadabhai, stepped into the breach. Wedderburn earnestly appealed to North Lambeth to send Dadabhai to St. Stephen's. A series of views of India, ancient and modern, was then presented to the audience, accompanied by a descriptive lecture by Mr. Parikh.

Within a fortnight Dadabhai was fit again to address a meeting held under the auspices of J. P. Heath Lodge of the Sons of Temperance, at Clapham Park. "British Rule in India—Promises and Performances," was the subject of this address. He appealed to the people of Great Britain to compel the Government to redeem the promises so often made and to secure self-government for India.

The Reception Committee of the Indian National Congress sent a pressing invitation to Dadabhai to attend the twentieth Congress. He could not go, but at his request Sir Henry Cotton accepted the Presidentship of the Congress, and Wedderburn, too consented to visit India once more and to assist at the Congress.

In proposing their toast at a dinner organised in their honour, Dadabhai said that they had requested the two Englishmen to go to India to prove to the Indian people that they should not yet despair, as the British conscience was not altogether lost. Repressive, restrictive, and reactionary measures had been resorted to in India; resulting in widespread discontent. He wished that the rulers would take note of that fact and consider what it meant.

An Empire like that of India could not be governed by petty minds. The rulers must expand their ideas and adopt measures to undo the mischief.

"Home Rule in India—Past and Future" was the subject of another discourse at St. Albans in February 1905. This was followed by another on March 16, at the North Brixton Gladstone Club, Kennington. Before the lecture there was an exhibition of lantern-slides, presenting from photographs die state of misery existing in India through famine. One of the slides reproduced upon the screen the memorable words of the Government of India Act of 1833:

That no native of the said territories nor any natural-born subject of His Majesty resident therein shall, by reason only of his religion, place of birth, descent, or any of them, be disabled from holding any place, office, or employment of the said Company. Dadabhai sounded a warning that some great catastrophe would take place if India were not placed in the position of self-governing Colonies. That was New India's aim and claim.

Lord Curzon became more and more unpopular. The division of the ancient historic Province of Bengal into two separate provinces with separate capitals antagonised the entire population. A great protest meeting of Indians resident in the United Kingdom was promoted in London. Dadabhai presided. His address was one of the most stirring and inspiring he had ever delivered during his residence in England.

Indians (he said) have unanimously, earnestly and emphatically declared that the system of rule they are now under should not continue to be. Let us consider what that means. More than 50 years ago—I will not go back to an earlier period of our history—Mountstuart Elphinstone said: "It is in vain to endeavour to rule them (the Indians) on principles only suited to a slavish and ignorant population." And 40 years after in the last 10 or 12 years—we find, not only a continuance of the same old system, but we find it brought to bear on the people with even more energy and more vigour. Some years ago, Sir Henry Fowler distinctly and decidedly showed us that India was to be governed on the principles condemned by Elphinstone. . . . Then followed Lord George Hamilton as Secretary of State. ... He said, "Our rule shall never be popular. Our rule can never be popular' . . . and he has taken very good care that his prophecy shall be fulfilled. ... But then comes Lord Curzon, and he out-Herods them all. ... Here, then, we have a clear and distinct issue. Our rulers—the officials—tell us we shall have no chance of ever becoming a self-governing country—that they will not give us an opportunity of preparing ourselves for it. Undoubtedly, the character of the whole of the measures passed within the last 10 years points towards such an intention. . . . Now the Indian people have, for the first time, risen and declared that this thing shall not be. Here is a clear issue between the rulers and the people: they are come face to face. The rulers say, "We shall rule, but only as foreign invaders with the result of draining the country of its wealth, and killing millions by famine and plague, and starving scores of millions by poverty, and destitution." While the ruled are saying for the first time, "that shall not be." I regard the day on which the first Calcutta meeting was held as a red-letter day in the annals of India. I am thankful that I have lived to see the birthday of the freedom of the Indian people.

The question arose: "What would be the consequence of this open declaration of war between the rulers and the people?"

Instead of giving his own views, Dadabhai quoted the words of eminent authorities. John Malcolm had prophesied that "the evil" carried with it the seeds of the destruction of the Empire itself. Thomas Munro had said that it would have been more desirable that they should have been expelled from India altogether than that the result of their system of government should be such an abasement of a whole people. John Bright had warned his countrymen: "If there be a judgement of nations, as I believe there is as for individuals, our children, in no distant generations, must pay the penalty which we have purchased by neglecting our duty to the populations of India." William Hunter had summed up the gist of one of his lectures in the words: "We should have had an Indian Ireland multiplied fiftyfold on our hands." Lord Harrington had pointed out that the only consequence of exclusion of Indians from the government of their own country could be to make them "desirous of getting rid, in the first instance, of their European rulers."

That is the position (said Dadabhai) in which we are at the present time. Either that evil system must cease, or it must produce disastrous results to the British Empire itself.... There is a duty on Indians themselves. They have declared that they will not be governed as slaves; and now let them show a spirit of determination, for I have very little doubt that, if the British public were once satisfied that India is determined to have self-government, it will be conceded. I may not live to see that blessed day, but I do not despair of that result being achieved. The issue which has now been raised between the governors and the governed cannot be put aside.

There was no need, continued Dadabhai, for him to refute what Lord Curzon had said in a spirit of peevishness against the character and religion of the East. He had performed that task before. He rather preferred to give illustrations of the political hypocrisy of British statesmen and administrators and to remind them that they were living in glasshouses and should not indulge in the pastime of throwing stones. On one aspect of Lord Curzon's conduct he had, however, something to say.

He does not seem to realise (said Dadabhai) the responsibility of die position in which he has been placed. He is there representing the sovereign of the Empire—as Viceroy or Second King—the head of a great people, 300 millions in number, who had possessed civilization for thousands of years, and at a time when his forefathers were wandering in the forests here.... His duty as

Viceroy is to attract as much as possible and to attach the good feeling of the Indian people to the rule of the British Sovereign. What does he do ? By his Acts he deals a deadly blow to British rule, and then, by a peculiarly ignorant and petulant speech, he creates almost a revolution in the whole Empire.

Dadabhai was always ready to give every one his due; indeed, he was sometimes blamed for overdoing it in the case of British people and officials. While condemning Lord Curzon, he recalled that the Viceroy had claims to the gratitude of the people for what he had done during the early period of his administration.

I will certainly mention one circumstance in his favour and to his credit. He made a very firm stand against any brutal treatment of the Indian people by Europeans, and, in so doing, caused dissatisfaction to his own countrymen. In that he really did a service, not only to Indian but also to the whole British Empire.

That one act of his shall not be forgotten by Indians. .. . The crisis has come (added Dadabhai), the people and the rulers are face to face. The people have for 150 years suffered patiently, and, strange to say, their patience has been made a taunt as well as viewed as a credit to them. Often I have been taunted with the fact that 300 millions of Indians allow themselves to be governed like slaves by a handful of people. But the spell is broken. The old days have passed and the Indian of today looks at the whole position in quite a different light. Now India is becoming restless, and it is desirable that the Government should at once realise it.

In order that India's restlessness may be more pronounced, Dadabhai encouraged Bengal to keep up the agitation.

The responsibility and the opportunity (said he in his message to his Bengali friends, published in the Bengali, January 5, 1906) that has fallen to your lot is to show that Indians have a backbone—the staying power to the last. If we can once establish this reputation, half of our fight for self-government will be fought and won. I don't care—I am prepared for ultimate failure—Bengal may remain partitioned—the boycott may at last end but it will be a great gain if we can once establish the character for organised union and self-sacrifice. One more important result I am looking forward to. It is the rousing up of the masses, and the present is just the kind of struggle which can accomplish this object. If the people are once roused, they will always be ready to follow their leaders.

Interviewed by a representative of the Daily News, in August 1905, Dadabhai said he had known Lord Curzon when he was in Parliament.

I don't deny that he is a brilliant man, but he and Lord George Hamilton have wrought infinite mischief in India, their whole policy being to break down the rising spirit of the Indian people. Now India is quite different from the India of the past. The country is ripe for steps towards self-government.

On November 10 the Indians resident in the United Kingdom, entertained Dadabhai and Gokhale at dinner. W. C. Banerjee proposed the toast of the evening. In responding to the toast, Dadabhai harped on the same theme. The Colonies were prospering with self-government, India was perishing without it.

But, he said, he was "generally of an optimistic nature." The work of the last 52 years has not been thrown away. Though it may not be my fortune—perhaps it may be—to see our efforts crowned with success, many of you may live to see the dawn of the day of self-government and prosperity for India.

As one of the grounds of his hope for the future, he referred to the declarations of Liberal statesmen such as Sir Henry Campbell-Bannerman and Lord Rosebery, who had declared that freedom was the essence of the British Empire.

After all (he added) great events have been happening abroad, in Japan and Russia, and I do not think our present statesmen will shut their eyes to the obvious result of these great events. In the House of Commons I was supported by the Irish, the Radical and Democratic parties. Outside, we have at present very widely the sympathy and support of the Irish, and what I may comprehensively call the People's party. But I depend most of all upon what I see today before me—the union of all classes of my fellow countrymen working together with one heart and with one mind for the great common end. If the whole population of India said once for all they were determined to have self-government—theirs by birthright as well as theirs by pledge—their claim would not be and could not be made in vain.

Dadabhai had spoken (said Gokhale) with that overmastering force of conviction which comes from a lifelong and strenuous exertion on behalf of his countrymen. He is the only man who is entitled to speak in the terms in which he has addressed us. ...It never will be given to another—at any rate for some time to come—to occupy so large a place in the hearts of the people of India and that for more than half a century.

Little could Gokhale have dreamt at that time that it would not take long before there arose another high-souled son of India to fill that place and to lead his countrymen manfully towards the goal of self-government—and that none other than the hero whom he and Dadabhai both, admired and encouraged as the intrepid commander of the forces of Satyagraha in South Africa, the spirited young barrister of the day, Mohandas Karamchand Gandhi.

A plea for a better understanding between India and England was then put forward at Leicester by Dadabhai in his address on the "Needs of India" at a meeting held on November 24, under the auspices of the Leicester Women's Liberal Association. Millions in India did not know, lie sighed, what it was to have a full meal. The fundamental need of India was that she should live free from the yoke of the stranger. Self-government she must have. English pledges and English honour, as well as the birthright of Indians, demanded it. He hoped England would give it with good grace, without loss of time.

3

Select Writings

(Articles)

More European Leeches

April 17, 1905.

In a "Memorandum on a few Statements in the Report of the Indian Famine Commission of 1880," which I submitted on January 4, 1881, to Lord Harrington, then Secretary of State for India, I said:—India does not get a moment to breathe or revive. "More Europeans, more Europeans" is the eternal cry, and this very report itself of the Commission is not free from it. ...

When any question of reform arises, the only remedy that suggests itself to British officials' minds is, "Apply more European leeches, apply more European leeches." Now the Police Commission Report is out, and other Commissions, resolutions, and Reports for "Reforms" (?) (Heaven save us from those "Reforms") have been coming out, with the same eternal cry, "More European leeches, more European leeches," and add to that hideous drain of £30,000,000 or more, as if India had no people of her own, and, if she had, as if they existed only to be "bled" and "plundered," with all the ghastly consequences of famine and plague—deaths of millions and starvation of scores of millions! When will this curse end?

To Maintain British Supremacy

I

May 20, 1905

The question of military expenditure in India is much under discussion at present. And it is being all thrown on wretched India. Let us see what it is for that all the expenditure is incurred. I would give only one extract out of several from the statements of the Government of India itself (despatch March 25, 1890):—

> "Millions of money have been spent on increasing the army in India, on armaments, and on fortifications to provide for the security of India, not against domestic enemies or to prevent the invasions of the warlike peoples of adjoining countries, but to maintain the supremacy of British power in the East."

Now, may I ask whether it is just and worthy of the British name, conscience, and wealth, to burden India with this expenditure ? India, impoverished, bleeding, and perishing by England's own draining of its wealth of over thirty millions every year, and thereby afflicted with famine and plague! Is it not cruel in the extreme?

II

June 1, 1905

Regarding military expenditure in India being of Imperial necessity, I now give the view of the India Office Sir James Peile was a member of the Council of the Secretary of State for India, and represented the India Office on the Royal Commission (Welby's) on Indian Expenditure, Sir J. Peile, after pointing out that the military policy which regulated Indian military expenditure was not exclusively Indian, urged that, "It is worthy of consideration how far it is equitable to charge on a Dependency the whole military cost of that policy, when that Dependency happens to be the only part of the Empire which has a land frontier adjacent to the territories of a great European Power."

Thus, it is the view of the India Office also (though it falls much short of the reality) that the expenditure is for Imperial purposes, and "not exclusively Indian." And yet the rulers go on heartlessly and meanly, imposing the whole expenditure upon the famine and plague-stricken and starving Indian people...

Is this the blessing to India of British rule 2

III

June 20, 1905

I now give the declaration of a Secretary of State for India himself as to the entire British interests in India for which European civil and military expenditure is incurred. Lord Kimberley (The Times, June 13, 1893) at the Mansion House, said:—

> "There is one point upon which, I imagine, whatever may be our party politics in this country, we are all united; that we are resolutely determined to maintain our supremacy over our Indian Empire. That, I conceive, is a matter about which we have only one opinion."

Then, as to the means, among others, he mentioned, "Our European Civil Service" and "the magnificent European force," and then he concluded: "Let us be thoroughly armed as to our frontier defences ... to support our supremacy in that great Empire. Now, can anything be more unjust, more tyrannical, more barbarous and unrighteous than to make the wretched Indians pay the whole expenditure of these European services, which are entirely for British interests.

The Bargain With India

June 27, 1905

Mr. Brodrick, in his Budget speech, said: "I am prepared to maintain the importance of India's carrying out to the full her share of the bargain which has been laid down on condition that Great Britain is ready to adhere to her share of it." The Indians are also often told that they are partners in the Empire and that they must take their share of the responsibility. What, then, should this "bargain" or partnership mean?

I take the figures which Mr. Brodrick gives. He says India spends 2½ millions for the Army, and Great Britain spends £29,800,000 on the Army and £33,400,000 for the Navy, and, with some extras, equal altogether to 71 millions, making a total, say, of 92 millions. Say the Indians should be ready to contribute half, or 46 millions. Then the essential condition of such true partnership or bargain is that the Indians should share in all the benefits, employments, profits, etc. of all the Army and Navy expenditure to die extent of their share.

Now, I ask Mr. Brodrick whether this is the only true and just "bargain" or partnership, and should be honourably carried out? Or does Mr. Brodrick mean that the Indians should contribute 46 millions, but the English should grasp and plunder the whole benefits, employments, profits, etc. of the expenditure of these 46 millions also? In other words, whether he means the "bargain" of two true partners, or does his "bargain" mean the tyranny of the tyrant slaveholder over the slave ? May I request Mr. Brodrick to give a straight, honest answer to this question?

And what is the "bargain" with the Colonies, which form a part of the Empire ?

Nothing but Greed

August 14,1905

Now that the Curzon-Kitchener fight is over, may I ask:

What about the people of India? Where do they come in? They had not the slightest voice whatever in the matter; the main object of the European military expenditure in India is to secure from Russian attack British power, British prestige and British exaction of forty to fifty millions a year for British interests.

As Mr. Frederick Shore has said: "The fundamental principle of the English had been to make the whole Indian nation subservient, in every possible way, to the interests and benefits of themselves." ... Is British rule to be nothing but greed, injustice and unrighteousness ? I still hope not.

Partition of Bengal

August 21, 1905

It is said, "those whom God has a mind to destroy, He first deprives of their senses" I wonder whether the Indian authorities have taken leave of their senses. Do they really think that a deep national feeling, sentiment and interest of a whole and vast people can be flouted and treated with disregard by the British rule, whose whole strength, as has been repeatedly urged by Englishmen and Anglo-Indians themselves, must depend solely and ultimately upon the satisfaction and contentment of the people?

No mean English and Indian military authority—Lord Roberts—has said: "But however efficient and well equipped the army of India may be, were it indeed absolute perfection, and were its numbers considerably more than they are at present, our greatest strength must ever rest on the firm base of a united and contented India." This high-handed and narrow-minded project of rousing the estrangement and hatred of the vast Bengal population, by the partition of Bengal, cannot but be productive of mischief to the British rule.

4

Significant Speeches

India's Interest in General Election (1886)

[*Before a meeting of the members of the Bombay Presidency Association, held in the rooms of the Association on Tuesday evening, the 29th September 1885. Mr. (now Sir) Dinsha Maneckji Petit in the chair*].

The Hon. Dadabhai Naoroji proposed: — "That the following candidates, on account of their services and opinions publicly expressed by them on Indian questions, are deserving of the support of the Indian people: — The Right Honourable Mr. John Bright, the Marquis of Hartington, Mr. J. Slagg, Sir J. Phear, Mr. L. Ghose, Mr. W. Digby, Mr. W. S. Blunt, Mr. S. Keay, Mr. S. Laing, Captain Verney, and Mr. W. O. Plowden. That the views regarding Indian questions publicly expressed by the following candidates cannot be approved by the people of India, and these candidates cannot be accepted as representing Indian interests: — Sir Richard Temple, Mr. J. M. Maclean, Mr. A. S. Ayrton, Sir Lewis Pelly, and Sir Roper Lethbridge." He said: — I speak to the motion which is placed in my hands with a deep sense of its importance.

Hitherto it has been, and it will be so generally, that the English people can mostly derive their information about India from Anglo-Indians, official and non-official, but chiefly from the former. But there are Anglo-Indians and Anglo-Indians. Some, but their number is small, have used their eyes rightly, have looked beyond the narrow circle of their own office, have sympathised with the natives, and tried to understand them and to find out their true wants and aspirations.

Unfortunately the larger number of Anglo-Indians do not take such wide views, or such interest in the natives as would enable them to judge rightly of the actual condition of India. Now when we consider of what extreme importance it is to us that the people of England should have correct information of our condition and wants; how almost entirely we have to depend upon the people and Parliament of England to make those great reforms which alone can remove the serious evils from which we are suffering, it is no ordinary necessity for us that we should take some steps, by which we may inform the great British public, on which sources of information they could rely with any confidence. As I have sad, the number of those who have the necessary true experience and interest in the natives is very small.

It is extremely necessary that such should be pointed out by us. We also find that several Englishmen visiting India, as impartial observers, without any bias or prejudices, have often formed a more correct estimate of the position and necessities of India than many an Anglo-Indian of the so-called experience of twenty or thirty years. Even some, who have not been here at all, form fair and just estimates. It is not always that we can approach the British people in a way so as to secure the general attention of the whole nation at the same time. The present occasion of the new elections is one of those rare occasions in which we can appeal to the whole nation, and especially in a way most useful for our purpose. It is in Parliament that our chief battles have to be fought. The election of its members, especially those who profess to speak on Indian matters, requires our earnest attention, and we should point out clearly to the electors, which of those candidates who make India a plank in their credentials, have our confidence. We do not at all intend to influence the electors in any way in matters of their choice of the representatives that suit them best for their local politics. What we desire to impress upon them is, that so far as the important element of the deliberations on Indian questions is concerned, we desire to name those candidates who are deserving of our confidence and support, and on whom we can rely as would fairly and righteously represent our real wants I and just rights before Parliament. It is with this object that I ask you to adopt the resolution before you. The first name in our resolution is the bright name of The Right Honourable Mr. John Bright. Now I do not certainly presume that I can say anything, or that our association can do anything that can in the least add to the high position Mr. Bright occupies. What I say, therefore, is not with any view that we give any support to him, but as an expression of our esteem and admiration, and of our gratitude for the warm and righteous interest he has evinced on our behalf. I would not certainly take up your time in telling you what he is and what he has done. His fame and name are familiar to the wide world. I may simply refer to a few matters concerning ourselves.

Our great charter is the gracious Proclamation of the Queen. That proclamation is the very test by which we test friends or foes; and it is Mr. Bright who first proposed and urged the duty and necessity of issuing such a proclamation, at a time when the heads of many were bewildered and lost, in his speech on the India Bill in 1858. I should not tarry long on the tempting subject, for if I went on quoting from Mr. Bright's speeches, to show what he has done more than a quarter of a century ago, asking for us what we have been only latterly beginning to give utterance to, I might detain you for hours.

I must, however, give you a few short extracts, showing both the earnestness and the intense sense of justice of the man. The people of India," he said, ' have the highest and strongest claims upon you — claims which you cannot forget — claims which if you do not act upon, you may rely upon it that, if there be a judgement for nations — as I believe there is, as for individuals our children in no distant generation must pay the penalty which we have purchased by neglecting our duty to the population of India." In his speech of 1853, on the occasion of the renewal of the E. I. Company's charter, referring to the miserable condition of the masses of India, he said: — " I must say that it is my belief that if a country be found possessing a most fertile soil and capable of bearing every variety of production, and that notwithstanding, the people are in a state of extreme destitution and suffering, the chances are that there is some fundamental error in the government of that country." When, may I ask, will our rulers see this "fundamental error ?" I have purposely confined myself to his older utterances so far, that we may fully appreciate the righteous advocacy at a time when our own voice was feeble and hardly heard at all You will allow me to make one reference to his later words, and you will see how he is yet the same man and the same friend of India. In his Public Letters," in a letter written by him last year to a gentleman at Calcutta, he says: — " It is to me a great mystery that England should be in the position she now is in relation to India. I hope it may be within the ordering of Providence that ultimately good may arise from it. I am convinced that this can only come from the most just Government which we are able to confer upon your countless millions, and it will always be a duty and a pleasure to me to help forward any measure that may tend to the well-being of your people."

The Marquis of Hartington also occupies a position to which we can hardly add anything. But as we have during his State Secretaryship of India observed his disposition towards a due appreciation of and fulfilment of the noble principles of the proclamation, and his emphatic identifying himself with the righteous Ripon policy at a time of crucial trial— during the excitement of the Ilbert Bill — we cannot but take this opportunity of expressing our thanks and our confidence in him.

To assure you the more fully of this duty upon us, you will permit me to read a few words on this very topic from his speech of 23rd August, 1883. After pointing out the insufficiency of the administration, and the inability of India to afford more for it he said: — 'If the country is to be better governed, that can only be done by the employment of the best and most intelligent of the natives in the service. There is a further reason, in my opinion, why this policy should be adopted, and that is, that it is not wise to educate the people of India, to introduce among them, your civilization and your progress and your literature, and at the same time to tell them, they shall never have any chance of taking any part or share in the administration of the affairs of their country except by their getting rid, in the first instance, of their European rulers." I Cannot refrain myself from expressing my deep regret that we are not able to include in our present list a name that stands pre-eminently high as one of our best friends — I mean Mr. Fawcett. But I trust you will allow me to give a few short extracts, as a warning and a voice from the grave, of one who had the welfare of the poor and dumb millions at heart.

Though he is dead his spirit may guide our other friends, and our rulers. I give these extracts as specially bearing on the present disastrous move of imposing a permanent additional annual burden of some two to three crores of rupees upon us, and on the whole Indian problem. With reference to the Afghan policy he said in 1879: — " It cannot be too strongly insisted upon that in the existing financial condition of India, no peril can be more serious than the adoption of a policy, which, if it should lead to a large additional expenditure, would sooner or later necessitate an increase of taxation. . . The additional taxation which must be the inevitable accompaniment of increased expenditure will bring upon India the gravest perils." Again — " The question, however, as to the exact proportion in which the cost of pursuing a forward policy in Afghanistan should be borne by England and India respectively will have again to be considered anew, now that it has become necessary to renew hostilities in Afghanistan." These words apply with equal force today when we are threatened with a large unnecessary additional burden. On the subject of the whole Indian problem, he said: — " Although there is much in the present financial condition of India to cause the most serious apprehension, yet there is one circumstance connected with it which may fairly be regarded as a most hopeful omen for the future. Until quite lately, India was looked upon as an extremely wealthy country, and there was no project, however costly, that India was not supposed to be rich enough to pay for. Now, however, juster ideas of the resources of the country and of the condition of the people prevail. The recurrence of famines have at length led the English public to take firm hold of the fact that India is an extremely poor country, and that the great mass of her people are in such a state of impoverishment that the Government will have to contend with exceptional difficulties if it becomes necessary to procure increased revenue by additional taxation." "Without an hour's delay the fact should be recognised that India is not in a position to pay for various services at their present rate of remuneration. A most important saving might be effected by more largely employing natives in positions which are now filled by highly paid Europeans, and from such a change political as well as financial advantages would result." " The entire system in which the Government of India is conducted must be changed.

The illusion is only just beginning to pass away that India is an extremely wealthy country." " The financial condition of India is one of such extreme peril that economy is not only desirable but is a matter of imperative necessity." " No misfortune which could happen to India could be greater than having to make her people bear the burden of increased taxation. " In order to restore the finances of India and prevent them drifting into hopeless embarrassment, it is absolutely essential that the policy of rigid economy in every branch of the public service' which has been recently announced by the Government should be carried out with promptitude and thoroughness." This policy was announced by the Conservative Government, and now all this is forgotten and the Conservative Government are proposing to burden us with additional expenditure of two or three millions, or may be more ! We cannot too strongly protest against this. In all the extracts I have read you will perceive the kind of policy which our friends have urged, and this test, or as I may shortly call, the Royal Proclamation policy, is the principal one by which we may discriminate friends from those who either from ignorance or narrow-minded selfishness advocate a different policy. Judging by this test, I may say that all the other names in the first part of the resolution are fairly entitled to our confidence and to an appeal from us to the constituencies to return them to Parliament as far as our interests are concerned. Their writings show that they have a good grasp of our position and wants. I may refer to Mr. Slagg's views and efforts to abolish the India Council Nothing can be more absurd than that in the nineteenth century and in England itself, the first home of public and free discussion upon all public matters, there should exist a body to deliberate secretly upon the destinies of a sixth of the human race ! It is an utter anachronism. Mr. Blagg laudable and persistent efforts to get an enquiry into the Government of India promises to be successful. Messrs. Slagg,

Digby, Keay, Blunt, and Verney's writings show that they understand us and have done us good service. About Mr. Lal Mohan Ghose I need not say more than that he is the only one through whom the Indians will now have a chance of speaking for themselves. I have every hope that he will do justice to himself, and fulfil the expectations which India has rested on him by honest and hard work for the welfare of his country. We must feel very thankful to the electors of Greenwich for giving him such welcome and sympathy as they have done. They have shown remarkable liberality, vindicated the English spirit of justice and philanthropy, have held out a hand to us of equal citizenship, and nobly confirmed the sincerity of the Royal Proclamation, by their action as a part of the English nation. Mr. Laing has, I pm afraid, some incorrect notions about the balance of the trade of India, but we know that he understands India well and will continue to be useful in promoting our welfare.

Sir John Phear and Mr. Plowden are known to us for their sympathies with us. Sir John Phear's book "The Aryan Village" shows much sympathetic study of the country and its institutions, and he proved our friend at the time of the Ilbert Bill. He said: — We have a higher duty to India than to consult the prejudices of this kind of a few thousands of our own countrymen, who are there today, but may be gone tomorrow. We have to govern that vast Empire in the interest of the millions who constitute the indigenous population of the country."

Mr. Plowden says, with reference to Lord Ripon's policy: — " I know it to be just, I know it also to be honest and earnest, I believe it to be sound and thoroughly practical." I next come to our second list. As I have already said, we do not ask the constituencies not to return them if they are suitable to them on other grounds. We only ask that whatever weight the electors may give to their other qualifications, they would not take them as fair exponents or trustworthy interpreters of India's wants and just wishes, and as favouring us by electing them. With regard to Sir R. Temple I need say nothing more than that he endeavours to produce the wrong and mischievous impression upon the minds of the English people that India is prosperous and increasing in prosperity, in the teeth of the early and latest testimony of eminent men and in the teeth of facts.

Mr. Fawcett told that the illusion was passing away, while Sir Richard keeps it up ! I do not advert to some of his acts in India, such as the strange contrast of 2 lbs. rations in Bengal and the disastrous 1 lb. ration famine policy here, probably to please higher authorities his high-handedness, his treatment of the local funds, etc., I confine myself to an utterance or two of his after leaving India. It is strange that a quarter of a century ago Mr. Richard Temple was able to take and express a remarkably intelligent view of the Indian problem. In connection with the Punjab he expounded the causes of Punjab's poverty and revival in his report of 1859 in these significant and clear words:— In former reports it was explained how the circumstance of so much money going out of the Punjab contributed to depress the agriculturist. The native regular army was Hindustani, to them was a large share of the Punjab revenue disbursed, of which a part only they spent on the spot and a part was remitted to their homes. Thus it was that year after year, lakhs and lakhs were drained from the Punjab, and enriched Oudh.

But within the last year, the native army being Punjabi, all such sums have been paid to them, and have been spent at home. Again, many thousands of Punjabi soldiers are serving abroad. These men not only remit their savings, but also have sent quantities of prize property and plunder, the spoils of Hindustan, to their native villages. The effect of all this is already perceptible in an increase of agricultural capital, a freer circulation of money and a fresh impetus to cultivation. Now, gentlemen, am I not justified in saying that it is strange that what Mr. Richard Temple of twenty-five years past saw so intelligently, about Punjab, Sir Richard Temple of the present day does not or would not see about India, whence, not merely lakhs and lakhs" but hundreds and hundreds of lakhs — thirty hundred or so lakhs are drained to England. He cannot, it appears, now grasp the problem of India as he did that of the Punjab. I cannot undertake to explain this phenomenon. What may be the reason or object? He alone can explain. As he is presently doing mischief by posing as a friend, I can only say " save us from such a friend." We cannot but speak out, however unwillingly, that Sir Richard Temple is not a safe and correct guide for the people of England for India's wants and wishes. While Bright in '63, Lawrence in '64 and '73, Fawcett in '79, the London Punches grand cartoon of Disillusion in '79 portraying the wretched Indian woman and children, with the shorn pagoda tree over their heads, begging alms of John Bull, Hunter in '80, Baring in '82, deplore the impoverishment of the masses of India, Sir Richard in a fine phrenzy talks in '85 "of their homes becoming happier, their acres broader, their harvest richer." India is prospering, that there is no lack of subsistence, no shrinkage of occupation, no discontent with the wages at home, and in consequence no searching for wages abroad."

And yet some light-hearted people coolly talk of sending him as a Viceroy here ! No greater misfortune could befall to India ! About Mr. Maclean I need not say much as you are all well aware, that he has been throughout his whole career in India a thorough partisan and an avowed and determined anti-native, with a few rare intervals of fairness. He can never be a fair and trustworthy interpreter of our views and wishes. He off-handedly says in his letter in the Bombay Gazette of 9th June last: " Mr. Slagg recited the usual rubbish about the deplorable poverty and overtaxation of the Indian people." So you see, gentlemen, who Mr. Maclean is. He is a great man before whom the views of such persons as Bright, Fawcett, Lawrence, the Punch and Baring are all mere rubbish ! Mr. Ayrton's whole policy can be summed up in a few words — treat natives gently, but give them no posts of power or responsibility, have no legislative councils with non-official element, and if you have, put no natives in them. He says:

The power of governing must remain, as it had hitherto been, solely and exclusively in the hands of British subjects going out of this country." Why were we to teach the natives, what they had failed in discovering for themselves, that they would one day be a great nation." This un-English narrow-mindedness and pureblindness is the worst thing that can happen to England and India both, and according to it all that the best and highest English statesmen, and even our Sovereign have promised and said about high duty, justice, policy, must become so many empty words, hollow promises, and all sham and delusion. My personal relations with Sir L. Pelly at Baroda were, as you know, friendly, but the reason of his name appearing in this list, is that he was an instrument of Lord Lytton's Afghan policy, and that as far as his views may have coincided with the Lytton policy, he cannot fairly represent our views against that policy. About Sir Roper Lethbridge, I was under the impression that when he was Press Commissioner, he was regarded as one sympathising with the natives. But when the day of the crucial trial came, the Ilbert Bill and the Ripon policy, he was then found out that his views were anything but what would be just, fair and sympathising towards the natives of India.

In addition to the names I have mentioned, I am required to mention Sir James Fergusson, and I cannot but agree to do so though with some reluctance. I have personally much respect for him, and I do not forget that he has done some good. In the matter of the native Princes he enunciated a correct principle some eighteen years ago when he was Under-Secretary of State for India. Presiding at a meeting of the East India Association, 1867, he said: — "It is earnestly to be hoped that the Princes of India look upon the engagements of the British Queen as irrevocable, and I believe he consistently carried out this principle when here with the Princes of this Presidency, We cannot also forget that when acting upon his own instincts he did good in matters of education and social intercourse, and nominated to the Legislative Council our friends the Hon. Budroodeen and the Hon. Telang as representatives of the educated class, retaining also the Hon. Mundlik. You can easily conceive then my reluctance to speak against him, notwithstanding some mistakes and failures in his administration as Governor under official misguidance.

But when I see that after his arrival in England he has made statements so incorrect and mischievous in results, in some matters most vital to India, it is incumbent upon us to say that he does not know the true state of India. Fancy, gentlemen, my regret and surprise when I read these words from the latest Governor of Bombay: — At the present time her (India's) people were not heavily taxed, and it was a great mistake to suppose that they were." This is a matter of easy ascertainment, and the heaviness of taxation is repeated by acknowledged eminent men. Here are a few figures which will tell their own tale. The income of the United Kingdom may be roughly taken at £1,200,000,000 and its gross revenue about £87,000,000, giving a proportion of about 17½ per cent, of the income. Of British India the income is hardly £400,000,000 and its gross revenue about £70,000,000, giving 17½ per cent, of the income, and yet Sir James tells the English people that the people of India are not heavily taxed, though paying out of this wretched income, a gross revenue of more than double the proportion of what the people of the enormously rich England pay for their gross revenue.

Contrast with Sir James's statement the picture which Mr. Fawcett gives in his paper in the Nineteenth Century of October, 1879: —"If a comparison is made between the financial resources of England and India, it will be found almost impossible to convey an adequate idea of the poverty of the latter country an consequently it is found that taxation in India has reached almost its extreme limit." Again he says: " It is particularly worthy of remark that the Viceroy and Secretary of State now unreservedly accept the conclusion that the limit of taxation has been reached in India, and that it has consequently become imperatively necessary that expenditure should be reduced." (The italics are mine). Now, gentlemen, mark this particularly. When in 1879 the Conservative Viceroy and Secretary of State had, as Mr. Fawcett says, unreservedly accepted that the limit of taxation had been reached in India the gross revenue was only £65,000,000, while the budgeted revenue of the present year is already £72,000,000, and we are now threatened by the same Government with an addition of £2,000,000 or £3,000,000 more permanently.

This is terrible. Change the entire system as Mr. Fawcett says, substitute far the present destructive foreign agency, the constructive and conservative native agency, except for the highest posts of power, and you can have a hundred millions or two hundred millions with ease for purposes of government or taxation. This is the difference between Fawcett and Fergusson. Both are gentlemen, but the former speaks from careful hard study, the latter without it. Mischievous as such statements generally are, they are still more so when delivered before a Manchester audience, who unfortunately yet do not understand their own true, interests, and the interests of the English workmen. They do not understand yet that their greatest interest is in increasing the ability of the

Indians to buy their manufactures. That if India were able to buy a pound worth of their cotton manufactures per head per annum, that would give them a trade of £250,000,000 a year instead of the present poor imports into India of £25,000,000 of cotton yarn and manufactures from all foreign countries of the world. Sir James, I think, has made another statement that all offices in India are occupied by the natives except the highest. I am, not able to put my hand just now upon the place where I read it. But if my impression be correct, I would not waste words and your time to animadvert upon such an extraordinary incorrect statement, so utterly contrary to notorious facts. Why, it is the head and front the very soul of all our evils and grievances that the statement is not the fact or reality as it ought to be. This is the very thing which will put an end to all our troubles, and remedy all our evils of poverty and otherwise. Let Sir James bring it about, and he will be our greatest benefactor and England's best friend. In concluding, I may lay down a test for our appeal to the electors, that whichever candidates are not in accord with the Royal Proclamation, and with the lines of the Ripon policy, they are those whom we ask to be not regarded as trustworthy and fair interpreters of our views and wishes.

The resolution has Mr. Blunt's name in the first list and Mr. Aryton's in the second. This will show that we are not actuated by a spirit of partisanship. Whoever are our real friends, be they Liberal or Conservative, we call them our friends- Differences of opinion in some details will no doubt occur between us and our friends, but we are desirous to support them, because the broad and important lines of policy, which India needs, such as those of the Proclamation and the Ripon policy, and the broad and important facts of our true condition, are well understood and adopted by those friend for their guidance in their work for the welfare of India. (Applause.)

Election Speeches in England

[*Before various meetings in support of his candidature as the Liberal candidate for the Holborn Division of Finsbury in the General Election of 1886*].

Hon. Dadabhai Naoroji's Great Speech

[*At a meeting of the Electors of the Holborn Division, held on the 27th June 1886, in the Town Hall, Holborn. Mr. W. Percy Bunting in the chair*].

Mr. Dadabhai Naoroji, (on rising to address the meeting, was received with prolonged cheering, the audience rising and waving hats and handkerchiefs,) said: I really do not know how I can thank you from the bottom of my heart, for the permission you have given me to stand before you as a candidate for your borough. I appreciate the honour most highly, I will not take up more of your time on this point because you may believe me when I say that I thank you from the bottom. It was a very crowded meeting of the Electors of the Holborn Division, and on the crowded platform were Mr. Bryce, M. P., Under-Secretary for Foreign Affairs. Mr. Wilfrid Blunt, Mr. B. Molloy, M. P., the Rev. Stewart Headlam, Mr. Hodgson Pratt, Major Evans Bell, Mr. W. Martin Wood (late editor of the Times of India and others. Letters from Lord Ripon, Mr. Charles Harrison, Mr. Samuel Smith, M. P., Professor Hunter, M. P., Lord Hobhouse, Mr. John Slagg, Mr. Chesson, Mr. Arnold Morley, M. P., and others, warmly approving of the candidature of Mr. Dadabhai, were read. Lord Ripon wrote: —I have learnt with much pleasure that you contemplate offering yourself as a candidate for a seat in Parliament at the approaching General Election. Your intimate acquaintance with the feelings and wishes of the people of India, particularly in the Bombay Presidency, would enable you to give very valuable assistance in the discussion of Indian questions in the House of Commons. Your experience in the Bombay Council would be useful to you, and I am quite sure that your election to Parliament would give great satisfaction to your compatriots in India."

At a fully attended Meeting of the Executive Committee of the Holborn liberal Association, held on Friday, the 18th of June, 1886, it was unanimously resolved

> "That this Meeting, having heard the political views of The Honourable Dadabhai Naoroji, earnestly commends him to the Electors of Holborn as a fit and proper person to represent the Liberals and Radicals

of the Borough in Parliament."— Thos. Johnson, Chairman Harry T. Eve, Hon. Secretary.

The followings Mr. Dadabhai's Manifesto to the Electors of the Holborn Division of Finsbury.

Gentlemen, I am greatly honoured by an invitation to contest your Borough as the Liberal Candidate. To many of you I am a man of strange name and race. This fact must plead as my excuse for a few remarks about myself. I am an Indian subject of the of my heart. It is really and truly so. (Cheers.) Standing as I do here, to represent the 250,000,000 of your fellow subjects in India, of course I know thoroughly well my duty; for if I am returned by you, my first duty will be to consult completely and fully the interest of my Queen. The best years of my life have been spent in mercantile pursuits in this country. With English life and English politics I am familiar; I have voted at British Elections; I have worked for Liberal Candidates. Now, by your favour, I aspire to a seat in thc British Parliament. In my own country I have been largely concerned with important affairs. I was Prime Minister of the Kingdom of Baroda. I have done my share of municipal work in the Town Council and Municipality of Bombay. At this moment I am a Member of the Bombay Legislative Council. On the condition of my country I have frequently written, having given special study to economic questions affecting my countrymen; I have not the less given my best attention and consideration to subjects gravely affecting the welfare of my English fellow subjects.

I am a Liberal in politics, prepared to support the great measures of Social Reform, including a change in the Land Laws affecting dwellers alike in town and country, which have been announced by the Great Leader of the Party. Upon the momentous issue now before the Electors of Great Britain and Ireland, I am at one with Mr. Gladstone in his noble-hearted and heroic effort to satisfy the just aspirations of the Irish people to control their own affairs while-yet remaining a part of the great British Empire. The Irish problem must be solved.

To my mind a measure of Irish Self –Government, embodying the principles of Mr. Gladstone's Manifesto to his Constituents, far from disintegrating the Empire, as some wrongly allege, is, in my humble opinion, calculated to produce a real and lasting union between Great Britain and Ireland in place of the sham, or worse than sham, union which at present exists. Further, I am of opinion that when Ireland gets her own Parliament, the material advancement of the Irish people will be ensured. It is with especial pride and pleasure that I, an Indian, address a Metropolitan Constituency as a candidate for the suffrages of the Electors. I remember that it was a neighbouring Constituency to your own that elected my friend Henry Fawcett, when he was rejected by Brighton, and retained him as its representative until his lamented death. I will not, here and now, set forth the features of Indian Reform which I hope to be privileged, by your kind favour, to advocate in the House of Commons. In due course I hope to take counsel with you on these matters.

I pray you, members of the race which rules India, to remember the condition of that Empire, and to give me the opportunity of serving my countrymen in Parliament.

By favour of the Executive Committee of your Liberal Association, I have the opportunity of appealing to the Electors of your Borough, and I appeal to your generous spirit, which is always prepared to do what is good and right, to give me your votes, enable me to enter Parliament, and there demonstrate the pressing need of my country and countrymen for a consideration of Indian affairs from their standpoint. At the same time I need hardly add that I should give my best and fullest attention to the interests of my constituents.

The time for fighting is short. I may not be able to see all the Electors before the day of polling; but by public meetings, and in other Ways, I hope to be able to make myself acquainted with you, and to lay my views in detail before you.

Speech at the Store-street Hall

[*Before a large number of Electors in the Store-Street Hall on Monday night, 28th June 1886. Mr. Newton Wilson in the chair*].

The Hon. Dadabhai Naoroji, in the course of his speech, said he thanked them most sincerely for the honour they had done him in allowing him to stand for their constituency. (Hear, hear.) The chairman had very kindly said something about him, and he would not trespass much upon their patience by dwelling more upon that point.

He would only say that he stood before them representing 250,000,000 of their fellow-subjects in India, and he stood before them as a fair representative of India. He appealed to the people of England to allow a single voice or two to be heard in the British Parliament on behalf of these 250,000,000 people, yet he did not forget that his first duty would be to the constituency itself, and he should feel it his duty, if returned, to represent the interests of the constituency to the fullest extent before even representing the interests of India. He was not altogether a stranger in this place. The first time he had ever put his foot in this country was in 1855, and he had been altogether more or less a resident in this country since. He had resided in England during the past twenty years, only going to his own home at short intervals. Under these circumstances he could claim fairly on one hand to represent his own countrymen, and on the other hand he hoped he should fulfil his duty to his constituents if he was honoured with their representation in the House of Commons. (Loud cheers.) He could tell them that the Indians felt a keen interest in this question of the election of Indians in the House of Parliament here. Two or three days ago, on the wings of lightning, a message from that vast assemblage — a telegram to the people of this country — stating that they were watching, with keen interest, the candidature of the Hon. Dadabhai Naoroji and Lal Mohan Ghose, and a desire was keenly felt and universally expressed for their success, and much gratitude was felt to Holborn for supporting the candidature of Mr. Naoroji, and also that a public meeting, expressing confidence, would soon be held. (Cheers and applause).

That telegram bad been despatched from India since it was known that Holborn Lad honoured him with their acceptance. This was not the time or the place for him to enter into the wants of India, which his countrymen were desirous he should represent in the House of Commons. This was the time to consider a far more immediately urgent question — the question of Home Rule for Ireland. (Cheers and applause)

After dealing at length with the question, the speaker went on to say one word on behalf of his own country. Miss Nightingale had written him a letter in which she appealed to the English nation on behalf of India, and expressed her pleasure at the success of the meeting in the Holborn Town Hall, and her ardent hope that the electors of Holborn would return Mr. Naoroji to the House of Commons, Lord Ripon had also written him a letter since the meeting in the Town Hall, congratulating him on the success of that meeting, and expressing the hope that he would be returned; a fact which would give great joy to his compatriots in India. (Cheers and applause.) The speaker concluded by making an earnest appeal on behalf of the five millions in Ireland and 250,000,000 of India, and resumed his seat amid cheers.

Speech at the Old Friends' Hall

[*Before a Meeting of the Electors of the Holborn Division in the Old Friends', St. Martin's Lane, on Tuesday night, 29th June 1886. Mr. J. P. Murrough in the chair*].

The Hon. D. Naoroji, on rising, was received with rapturous applause. After some few preliminary remarks the speaker said, amid cheers, that England had shown herself to be the friend of struggling nationalities all over the world, and it was a great pity that when she came to Ireland she should stop there. He did not think, however, that England would stop at the case of Ireland, which had now spoken with a firm voice her demand for Home Rule. - Much had been said that this question had not been formally brought before the country, but times and circumstances produced the man fit for the purpose. A great deal had been made of the heated expressions of the Irish members when the battle was raging. No doubt words had been uttered which in cooler moments would be heartily condemned, but when men were in the thick of the fight they did not care how or where they hit. (Cheers.)

Now, however, in peaceful moments, a better tone and temper prevailed. It was an Irish poet who said that failure was rebellion, and success patriotism. Well Mr. Gladstone had converted rebellion into patriotism, and the rebels of yesterday were the patriots of today. (Cheers and applause.)

He had no doubt whatever in his mind, that the Irish people would justify the confidence of the Grand Old Man — (cheers) — and the English people at the present juncture would also, he believed, justify the confidence to be placed in them to return him to power to do this great act of justice for Ireland. (Loud cheers.). On the motion of Mr. Campbell, a vote of confidence in the Hon. D. Naoroji's candidature was unanimously passed. A vote of thanks to the chairman brought the proceedings to a close.

Speech at the Phoenix Hall

[*Before a crowded meeting of the Electors in the Phoenix Hall, Hatton Hall, on Wednesday night, 30th June 1886. Mr. T. Johnston in the chair*].

Mr. Dadabhai Naoroji, who was received with ringing cheers, thanked the electors for the kind reception they had accorded to him. He had come there from a distant land, which under the dispensation of Providence, was ruled by a race distinguished for its love of liberty and justice, and he appealed to that race that they should grant that liberty and justice to India which they so highly esteemed themselves. He had received a telegram stating that on the previous day a meeting had been held in Bombay, thanking Holborn and Deptford for having chosen as Liberal candidates Mr. Lal Mohan Ghose and the Hon. Dadabhai Naoroji. It was also stated that meetings were being held throughout the length and breadth of the Bombay Presidency, in which the most lively interest was exhibited in the elections for these two constituencies. He could assure them that it was not for the simple ambition of placing the letters M.P. after his name that he sought their suffrages, but because lie wished to continue a worker in the good cause. If he were honoured with their representation, he could assure them he would do justice to their choice. (Hear, hear and applause.) During his whole life he had always made it a point to work for the amelioration of the poor, distressed and ignorant, and he hoped to pursue that course to the end of his days. He would consider it to be the crowning work of his life to get into the British Parliament to endeavour to serve 250,000,000 of his countrymen, and of their fellow subjects in India. After stating his opinion of the Irish question, the speaker said it would be for the people of England to choose the good and reject the evil. (Hear, hear.)

The good was to do justice to Ireland, and by doing that they would be rejecting the evil. (Loud and prolonged cheers and applause.)

Speech at the Town Hall

[*Before a crowded meeting of the Electors on Friday, July 2nd, 1886, in the Town Hall, Holborn. Mr. Eve, B. L., in the chair. This meeting was a most enthusiastic one*].

Mr. Dadabhai Naoroji, (who was received with loud and prolonged cheers and applause, which lasted for several minutes), said: — He had before the honour of addressing them in that hall. He referred to the object of his standing before them, viz., to ask for justice for India; and he was not going to dwell longer on the point, except to read to them the substance of three telegrams he had received from that country. The National Telegraphic Union, which represented all parts of India, had sent a telegram to Holborn and Deptford to assist Lal Mohan Ghose and himself in getting seats in Parliament, and also thanked them for accepting their candidature. On the subject of Home Rule he had already addressed to them certain arguments, but he would now take up the thread of those arguments, and answer certain objections. He would not enter into details, for the simple reason that the principle of a measure should be first agreed upon, and if they agreed in adopting the principle it was time enough to discuss the details, but if the principle was not agreed upon, it would be simple waste of time discussing the details. (Hear, hear, and applause.) He had, therefore, dwelt upon the consistency of the moral courage of Mr. Gladstone in acceding to the demands of the expressed wish of the Irish people. In sending his message of peace to Ireland, amid the turmoil by which he was surrounded, he had kept his temper and pursued the even tenor of his way, confident- in the strength and of the righteousness of his cause. He did his utmost to meet the views of his party, which proved how great and good a man he was. There were persons who called themselves Unionists, but really it was the Gladstonians who were the Unionists, and the opposition was the sham Unionists, because the Union they were defending was a sham union, and not one of hearts and affections. (Cheers and applause.) They could not say there had been a real union during the past eighty-six years, or that it had produced any good result (Hear, hear, and applause.) The union between the two countries had really been brought about by the basest corruption; in fact, so mean were the ways by which it was brought about, that Lord Cornwallis was so utterly disgusted that he said, " Would to God that I had never put my hand in this dirty business." (Applause.)

"Were they afraid that Empire would be broken up simply because Ireland had a Home Rule Government ? In India there was a number of native states which possessed Home Rule, the only connection that they had with the British rule being that they paid a small tribute to the British authorities. These native states proved a strength to the British Empire, for in 1857, at the time of the Indian Mutiny, these states formed contingents to restore peace to the country; and again, at the scare of Russian invasion, these states, thoroughly independent, came forward ready to assist the British forces in repelling that invasion. A great deal was said about the exclusion of the Irish members, and that taxation should not go without representation; but if the Irish people, whose right it was to be represented in the Imperial Parliament of their own free will, wished to forego that chance, why should others complain? (Hear, hear, and cheers.)

Speaking of the opposition to the measure expressed by certain persons in Ireland, the Speaker said that all classes, after the passing of the Bill, ought to unite in doing the best they could for their country; and the gentlemen who had spoken on behalf of the Protestant Home Rule Association had shown there was no danger whatever in their- minds on the score of persecution of the minority. He had not the least doubt in his mind, although in the present excitement opposition of this kind might be raised by those who enjoyed certain privileges, still the time must come when these very gentlemen would be foremost in taking advantage of the privileges conferred upon Ireland, and would be glad that they had been conferred upon her. He had not the least fear that any one in Ireland would have reason to complain of the effect of opening a new Parliament there. (Hear, hear.)

At one time Home Rule was synonymous with rebellion, but the Irish leaders had managed their affairs in such a way that it was now synonymous with patriotism. The time had come when the greatest statesman of the age held out the hand of fellowship to them, gave them a message of peace, and they thankfully accepted the offer made to them and said now will begin the regeneration of the country. They showed that if they knew how to fight they also knew how to make peace. Having shown this capacity on their part, they might rely upon it they would justify the confidence which Mr. Gladstone was willing to put in them. Much was said about the curtailment of the powers of the Imperial Parliament.

Mr. Bright said that any laws which Parliament passed they could also repeal. Some said if the Irish had a Parliament they would enact laws which would be oppressive and contrary to the wishes of the English people, and which would end in civil war. Suppose the Irish were so foolish to do such a thing, as Englishmen, had they never known what civil war was — they who refused to take the laws from their own sovereign, and said they would not have them, as they were not made by the people themselves. They should not forget that love created love, confidence produced confidence, thistles produced thistles, and evil was never productive of good except Providence turned it in some way or other. They had no confidence in the Irish.

Lord Salisbury, in speaking before the Worshipful Company of Grocers, said, " In respect to institutions and property, we have again and again the fact forced upon us that confidence will create greater riches than by confiscation can ever be gained. If you destroy confidence, no confiscation will repay you." He would only ask the same thing from Lord Salisbury. Let them have confidence in the Irish, and the Irish would rise and prosper. One of the great arguments used against the Irish was the outrages and murders and assassinations that took place there. But did they suppose that a nation who, in physical endurance, was as good as any on the face of the earth, and whose mental calibre distinguished them amongst men, did they think they would take a blow without giving another. It was absurd to expect such a thing. He did not want for a moment to justify the outrages or any violence that might have taken place in Ireland, but he would say in the nature of things, they could not expect any other result. Those who opposed the measure because there were outrages committed in Ireland, were using that as a shift, because they had no other argument. See what Mr. Bright says: — "The first thing that ever called my attention to the state of Ireland was the reading on account of one of these outrages. I thought of it for a moment, but the truth struck me at once, and all I have ever seen since confirms it, when law refuses its duty, when Government denies the right of the people . . . those people are driven back from law and from the ways of civilization to that which is termed the law of nature, and if not the strongest, the law of the vindictive." After referring to the decision of the population in Ireland, he said he hoped that the measure would be accepted with gratitude, and that it would be given not only as a matter of justice, but of reparation of the past. By giving this boon to Ireland, England would add to its history a brighter chapter than any it at present contained. Their greatest man had been inspired to do that act. Let them feel that inspiration and help him in the struggles which he was now undergoing, carrying him on their shoulders to victory, and not only would they earn the blessing of five millions of Irishmen, but they would also earn the blessing of fifty times five millions of the inhabitants of India. (Cheers.)

In the above meeting the following resolution was passed — "That this meeting of Holborn electors having heard the expression of the Hon. Dadabhai Naoroji's political opinions, cordially accepts him as the Liberal candidate for this borough, and pledges itself to use every legitimate effort to secure his return.

Speech at the Reception Meeting in Bombay

[*Before the public meeting of the inhabitants of Bombay called by the Bombay Presidency Association at the Framjee Cowasjee Institute on Sunday, the 13th February 1887, to pass a vote of thanks to the Hon. Dadabhai Naoroji and Mr. Lal Mohan Ghose for their exertions on behalf of India at the Parliamentary elections of 1886 in England. Mr. (now Sir) Dinshaw M. Petit in the chair*].

The Honourable Dadabhai Naoroji (amidst long and immense cheering), said: — Mr. Chairman, Ladies and Gentlemen, — I feel extremely obliged by the very kind reception you have given to my friend Mr. Ghose and myself, and for the confidence you have reposed in us. Such hearty acknowledgments of my humble services and of my friend's arduous exertion cannot but encourage us largely in our future work. (Cheers.) As natives of India, we are bound to do whatever lies within our power and opportunities. In undertaking the work of trying to get a seat in Parliament, the first question that naturally arose was whether it would be of any good to India and whether an Indian member would be listened to. The first thing, therefore, I did on arriving in England was to consult many English friends, several of whom are eminent statesmen of the day and members of Parliament.

I was almost universally advised that I should not hesitate to try to carry out my intentions, that it was extremely desirable that there should be at least one or two Indians in Parliament to enable members to learn the native view of questions from natives themselves. (Cheers.)

That if I could by any possibility work way into the House, I would certainly be doing a great service not only to India, but to a large extent to England also. (Cheers.)

Several fundamental important questions of policy can be fought out and decided in Parliament alone as they depend upon Acts of Parliament, and Parliament is the ultimate appeal in every important question in which Government and the native public may differ. To get direct representation from India was not at present possible.

An indirect representation through the liberality and aid of some British constituency was the only door open to us. I undertook to contest Holborn under many disadvantages. I was just occupied in making acquaintances and feeling my way. I had no time to find out and make the acquaintance of any constituency; I was quite unknown to the political world, when of a sudden the resolution came on upon me. The Liberal leaders very properly advised me that I should not lose this opportunity of contesting some seat, no matter however a forlorn hope it might be, as the best means of making myself known to the English constituencies, and of securing a better chance and choice for the next opportunity.

That I could not expect to get in at a rush, which even an Englishman was rarely able to do except under particularly favourable circumstances. I took the advice and selected Holborn out of three offers I have received. I thus not only got experience of an English contest, but it also satisfied me as to what prospects an Indian had of receiving fair and even generous treatment at the hands of English electors. The elections clearly showed me that a suitable Indian candidate has as good a chance as any Englishman, or even some advantage over an Englishman, for there is a general and genuine desire among English electors to give to India any help in their power. (Cheers.)

I had only nine days of work from my first meeting at the Holborn Town Hall, and sometimes I had to attend two or three meetings on the same day. The meetings were as enthusiastic and cordial in reception as one's heart could desire. Now the incident I refer to is this. Of canvassing I was able to do but very little. Some liberal electors, who were opposed to Irish Home rule, intended to vote for the conservative candidate, but to evince their sympathy with India, they promised me to abstain from voting altogether. Unknown as I was to the Holborn electors, the exceedingly enthusiastic and generous treatment they gave me, and that nearly two thousand of them recorded their votes in my favour, must be quite enough to satisfy any that the English public desire to help us to have our own voice in the House of Commons. (Cheers.)

Letters and personal congratulations I received from many for what they called my " plucky contest." Lord Ripon — (cheers) — wrote to me not to be discouraged, as my want of success was shared by so many other liberals as to deprive it of personal character; that it was the circumstances of the moment, as it turned out, that worked specially against me, and he trusted I would be successful on a future occasion. Now it was quite true that owing to the deep split among the liberals in the home rule question, it was estimated by some that I had lost nearly a thousand votes by the abstention of liberal voters. In short, with my whole experience at Holborn, of both the manner and events of the contest, I am more than ever confirmed in my opinion that India may fairly expect from the English public just and generous treatment. (Cheers).

I have no doubt that my friend Mr. Ghose — (cheers) — with his larger electioneering experience of two arduous contests, will be able to tell you of similar conviction and future hopefulness. There is one great advantage achieved by their contests, which in itself is an ample return for all the trouble — I mean the increasing and earnest interest that has been aroused in the English public about Indian matters.

From everywhere you begin receive expressions of desire to know the truth about India, and invitations come to you to address on Indian subjects. The moral effect of these contests is important and invaluable. (Hear, hear.) A letter I received from an English friend on the eve of my departure for India.

5

Important Letters

Letters to Dadabhai

Sir John Budd Phear to Dadabhai

July 7,1887

I wish very much that I could have been personally present at this great national gathering. The event is most significant and instructive, and I trust that the lessons deducible from it will be rightly apprehended and understood by the governing classes in this country. As to this, however, I am not very sanguine. Those whose influence is at this time paramount in controlling the Government are the Jingo classes of the people, admirers of liberty and right in all wherein they are themselves concerned, but ever ready to override and assert authority whenever their own will is disputed by those over whom they are able to domineer. A crucial example of this is the treatment which the Irish question is receiving at the hands of the present House of Commons. From the columns of The Times, you may judge how the English "classes" look upon the political aspirations of the Indian people.

And I have no hope that these can be realised without more than one repetition of struggles of the Ilbert Bill type. But, of course, the cause of the people must prevail ultimately; and the sooner our home democracy learns its power and exercises it, the better will it be for at least the Indian portion of the Empire.

Hyndman to Dadabhai

February 2, 1905

Whether you survive me, or I you, it is certain that so long as my pen can write and my tongue can speak, the many scores of millions who are being ground down to death under our merciless rule will not lack a champion, such as he is, in this country. I live now in the hope of seeing the overthrow of our infamous system.

Bishop of New York to Dadabhai

May 28, 1900

I am bound to add that I do not find myself in agreement with the positions you maintain with reference to the English occupancy of India. There was no order, nor safety for life or property, nor freedom of person in India until England went there. As a native Indian of high rank recently said to me in Madras, "We have all that you Americans fought for—life, liberty and the pursuit of happiness; and if British power were to take itself away from India tomorrow, we should have bloodshed, chaos and internecine warfares in endless varieties." I confess, for myself, that the people who are saved from these things should, in my judgement, pay the bill for them.

Robert Pedlar to Dadabhai

August 15, 1887

The subject is one of the deepest interest and importance for the future welfare of Britain as well as of India. ... I shall place the report (of the Congress) in the Reading Room of our Liberal Club (Perth).

G.J. Day to Dadabhai

August 16, 1887

It is extremely difficult in Indian affairs to know how far to encourage volunteering; it would be most disastrous to England to find a fresh Indian Mutiny spring up and, at the same time, it is most illiberal to prevent by force a people fit to govern themselves from so doing; officering the volunteer forces with Englishmen might do some good; crushing a martial spirit out of a people is a great wrong. We as a nation in our early Roman age suffered terribly from it, and your country would suffer in like manner.

The Rev. Fred. Trestrail to Dadabhai

January 3, 1888

The enthusiasm so manifest astonished me. A people hitherto so quiet and impassive to be roused to such energy seems like life from death. . . . I trust this grand debate will put to shame those English residents in India who are so apt to treat her people with scorn and contempt, as if they were an inferior race. Against this spirit I have vehemently protested ever since I had, as Secretary of the Baptist Mission, to do with India.

Within a short time a cousin of Hume, Robert Mullet, M. D., Surgeon-Major on the Retired List of the Bombay Army, became a supporter of the Congress. In a letter to Fram Desai, dated December 3, he wrote:

Will you please tell your uncle (Dadabhai) that I am the 2nd cousin of Mr. Allan Octavian Hume. (late Secretary to the Government of India in the Agricultural Department), that until Mr. Charles Forjett sent me some copies of the Homeward Mail I did not know anything about die Indian Congress—that if there be an Englishman more than another who considers the Government of India to be "a Despotism"—I am that man! And if he will please to send me all the papers connected with the movement, he may find me to be one of the most energetic supporters of the movement.

Dadabhai's Letters

To Malayan

January 30,1887

Sir W. Hunter takes a kindly and lively interest in the Congress and intends to write to disprove the statement that Mahomedans do not join the Congress. The Times correspondent from Calcutta grossly misrepresents everything. . . . The Congress is exciting much interest here and, if it is carefully and perseveringly continued, will do a great good in creating a permanent and effective interest in India in this country.

How great an interest Congress was really exciting in England about this time, due to Dadabhai's single-handed but gigantic propaganda, is evident from the following extracts from some of the letters received by him concerning the proceedings of the Calcutta Congress over which he had presided. By wide distribution of Congress literature he had succeeded remarkably well in eliciting the sympathy and support of a large number of people in England.

To Malayan

December 15, 1887

In the present number of the Indian Spectator you have three times hit the political reformers, "who are always for equality between themselves and the English." . . . Now, my dear fellow, what an amount of unnecessary mischief you are doing. By all means fight for the merits of your cause (social reform), but why unnecessarily discredit and discourage other important movements 2 One thing you may remember, that no people who are politically debased will ever be, and ever have been, socially high.

It is the political elevation which will give that backbone and stamina, that manliness which would give strength and courage to carry social reforms. ... I do beseech you to consider the matter carefully.

To Malayan

October 19, 1888

Now that the Congress will have a hard fight, I fully trust you will give it your most unflinching and strongest support. On such an occasion we must sink all our small differences. The Indian Spectator must take a prominent and marked share in the struggle. . . . No half-hearted work will do at present. Assure Hume that you will do all you can to support the Congress.

He feels somewhat disappointed with you. He is our best friend.

Give him every assurance and help you can. We cannot do less both in gratitude to him as well as for the sake of the great cause now at stake.

To Malayan

March 23, 1890

I have been feeling much depressed by the extracts from the Indian Spectator, sent by the Calcutta correspondent of The Times, against the Congress.

To Wacha

December 23, 1887

I think it would be better to confine the Congress to the natives of India in its wide sense of including domiciled Europeans and Eurasians. It would be better not to mix up the European element with it.

To Wacha

August 29, 1890

The more you can get Europeans of influence on your side as Presidents taking active part, the less will be the cry that your object was revolutionary and anti-British. Still, it would be desirable to have interspersion of Indian Presidents.

To Wacha

January 30, 1891

I am so glad Congress passed off successfully, but a grievous loss in Bradlaugh's death. . . .

To Wacha

February 27,1891

The projected delegation of 100 members of the Congress to London will do much good. . . .

To Wacha

July 3, 1891

Sir William asks: "Why does Mr. Wacha write on such horribly heavy papers ? He will ruin himself in postage."

To Wacha

December 23, 1891

Hume is discouraged for want of funds. It will be disastrous to India if he gives us up.

To Wacha

April 8, 1892

The Congress Committee prepared a rather strong resolution and sent it to The Times with a letter. I am distressed to have had to sign that letter after what Hume had done for us.

To Wacha

April 14, 1892

We cannot but expect that our opponents will make capital out of Hume's letters.

These references to Hume's letters and the resolution repudiating his views need elucidation. On February 16, 1892, Hume issued a circular letter addressed to Congressmen, marked private and confidential, which came to be published to the consternation of the writer and his colleagues. The burden of the communication was that the existing system of administration in India was not only pauperising the people, but also inevitably preparing the way for "one of the most terrible cataclysms in the history of the world." The people were patient, mild, and humble, but so were the people of France only ten years before they rose and murdered their Sovereign and practically the bulk of the better classes. It was Hunger and Misery, those great leaders and teachers, that changed at last, apparently in a day, that crowd of sheep into an army of wolves. To Hume, therefore, it appeared as certain as night follows day that a terrible rising must evolve, sooner or later, out of this state of affairs. He, therefore, warned the people, particularly the rich and the well-to-do:

Do not fancy that Government will be able to protect you or itself. No earthly power can stem an universal agrarian rising in a country like this. My countrymen will be as men in the desert, vainly struggling for a brief space, against the simoon.

Thousands of the rioters may be killed, but to what avail, when there are millions on millions who have nothing to look forward to but death—nothing to hope for but vengeance; as for leaders—with the hour comes the man—be sure there will be no lack of leaders. This is no hypothesis—it is a certainty.

There was not the slightest intention to incite people. Hume was merely articulating loudly the beliefs of those who had given earnest attention to the subject and was asking the well-to-do classes to realise betimes the internal danger that faced them.

It was an appeal to them to provide the Congress with the means to plead their country's cause and to flood Great Britain -with pamphlets and newspapers so as to awaken the British public as to the reality of the situation in India. The hostile Press, however, made capital out of Hume's speculations. To avert further harm from Congress, the British Committee passed a resolution on April i, expressing regret that such an injudicious letter should have been circulated and their entire repudiation of the "unjustifiable conclusions" to which Hume appeared to have been "driven in face of the consideration of the deplorable condition of large portions of the Indian people." Dadabhai was one of the unhappy signatories to the letter to The Times.

The British Committee of the Congress was another baby Dadabhai had to nurse. An annual sum had been voted for its support by the 1889 Congress; but it did not suffice to meet the expenditure on the journal India, which was started as its official organ, and on the other activities of the Committee. The means of Wedderburn were limited; Dadabhai's much more; yet the two devoted servants of India bore a very large part of the financial burden. Wedderburn's share was unquestionably the larger, and he bore the burden, as his biographer, S. K. Ratcliffe, remarks, "for many more years than he should have been allowed to carry it."

Despite his own slender resources and the heavy electioneering expenses, Dadabhai usually advanced small sums from £30 to

£200, whenever needed, and guaranteed losses on political breakfasts and other functions and publications. But there were larger contributions too. At a conference held on May 18, Sir Henry Cotton, Romesh Dutt, and S. H. Swinny, who had just returned from India, reported that the general feeling in the country was that India was a heavy burden upon the Congress.

Wedderburn thereupon submitted a note on the question (June 3, 1903) in which he stated that he had been primarily responsible for the whole expenditure on both the British Committee and India. In 1902 a deficit of £137 was left. For 1903 the estimated expenditure was £2,250, whereas till the middle of the year payment had been received for only 1,750 copies of India, out of the 4,000 circulation guaranteed by the Congress:

> On various occasions I have explained (he observed) that it was quite beyond my means to remain responsible for such large sums, and both India and the Committee would have come to an end in December 1901 had not Mr. Dadabhai, in order to give the Congress one more chance, deposited with me Rs. 25,000 Government paper as a material guarantee against loss. What we required from the last Congress was to provide a material guarantee in substitution of that now provided by Mr. Dadabhai, but this they have not done. . . . The financial position is thus of the most precarious kind, depending upon Mr. Dadabhai's willingness to continue his material guarantee from day to day; the period for which he originally granted it having expired when the Congress had met and passed its decision upon our proposals.

Such being the condition of affairs, I do not think we should be justified in asking Mr. Dadabhai to continue his material guarantee for the £2,250 under present conditions. The sum involved is very large, and there is no reason why he should sacrifice himself in order to continue an arrangement which has no element of permanence, and which we find to be personally well-nigh unendurable.

What was the remedy ? Financial separation of India from the Committee and from die Congress was one of the alternatives suggested by Dutt. If no one came forward to run the paper, he was prepared to accept all financial responsibility, bearing any loss and taking any profit that might accrue. The offer was not accepted for public and private reasons. Eventually financial assistance was received from other quarters, thanks mainly to the effort made by Gokhale and the Servants of India Society in collecting subscriptions.

India was thus kept alive and was discontinued only when the London organisation was shut down in the year 1921 for causes other than financial. The British Committee was at the time out of tune with the Congress executive. Moreover, the Indian leaders considered it useless to have a London organisation. The Congress, they held, should rely for success upon its work in India. Meanwhile, Indian Liberals, representing the

Hume-Wedderburn tradition, had already established the Indian Reforms Committee, at the formation of which Lord Carmichael presided. Mr. H. E. A. Cotton (later to become Sir Evan Cotton) and Mr. Douglas Hall were Secretaries, Lord Clwyd was elected Chairman and remained Chairman until the Committee was dissolved, mainly owing to lack of support from India.

So much for Dadabhai's concern for the Congress as reflected in his letters. The following letters written by him during the period deal with general topics.

To Wacha

October 14, 1887

The opium profits happen to be large and Government finds it convenient to intercept them as so much indirect taxation. All profits of foreign commerce may be said to be paid by foreign countries. But they are India's property nevertheless, just as all profits of British exports are Britain's profits. ... As long as the present opium trade remains forced upon China, it is a curse to India.

To Wacha

October 27, 1887

If we can once get out of this ditch of the "drain," the rest will aU follow in the natural course of things. . . . Rest assured that mere reform of representation in the Legislative Councils would do little if the other reform of the stoppage of the drain is not carried out.

To Wacha

December 2, 1887

Sir Dinshaw (Petit)'s connection with the Presidency Association is a compliment to the Association. It has its advantages and also disadvantages.

To Wacha

April 27, 1888

If our educated friends would understand and perform their duty with some enthusiasm and sacrifice, either personal or pecuniary, it would be desirable to be as much independent as possible of the rich. ... If Sir D. (Dinshaw Petit) goes, then our friends (Telang, Mehta, Badruddin Tyabji, and others) will see their way to leave alone the rich gentleman and begin to stand upon their own strength. ... If our real intellectual and educated leaders determine to lead, the rich leaders will naturally fall in the background. This departure has to be managed with tact and care.

To Wacha

July 13, 1888

I very much desire that the Indian Press and Associations should first attack the report (of the Public Service Commission). My following the Indian opinion will be more effective than my leading it. The whole report is a monstrous, one-sided pleading—everything is twisted to a foregone conclusion. Simultaneous examination was the only solution of the problem and the pledges.

To Wacha

January 15, 1889

If I understand the Secretary of State's despatch to the Public Service Commission aright, the Statutory Service is lost. It is a corpse; its soul is gone. If it was anything at all and worth anything, it was part and parcel of the covenanted civil service with all its rights and privileges. By a stroke of the pen the Secretary of State has cut through the Act of Parliament. He is legally wrong and morally still worse. . . . The only condition justifying its abolition would be the introduction of simultaneous examinations.

To Wacha

February 21,1890

Sir T. Madhavrao is doing mischief by opposing the principle of election. What does he mean? Lord Cross's Bill is poor and no elective principle in it. Petitions must pour in for Bradlaugh's Bill. A great effort is necessary.

To Wacha

July 27, 1905

We are not yet quite prepared to bite, it is true, unless the vice of the rule so much intensifies as to lead people to nihilism. But our present weapon is to bark as loudly as we can and as frequently as possible. The demand that we must have self-government must be ever present and roaring all over India.. . . Another object it will accomplish is that the mass of the people will be trained in agitation and be educated in the evil and the remedy. We need to move the masses to an appreciable extent. . . . The more they try to keep us down, the louder must be our cry, and our cry must be clear and well kept directed towards self-government. Of course, all this is difficult, but it has to be done. A child is helpless, but it has a powerful weapon in crying. ... I am afraid some beginning of nihilism will not be very distant.

To Wacha

January 12, 1905

The very discontent and impatience it (the Congress) has evoked against itself as slow and non-progressive among the rising generation are among its best results or fruit. It is its own evolution and progress. .. . While there is great necessity for informing the people here, there is as much necessity that the true knowledge of their condition should widely spread among the Indian people themselves. The coordination of both is necessary to evolve the required revolution—whether it would be peaceful or violent.

The character of the revolution will depend upon the wisdom or unwisdom of the British Government and action of the British people.

To Wacha

July 12, 1906

I hope the next Congress will make a strong pronouncement as to the absolute necessity of self-government as the only remedy for all India's wrongs and needs. Congress should make a clear distinction between two aspects of its duties. The one, a complete change of policy as speedily as possible in the most suitable way, leading to self-government—this is Congress's main work—and the second, the hatefulness of the vagaries and failures of the existing administration. The most important of the two is the first.. .. The whole movement of the Congress must be managed to be backed by the masses.

To Wacha

October 19, 1905

I hope the Bengalees will keep up the Boycott Movement—and will now be awakened to the necessity of taking their Industries in their own hands and by their own capital. This Swadeshi movement must have proved very advantageous to the Bombay mills. The home consumption of India alone ought to supply an 1 Rs. 100,000 immense market for all that the mills can produce and will require many more mills. I wonder whether Lancashire being boycotted will retaliate by not providing India with machinery for new mills and repairs for old ones. Can India undertake to start factories to prepare the machinery?

To Wacha

December 20, 1888

I have been much distressed about the views some Parses are taking that we should dissociate ourselves from the Hindus and Mahomedans. Nothing could be more suicidal. We are India's, and India is our mother-country, and we can only sink or swim with, and as, Indians. If we break with the Indians, our fate will be that of the crow in peacock's feathers. The English will in no time pluck out those feathers. I shall be glad if you have taken many Parses with you.

To Wacha

January 28, 1889

I am sorry about the opposition (to the Congress) of some Parses. . . . The Kast Goftar is my greatest distress—the instrument that I had so fondly cherished (in the hope that it) would be for the progress of India and showing how thoroughly the Parses are faithful to the land of their birth and desirous to repay some of the debt to their asylum by doing whatever little good they can to promote the happiness and prosperity of its children, January 17, 1890.

To Wacha

I hear from Behramji (Malabari) that the Parsi opposition was faint and isolated. This is good news to me for the sake of the Parses themselves.

To Wacha

February 14, 1890

I am glad there were 36 Parsi delegates. . . . By numbers, merely, the Parses can have only one to 2,500 delegates.

To Wacha

February 9, 1888

My stay with Sir W. Hunter has been of some good in that he has seen more clearly than before the necessity of larger admission of natives into the Services. He will most probably write something to create greater sympathy for the Congress among the English public. ... He has left a hopeful impression upon me that he means well. I feel a little anxious about the next Congress. Sir Syed Ahmed will move Heaven and Earth to thwart the Congress.

To Wacha

September 21, 1888

Let the Mahomedans go ahead. This development of a new force will ultimately prove of use to India. It is good that they are roused to some activity.

To Wacha

July 27, 1888

I hope you will be able to do something about Digby's proposed Agency (for officially representing the Congress in England).

He is the best man we can have for the purpose and without some such worker here our labours will not fructify rapidly enough.

... He has time as well as energy and knowledge.

To Wacha

August 31, 1888

I hope that Telang, Mehta, and others will seriously take this matter into consideration. All this means money, and money must be found; for a time, self-sacrifice of a few becomes necessary.

Ever since the inauguration of the Congress, Dadabhai had been pressing on his colleagues in India the need for establishing a political agency to represent officially the Congress in England and to awaken the British public to a sense of the wrongs of India. The cost involved was a deterrent factor. Dadabhai volunteered in 1887 to act as Agent to the Congress, without remuneration, but even the funds for other expenses for propaganda could not be found. He, therefore, did what his own industry and limited resources rendered possible. Digby, however, took up the question earnestly and put forward a clear-cut scheme which led to an agency being set up, in the following year, with an office in Craven Street, Strand, under his personal direction. It served not only as the office of Congress in London but also did for unofficial India what the India Office was doing for official India, as regards presentation of Indian affairs to Parliament and the country. Its rooms became the recognised repository of information concerning India. The Gazette of India and the Gazettes of subordinate Governments, Blue Books relating to India and principal Anglo-Indian and Indian newspapers were filed there. Everything was freely rendered available to all persons interested in Indian affairs. Relations were established with the associations and organisations of both the great political parties in Britain, and a systematic and determined attempt was made to arouse British interest and to enlist British effort in Indian affairs.

The Agency freely circulated 10,000 copies of the report of the third Congress and many thousand copies of speeches and pamphlets among all the newspapers in the United Kingdom, members of both Houses of Parliament, various political organisations and leading public men. Huge posters, calling attention to Indian grievances, were printed and put up throughout the United Kingdom, and handbills were distributed at numerous meetings. Excellent propaganda was thus carried on by Digby under the general supervision of Dadabhai until the British Committee of the Congress was formed and associated with the Agency, in July 1889, with Wedderburn as Chairman.

To Wacha

August 10,1888

I shall be glad to see that the efforts made by Government to discourage Higher Education will awaken the people to the necessity of helping themselves. . . . Congress has now become a subject of debate in Parliament.

To Wacha

November 16, 1888

The opposition to the Congress is doing it incalculable good and will add much to its triumph and usefulness –The (questions of the) Services and Representation they (leaders of the Congress) must stick to most earnestly. Both are immensely important, but the latter without the former will be a burden.

To Wacha

November 25, 1888

Work steadily on your side, take good care about the important subjects—the Services and simultaneous examinations.

To Wacha

November 30, 1888

We cannot afford to let this great question (Services) flag in the least. If the Congress achieve this one reform only, it will have conferred the greatest benefit on India.

To Wacha

December 20, 1888

At the Congress all leading men must meet. I wish Telang and Pherozeshah to be there. I wonder why Kabraji and Bhownaggree should be against the Congress. . . .

To Wacha

January 11, 1889

What a relief to me that the Congress has been so successful!... I do not despair that Sir Syed Ahmed will also come over like Raja Bhawan Prasad, whatever is his present attitude. Events have so shaped themselves that neither Dufferin's attack nor Colvin's correspondence did much mischief—on the contrary some good.

To Wacha

January 18, 1889

This is a new epoch in the history of England and India—the exact bicentenary of the Revolution of 1688-89 to the very months November to February. If the Congress goes on discreetly, there is every chance of its complete success. But moderation is very much needed indeed. ... Sir Lepel Griffin has attacked me in The Times. Sir R. Watkin has attacked the Congress as having Russian gold. Opposition and misrepresentation are thus progressing. Our moderation will overcome all.

To Wacha

February 8, 1889

Mr. Digby is arranging to see all prominent statesmen and I have no doubt his utterances will add to the strength of the Congress. Mr. Gladstone having once expressed himself so strongly and emphatically, we may look forward for better results. . . . Above all, therefore, we should never forget moderation and quiet, but firm and steady work. We are still in the speaking stage. When that is carried on with discretion and temperateness, action and good result will soon follow in due natural course. We have to go through all the usual ailments of infancy and childhood. We have just got our two teeth out and may be able to digest more solid food.

To Wacha

March 1, 1889

I have got many invitations to address on India, but am obliged to decline as I have always to be ready for any call from Central Finsbury. I wish to make a tour of all the towns to address on India and make the Congress a familiar topic and an institution deserving and claiming support from all Englishmen.

To Wacha

May 31, 1889

Do not feel annoyed at Mr. Hume. . . .We must not forget what we owe him. ... If he writes to me twice as angrily or unreasonably as he has written to you, I would simply say, "My dear friend, there is some misapprehension on your part," and in a kind way give him the facts. Trust him as one with whose scoldings we must put up as we would do of an elder brother or father. We cannot repay him adequately for what he has done and is doing for us.

To Wacha

August 16, 1889

A Madrasi should be asked to preside over the Congress deliberations this year. I do not approve of the idea of there being a permanent President.

To Wacha

February 7, 1890

India is estimated to work with a deficit of about £300. We shall have here a very active year, this one, to be sure, in Indian matters.

It was, in fact, a memorable year in the history of Indian Reform. Dadabhai had been constantly reminding his friends in India that the power to introduce reforms was entirely in the hands of the British people and the British Government, and asking them to send frequent delegations to England to convince the British people that the Congress demands were just and fair.

He was equally enthusiastic in inducing British statesmen to go out in large numbers to India, to make the acquaintance of Indians, to study their character, to learn their aspirations, to show sympathy for their just demands, and to prove by their own example that the British conscience was still as sound as ever.

Following his advice, the Congress executive in India sent to England, during the summer of 1890, a delegation consisting of Surendranath Banerjee, R. N. Mudholkar, Allan Hume, and Eardley Norton, to tour the country and to appeal to the British public, on behalf of the unrepresented millions of India, to support the Congress in its demand for reform in the administration of their country. The meetings they addressed were well attended; in every case the audience manifested great interest in the reform proposals. Resolutions were enthusiastically adopted at several meetings in favour of the reforms, particularly for a system of representative government, and petitions were sent to the House of Commons praying for the acceptance of the Congress scheme for Council Reform. The most active and also the most eloquent member of the delegation was Banerjee. His powerful oratory excited unusual interest. Dadabhai, as an Indian resident in England, was also a welcome speaker. His services on this occasion were specially recognised by the British Committee in their resolution eulogising the work accomplished by the delegates. Perhaps the most interesting feature of this platform campaign was the series of lectures delivered in different parts of England by Bradlaugh on Indian questions.

To Wacha

December 10, 1890

I hope the Congress will pass off successfully. Its importance and necessity increase every day. I am very sorry, indeed, the Maratha is playing in our opponents' hands. Such are always the difficulties of every great movement. We must surmount them.

To Malabari

March 2, 1888

It will, indeed, be a good thing to bring about some reasonable understanding with the Muhammadan opponents. This split will retard our progress very much, indeed. There are difficulties enough to contend against the Anglo-Indians. . . . "God help India" is true, but we must go on doing what we can.

To Malabari

April 18, 1888

I hope Mr. Hume will be able to bring round Syed Ahmed and prevent the opposition to the Congress. The disunion among ourselves will do us very great harm. Here, interest in India is growing gradually, but this split will check it very much. What was the opposition to the Congress and what sort of a split was it that it had become a regular nightmare to Dadabhai ?

During the year 1888 there was an outbreak of anti-Congress fever of a virulent type throughout India among the Anglo-Indian and Muhammadan communities. Dadabhai was referring to that almost forgotten chapter in the early history of the Congress. If Allan Hume might be called the father of the Congress, the Marquis of Dufferin was the godfather. Not only did he, as Viceroy of India, welcome its formation,- but he also advised Hume not to restrict its scope to agitation on the social side of Indian life, as was Hume's original idea, but to widen its scope and definitely to aim at the political education of the people. He even went so far as to recognise the movement by inviting the delegates to the second Congress, held in the following year in Calcutta under the presidentship of Dadabhai, as distinguished guests to a garden party at Government House. His example was followed by Lord

Connemara, the Governor of Madras, at the time of the third Congress. There were other provincial Governors, such as Lord Reay in Bombay, and many officials, who also approved of the idea of having a sort of constitutional opposition to the Government of the day.

Soon after the Madras Congress, however, the bureaucracy fell foul of the movement. The growth of the infant Hercules had alarmed officialdom. To the Anglo-Indian community also it seemed to spell subversion of the established order of things, and some Parses and Muhammadans, too, took fright at the outcry that the Congress aimed at transferring the Government of India from the Crown to a "Native Parliament," in other words, at the substitution of Hindu for British raj.

Those who were against the Congress found a strange ally in the report of the Madras session of the Congress itself. To this report were appended two pamphlets, A Congress Catechism by Veera Raghavachariar, and A Conversation between Moulvi Fariduddin (a pleader of a district called Hakikatabad) and one Rambuksh (a headman of Kambakhtpur), showing by a parable the evils of absentee landlordism, howsoever benevolent, and urging that the way to escape the tyranny of a despotic Government is to seek a representative one such as that for which the Congress was contending. Thousands of copies of both pamphlets in various vernaculars were circulated freely. The hostile organs read in them nothing but revolt and quoted passages from them to show that the Congress was fast becoming an engine for sedition.

Pamphleteering was not, however, the sole sin of the Congress. Special efforts were made by its leaders to induce Muhammadans to join. The appeal to his co-religionists made by Badruddin Tyabji, as President of the Madras Congress, was followed by active propaganda in Urdu all over the country. A Muhammadan, named Bhimji, toured the provinces enlisting Muslim support.

This was a real danger in the eyes of the bureaucracy, more unnerving than all the patriotic froth of Congress speakers and writers. How could Government sit with folded hands when they saw good Muslims walking lightly into the Congress trap? Official and non-official influences were, therefore, at work to make the

Muhammadan subjects of the Crown see through the "seditious" movement and to inflame the whole community against the attempt to introduce a Hindu raj fatal to its interests.

The worst "crime" of the Congress, however, was the agitation carried on in England by Dadabhai, in the name of the Congress, on behalf of the people of India. He had succeeded in enlisting the sympathy and support of a man like William Hunter in the Congress cause. He had openly declared that the political forces represented by the Congress were so great that the British Government, if it sought to thwart them, would break itself in the attempt. Dadabhai's daily distribution of Congress literature and his daily appeal to the strong sentiments and cherished principles of justice inherent in the English race considerably influenced English opinion in favour of the national movement.

For Anglo-India that was the most disastrous phase of the agitation. Already, no less an authority than Gladstone had declared that the capital agent in finally determining the question whether the British power in India was or was not to continue, would be the will of the 240 millions of people who inhabited the country. "It would not do for us," he warned his countrymen, "to treat with contempt, or even with indifference, the rising aspirations of this great people."

There was a clamour in Anglo-Indian circles that the Congress should be checked from speaking on behalf of India and misleading the British people. Writers like Theodore Beck went so far as to suggest that the time had arrived to use once more the iron hand in the velvet glove, and to put down this kind of agitation. The officials, however, resorted to another device.

In their opinion the best way to kill the Congress was to have countrywide demonstrations against it. There were the numerous Islamia Anjumans ready to take the lead. Besides, several anti-Congress organisations had already been set on foot specifically for the purpose. There was the United Indian Patriotic Association, of which Sir Syed Ahmed was the Secretary; there was also the British Indian Association of Oudh, ready to give the Congress a bad name and hang it. They all combined and organised public meetings and hostile demonstrations in different parts of India, denouncing the Congress and challenging its right to speak on behalf of the people of the country. They also issued tracts and pamphlets, subsidised journals, and took special care to send anti-Congress literature to England for the information of Members of Parliament, English journals, and the people of the United Kingdom. With funds lavishly placed in its hands, the so-called Patriotic Association was the most active in carrying on such agitation. It issued several pamphlets, one of which was entitled "Showing the Seditious Character of the Indian National Congress and the opinions held by eminent Natives of India who are opposed to the Movement." Theodore Beck was the editor. Among the avowed contributors were some "Rajahs," intellectually cyphers, unable to write a single page of good English. There were, no doubt, able men too, such as Syed Ahmed and Syed Hosain Belgrami, but they were both tainted by a very powerful communal bias. The most important names on the list of opponents of the Congress were those of the Nizam of Hyderabad and Nawab Sir Salar Jung.

Such were the men who were behind the opposition which made Dadabhai very apprehensive about the future of the Congress. The clouds, however, soon dispersed. Despite the furious cannonade of inimical criticism the Congress forged ahead, and the so-called patriotic associations found an early grave.

To Malabari

October 5, 1888.

I am not much afraid of Sir Syed Ahmed's opposition. No doubt, political Agents will be privately putting pressure upon the Chiefs to help them. But the cause is bad and must sooner or later collapse, unless our own friends turn traitors and a division among ourselves ruin the Congress. . . . Upon the whole, the feeling here is in favour of it. ... We shall now have a far more heavy struggle about the Services than we have had hitherto.

To Malabari

May 20, 1889

It would be desirable at the next Congress ... to thank Mr. Smith and his supporters for their kind interest in India.

Every little or great success achieved here in Parliament must be well acknowledged. A good echo from India of what is done here will have a good effect in inciting further action.

To Malabari

December 20, 1889

I read in the Indian Spectator that there was an idea of making the Congress quinquennial, and I wrote my views against it in Dinsha's letter. Soon after, I learnt from Mr. Digby that Mr. Hume had contradicted this rumour and I was glad.

To Malabari

March 21, 1890

Sir W. Wedderburn gave an address last night on India at Toynbee Hall under the auspices of the University Settlement at die East End of London. It was very well and sympathetically received. One Mr. Thomson presented the opposition view of Sir Syed Ahmed's party, and I replied to him.

To Malabari

April 26,1889

I am sorry that the Native members of the Viceroy's Council do not understand the subject of the economic condition of India and their duty towards the poor masses of India. I am not surprised that they should vote for a salt duty and against income-tax.

On the Public Service Commission report, Mr. Digby and myself are now preparing a more complete letter to Lord Cross.

To Hume

October 14, 1891

The Congress meetings should not be stopped. Such an action will put back India's progress a generation, or at least for years. . . . You have already achieved a great deal in rousing up the people. Don't give them up now.

To Hume

January 5, 1888

It is desirable that Native States should be allowed to take an interest in, and help, the Congress and even, if they choose, to find delegates. The Native States have their own wants and grievances, and a body like the Congress and other public associations can alone take up political questions. ... A solidarity of this kind between all the people of India is a thing to be desired.

The interests of the Native States are intimately connected with those of the subjects of British India. Any improvement in Native States is a gain to all India, and the very success of Native States will by comparison shame and expose the failures in the British system. We must carry the Native Princes completely with us. It will add much to our strength. The very fact that Native States and Princes take an interest in the Congress will in itself give weight and consideration to the Congress in the opinion of the people here.

To M. J. B. Namjoshi

December 10, 1891

I need not tell you with what grief I read your opposition to the Congress. From you, who have been one of its supporters and workers from its very birth! What is the matter? Can we afford to be so divided against ourselves and can India ever progress under such circumstances ? Have we not difficulties and obstacles enough that we create more of our own? Poor India!

To J. H. Keene

September 3,1887

If Englishmen carry on the discussion in a fair spirit, truth will at last come out, and if I am found wrong I shall be more happy.

To J. H. Keene

September 16, 1887

It is not the incidence of taxation that is India's evil. It would still be of no consequence if as much Land Revenue as Akhar's were taken. The evil is in the drain of a portion of the revenue out of the country.

To Sir George Birdwood

November 23, 1887

He (Sir William Hunter) is a good friend of the Natives at heart, and I beseech both you and him to achieve our result, which is the chief aim of my life and the accomplishment of which will be the greatest blessing. . . I mean simultaneous examinations both in India and England for all departments of civil administration.

To the Secretary: Islington Conservative Association

January 1, 1888

There is no objection on my part to address a Conservative Association on Indian subjects. For India we need the help of both parties and we are indebted to both.

To A. K. Cornell

July 13, 1887

The plan of competition properly arranged so as to test the whole man—physically and mentally—would be the best and perhaps the only plan that can be adopted to give "a fair field and no favour."

I should not have cared one jot, had all the Anglo-Indian members of the Public Service Commission gone against us. It is the defection of the Native members that has done the most harm. . . . The progress is delayed—come it must, but we have to wait longer, though it was quite within grasp now.

To Robert Grierson

March 2, 1890

Taking the instance of Madras, where Government have a sort of monopoly, the cost of production (of salt) is about 5¼ d. per maund, equal to 82 lbs., which means about a quarter of a farthing per lb. Government sells this at nearly 12 times or 1,200 per cent of the cost or 5/- per maund, and thus draws from an absolute necessary of life from a very poor people a revenue of £6,700,000 per annum.

To Martin Wood

April 4, 1897

The fact is that had Englishmen any such or even a tenth of our grievances, they would not only have spoken hundred times harder words but. . . would have gone to hard deeds.

To Wedderburn

March 24, 1905.

You need not worry yourself about there being any idea among the young Indians of being able to use force. We have discussions often in the London Indian Society and it is well understood and admitted that use offeree is out of the question.

To Romesh Dutt

July 5, 1903

Lord George Hamilton has made a dead set to get the Indians out of the higher services. . . . Things are growing critical. I have every fear that the attempt which Lord Lytton's Government openly made to stop Indians from competing for the Civil Service here, and which Lord Cranbrook nipped in the bud under Sir Erskine Perry's inspiration, will be sooner or later carried out, if the present Conservative Government continue for any length of time. The time is come when an agitation must be begun for self-government under British paramountcy. The work will be slow, but every effort needs to be concentrated on this purpose. At my age it will not be my lot to take any long part in this great battle—and I am, therefore, the more anxious to see that younger hands and hearts set themselves to work.

To Hyndman

October i, 1904

If you write anything to attack and disparage the Congress, you will weaken and discourage the only body through whom India has to work out its redemption. This will be an injury to India which you do not want to do. I hope, therefore, you will not do anything to weaken the Congress. It has already much to contend against conflicting influences in India itself....

Whatever may be your opinion about the deficiencies of the Indian character, your course is to guide and help them to supply such deficiency. In our work, one factor is very necessary—Englishmen themselves to denounce the evils of the present system. One Englishman like you denouncing the system will produce more influence in the minds of the British public....

We have to convince and convert the British public and every help is progress towards the object.

To Thomas Bell

September 30, 1897

My idea is that all British India should be divided up into a number of such States administered by Natives generally. Then the people of British India will prosper like the people of the well-administered Native States. This is not merely my idea, but Lord Salisbury himself has said this as far back as 1867, when Mysore was restored.

To H. H. Ranjitsinhji

September 7, 1906

You are, I think, aware that it has always been my earnest desire to see Indian Princes ruling with predominant success for the welfare of their subjects. This is of great importance to the uprising of all India. The instances of successful administration of Indian Princes strengthen the promotion of reforms in India by showing . . . [illegible].

To Joseph Booth

July 5, 1905

You put in a condition for the right of a people to control their own affairs as when fairly able to do so. This opens a door for an excuse for the strong to interfere with the weak. Why should any people have any right to subject another people?

Every people have their right to enjoy their own and to control their own affairs in the way they best can. The duty of the more civilized is not to subject and plunder the less civilized, but to guide, help, and uplift them without depriving them of their independence.

To George Freeman

December 18, 1897

There is, indeed, a remarkable coincidence between the treatment of India and Canada. The same stupid mistakes and course. But in the case of India, persistence in this course of greed and injustice—the result will be an inconceivable disaster. . . . There is no remedy for all our evils till the fundamental evil of greed is remedied—either by a peaceful change of system or forced by a revolution—and a successful revolution in India means the annihilation of British India. Nature will have its revenge, or, as Salisbury says, "Injustice will bring the mightiest to ruin." The pity is that till any retribution comes India must continue in ever-increasing suffering.

To J. E. Ellain

July 9, 1898

I may say this only here that when you doubt "whether India would be better off under the government of any other European Power," you do not mean that as a justification of England's evils in India. Then, also, I do not know in what way or sense you use the words "better off." In its economic condition I do not see how India can be worse off. There are some features in connection with Russia, which she will make good use of in trying to make the people of India think that some of the bad features of English rule will not exist in Russian rule. Whether Russia or other Power must of necessity occupy India, when England is made to leave, and whether Russia by becoming worse than England will be able to maintain its power in India, are all questions which time alone will solve.

To C. J. O'Donnell

December 6,1901

The fight India has to carry on is not against one party but against both parties. The Liberal Government is as bad as the Conservative. It was the Liberal Government with which I had to fight, and had it not been for the unwillingness of several Irish members and the Radicals to defeat the Government, I would have defeated the Government with more votes than 8 with which I defeated them on one of my motions.

To Sir George Birdwood

December 30,1904

You think that, had we been closer in earlier days, you might have made me a Conservative. Perhaps it might have been the other way, and I might have made you a Radical!

To The Right Reverend Henry Codman Potter, Bishop of New York

May 14, 1900

In a telegram from New York you are reported to have said, at a meeting held at the Chamber of Commerce, that "the famine was in one sense due to good government. Great Britain had stopped tribal warfare and slaughter and, in consequence, population increased." This, Sir, is the usual Anglo-Indian romance. The reality is quite different—namely, that the fundamental cause of "the extreme poverty" of Indians, with its natural consequences of famines, plagues, and every kind of misery, is the destructive system of government of a bleeding foreign domination.

To Bishop of New York

June 10, 1900

Both you and the Madrasi gentleman do not seem to have studied and considered the other side. I must say a few words of facts with reference to your statement that "we should pay the bill." We should pay for having been forced to pay every farthing (excepting a very few part payments for very shame) for all the wars and other circumstances from the very beginning of the English connection, for building up and maintaining the British Indian Empire entirely at our own cost and mainly with our blood . . . with the reward of being reduced to helotry and beggary! We should pay for bleeding us and carrying away clean out of the country hundreds of millions and continue to drain incessantly and unceasingly, or we should pay for what the Viceroys and Famine Commissioners sanction.... We should pay for impoverishing us to an detent to which probably no nation has impoverished another! We should pay for all the consequences of such "other improvements" as famines, plagues. . . and a chronic state of starvation . . . ! We should pay for the security of our property which, in the most ingenious, scientific and unseen way, is taken away from us by the protectors! We should pay for the security of our lives, which are not left worth living, by providing us with starvation, famines, pestilence, etc.! We should pay for the full liberty we enjoy to starve and perish...! We should pay for official Europeans bleeding us, and non-official Europeans exploiting our land and labour and natural resources...! In short, we should pay for a destructive and dishonourable system of government violating Acts of Parliament and the most solemn pledges that ever a people gave to another.

To Major J. B. Keith

December 5,1901

You want to know "the approximate cost of Western civilization to India, say for about fifty years." Before I deal with this, we have to remember that till the year 1849, when Punjab was annexed, all the wars for the formation of the Indian Empire were paid for by the Indians, not to say anything about their bloodshed for the same. The maintenance of the Empire was also at the cost of Indians; and besides to these was to be added all the wealth that had been remitted by the East India Company publicly, and by all Europeans privately, to this country; and also what was consumed by all Europeans in India itself. All this, with interest, will mean thousands of millions and form no small part of the cost of Western civilization.

Now, coming to the cost, say, from 1850, this cost is best ascertained by the net exports, that is to say, the produce and wealth that goes clean out of the country without any material or commercial returns, and of these net exports we have official records. The cost can be divided into two parts:

1. All that is consumed by Europeans in. India to die deprivation of the Indians. Of this part, I do not know of any record as a very reliable estimate. This is sometimes estimated at £10,000,000 annually, or 10 crores of rupees annually.

2. All that produce or wealth of India that goes clean out of the country in various shapes as "net exports." I first give you the exports officially recorded for the fifty years, omitting a period of six years, the unsettled period of the Indian Mutiny, comes to about Rs. 664 crores. To this has to be added the profits of the total exports of merchandise, which is only 10 per cent and actually amounts to 310 crores of rupees. To this has to be added freight and insurance monies, all shipping being British. Generally 6 per cent.

To all the above items is to be added the debt held in the United Kingdom which, in 1900, is about 186 crores of rupees, besides the rupee paper held in England. In India, the debt is 132 crores, of which a portion is held by Europeans.

Lastly, there is the item of interest lost to India on this accumulated drain. If the ordinary Indian commercial compound interest of 9 per cent, or even 5 per cent, be added, the total cost of Western civilization will be very enormous indeed. The cost of "Western civilization" is summed up in the destruction of millions by famine, pestilence, etc. and the subsistence of crores of millions 011 insufficient food.

To Sir K. Seshadri Iyer, Dewan of Mysore

December 20, 1900

For some time past, I have been reading the Mysore Standard with some distress of mind. ... I did not, however, think of troubling you. But what has now determined me to write this letter to you is an article in the Hindu, in which I read with much regret that the Mysore State was departing from the very essence of the only true policy of a Native State, namely, that a Native State must be administrated from top to bottom by Natives themselves. Even the British Government itself had recognised this principle and, while the late Maharaja was a minor, the Government of India took special steps to reduce gradually the foreign element, so that when the Maharaja came to the Gadi, he should have as nearly as possible a Native Administration.. ..

The employment of Europeans in Mysore would be a triple curse: (1) Mysore will be subject to an economic "bleeding" very much like British India. (2) It will prove that Indians are incapable of governing and could not do without Europeans, the severest blow that can be inflicted on the Indians. (3) The Anglo-Indians, who have so persistently opposed the Restoration for more than 30 years, will be only too glad to find the excuse that direct British administration would be the best for Mysore and Native States generally.

With regard to the Gold Mines, or the mineral resources of Mysore, I hope the Mysore State itself, or the Mysore people, would work them and keep for themselves the wealth that Nature has given to them, instead of allowing a foreign people to take it away, leaving only a small royalty to the State and only labourer's wages to the people. ... I go even so far that Mysore should strain every nerve to prepare her own subjects to carry on the administration.

To J. N. Tata

September 16,1902

Pray do not be annoyed for troubling you again. Is it not possible for you to raise the million you want from the Indian Princes? To me it is a matter of grief that you should become the instrument of enabling foreigners to carry away the natural wealth of India with the only benefit of some thousands of Indians earning a livelihood. To my mind, it is a great injury to India.

I would rather that this wealth remained buried than that it should be carried away by other people. ... I hope you will take it in the spirit in which I am writing it.

Tata explained that he would be only too willing to follow Dadabhai's advice if Dadabhai and other Indian friends could help him in raising the required capital in British India and the Indian States at about the same rate of interest which he would have to pay in England. Dadabhai worked whole-heartedly in that direction.

I am so glad (wrote Tata on February 20, 1903) that once more I have your support in my Iron and Steel project and I thank you cordially for your kind letter. I am disposed to take the sanguine view of the Kaiser-i-Hind that it may not be impossible to find the whole capital in India—particularly as a Parsi gentleman has, unsolicited, asked me to put him down for a lakh. But I will not conceal from you my belief that in order to accomplish what both you and I hold desirable—namely, starting Iron Works with as far as possible Indian capital wholly—I shall need all the powerful support that men in your position and with recognised service to our country can extend. Things are still in an experimental stage; my experts are working, and I am determined not to invite subscriptions of capital, until by a trial-plant, costing something like 4 or 5 lakhs, I have felt sure of success.

It was not given to the greatest Indian industrialist of the day to see the results of his splendid scheme to raise India to the status of one of the greatest industrial countries of the world. He died before the scheme had passed through the experimental stage.

When, however, it materialised, and when capital was invited from the public (August 1907), the Tata offices in Bombay were besieged from early morning till late at night by crowds of investors. At the end of three weeks every rupee of the entire capital required at the time was contributed by Indian investors.

To F. M. Dadina

October 25, 1901

This currency legislation is, in my opinion, a pure fraud and has imposed a heavy taxation upon die people. The treasury here had understood it so, and have expressed their views clearly in their correspondence with the Secretary of State.

To Bal Gangadhar Tilak

April 16, 1897

I have read with much grief that some unfortunate collision has taken place between the Government and the Sarvajanik Sabha. It is a misfortune; we in our political condition cannot afford that an institution, built up by the efforts of the Puna people for more than a generation, should be swept away in a breath. ... I hope you will do all you can to save the Sabha from the blow that has come down upon it. It is not an impossibility—a continuance of that spirit of self-sacrifice with which you and your colleagues began their career of usefulness will enable you to overcome any difficulty.

To Surendranath Banerjee

August 23,1900

I wish to write to you, and I am writing the same to Mr. Motilal Ghose, that I am grieved to note the differences that are going on between the Patrika and the Bengali. We cannot afford such quarrelling among ourselves.

To A. J. Balfour

March 7, 1905.

I thank you for your very courteous letter of the 28th ultimo regarding the correspondence between the Viceroy of India and Sir Henry Cotton, as President of the Indian National Congress.

In it you say that Lord Curzon declined to receive the President of the Congress "for the purpose of discussing the resolutions." But with much respect I would point out that this is a misapprehension; as Lord Curzon was not asked to engage in any discussion. I enclose a printed copy of the Viceroy's reply, from which it will be seen that Lord Curzon understood that the object of Sir Henry Cotton's proposed visit was simply "to present to his Excellency personally a copy of the resolutions passed at the recent session of the Congress at Bombay." Lord Curzon refused to receive the visit for the purpose thus stated; and it is with reference to this refusal that the London Indian Society submitted their protest. It has been the ancient and invariable custom of Indian rulers personally to receive all properly worded petitions for the redress of grievances, however humble the petitioners may be.

To the Editor, Pearsons Magazine

Christmas Day, 1902

In my wretched country there is no peace and goodwill towards men, but an everlasting struggle. Millions perish by famine and pestilence and scores of millions "live on scanty subsistence" in good season or bad. Not a ray of hope anywhere. A new century and a new sovereign, but India as wretched as ever. No sign of faithful fulfilment of the most solemn pledges. The United States have already begun the elevation, the emancipation and self-government of their new conquered. Britain continues to hold India in bondage for nearly a hundred and fifty years!

To The Editor of the Daily News

April 3, 1905

In the Daily News of sist ultimo a correspondent, "A Reader," asks for information about the yearly drain of ^30,000,000 from India. Will you kindly allow me to give it? I have given this explanation two or three times before, but I now bring the figures up to date.

Any drain from, or addition to, the wealth of a country in connection with other countries takes place through the channel of commerce. I give an approximate calculation. In order to have a fair average, I take figures for ten years; but I leave out the years 1899-1900 and 1900-1901, as these two years were those of famine in India. I take United Kingdom for the same ten years, viz. 1892 to 1899 and 1902 and 1903. (The latest figures available are till 1903. Parl. Ret. Cd. 2192-1904.) The total imports of the United Kingdom for these ten years (merchandise and treasure) are £4,988,919,3 59. The total exports for the same period (merchandise and treasure) are £3,421,478,153. This shows an excess of imports over exports, or, in other words, the profits on the exports as £1,567,441,206; that is to say, the United Kingdom received back the whole amount of its exports (£3,421,478,153), and also over and above that £1,567,441,206 more as an addition to its wealth by all its international transactions with foreign countries during the ten years. Thus the United Kingdom made a profit of 45.8 per cent over its exports.

I would make, however, the following allowance: The total profit of £1,567,441,206 includes, taking roughly £300,000,000 in ten years of the political drain of India. Deducting this £300,000,000 from the above profit leaves the net profit of its transactions with other countries as £1,267,441,206 independently of the drain from India. This deduction reduces the percentage of the profit of the United Kingdom from 45.8 to 37 per cent on its own exports.

I now take India. (Parl. Ret. Cd. 2299-1904.) The total exports (including Native States) of merchandise and treasure during the ten years are Rs. 1,180,665,000. To this must be added freight and insurance on exports to the United Kingdom, because they are paid in the United Kingdom, and not included in the invoices and official returns. This was the case when I was in business in the City. I do not know how the case is for exports to other countries, so I do not add this item. I take roughly for freight and insurance on exports to the United Kingdom from India for the ten years at 5 per cent. The amount of exports is Rs. 364,948,240, and 5 per cent on it will be Rs. 18,247,412. This addition will make the total of exports from India to be Rs. 1,180,665,000, plus Rs. 18,247,412 = Rs. 1,198,912,412.

The next item to be considered is the profit on the total exports. Though the profits of the United Kingdom, as stated above, are 37 per cent, I take for India a profit of only 20 per cent. The total, therefore, of exports and profit will be for the ten years Rs. 1,198,912,412, plus profit Rs. 239,782,482 = Rs, 1,438,694,894. This, then, is the amount equal to which India ought to have imported under normal circumstances like those of the United Kingdom. But India has imported only an amount of Rs. 923,205,000, leaving a drain or deprivation of Rs. 515,489,894 during the ten years.

Taking the present exchange of Rs. 15 to £i, this drain in ten years amounts to £343,659,920, or, say, average of £34,000,000 every year.

If the exports and imports of the Native States are excluded, the drain from British India will be larger than £34,000,000 a year. Besides this, there is the burden of foreign debt inflicted on India without India's voice. . . .

Here, then, is a strange and sad contrast. The United Kingdom and India are governed by the same Government, with the result of bringing to the United Kingdom an addition to its wealth, as profits of its exports, in ten years, of £1,267,441,206, and, on the other hand, causing to India in the same ten years a deprivation and loss of £343,659,920.

Not only this. The loss to India must be measured by how much more India would have benefited, had this enormous drain of the ten years and all drain of previous years been at India's own disposal and fructified in the Indians' pockets. It must be further remembered that what Europeans consume in India itself, to the deprivation of the Indians, is not included in this drain.

To the Manchester Guardian

March 1, 1906

Now the debate in the House of Commons last week has as fully as possible asserted that the army in India was for defending and maintaining British power, British prestige in the East, and British possession of India. . . . And yet it is extraordinary that not one of the speakers, in his conscience and sense of justice (which, I hope, have not vanished from the English heart), asked himself and the House the simple question why wretched India should be despotically and mercilessly compelled to pay for an army which is required entirely for Britain's own Imperial purposes, or at least why Britain should not pay a large portion of it. May I ask honourable M.Ps this question!

The most memorable correspondence of the period, however, was that initiated by Dadabhai with Lord George Hamilton in the year 1900. The miserable condition of India, her economic difficulties, and the frustration of hopes engendered by intercourse with the West and fostered by the promises of Government, impelled him to appeal for justice to Lord George, who was then Secretary of State for India. Together with his letter of October 12, 1900, he sent a cutting from the Kaiser-I-Hind, of September 16, in illustration of the strong feeling in India against the violation of promises of equality as regards admission to the service of the State.

New generations have received the blessings of education (he said) and they now realise the present un-British violation of all pledges, however masked it is by misleading, plausible statements. You will see that there is a panic that die authorities were tending towards stopping even in England the competition of Indians for the Civil Service and that the subtle encroachments on the various other services are but a prelude to that disaster.

He was writing that letter not in anger but in agony, and he appealed to Lord George Hamilton to reconsider "the unfortunate retrograde steps which had been lately taken, as well as the injustice and injuries of the past." In the letter that followed (November 28), he recalled the royal proclamations ignored by the executive and added that "notwithstanding the sword of the new foolish and suicidal sedition law that was hanging over their heads,

Indian newspapers were freely giving vent to their feelings of bitterness and despair." Then he humbly gave a warning: "The rising and coming generations would not stand, as patiently as the passing generations, the accumulating injustices with their dire consequences of famines, plague, etc. and material and moral degradation and deterioration."

Lord George's reply to the first letter (November 27) had been in Dadabhai's hands before the second letter reached him.

The gist of it was that so long as India was governed by the British Crown it was indispensable that a minimum proportion of the Indian Civil Services should be European. That principle, he maintained, was in no way opposed to the admission of Indians, as they became qualified, and as the conditions of the country permitted, to a very large number of offices in the administration.

Such an interpretation of the royal proclamations entailed a fuller recital by Dadabhai of all the "solemn pledges" given up to Queen Victoria's Jubilee year (1887). When those pledges were given, urged Dadabhai, all considerations, even that of losing India, had been thoroughly gone into by Conservative Secretaries of State and Conservative Governments. It was of the first and highest importance that that issue should be fairly faced.

Lord George, in turn, was brutally frank in his reply

(December 6):

You advance various contentions, all of which seem to me to be based upon a curious misinterpretation of language or disregard of acknowledged and existing conditions. You announce yourself as a sincere supporter of British rule; you vehemently denounce the conditions and consequences which are inseparable from the maintenance of that rule.

As regards the declaration of policy, his Lordship said they were announcements of the policy that in the government of British India the officials who should take part in its administration should not be exclusively European but an admixture of the inhabitants of Great Britain and the Natives of India.

You allude in passing (he added) to "the foolish and suicidal Sedition Law." Again you seem to be under a hallucination. The law of sedition in India is the same as the law of sedition in this country; and milder in its definition and application than those of any of the great Governments of Europe. You seem to think that a free press means that pressmen are free from the restraint of the ordinary law of the land and at liberty, through their newspapers, to advocate assassination, outrage and racial disturbance and riot. For these offenders alone have prosecutions been instituted. You speak of the increasing impoverishment of India and of the annual drain upon her as steadily and continuously exhausting her resources. Again, I assert, you are under a delusion. Except that during the last five years the rainfalls have thrice failed, and created droughts of immense dimensions, there is not a fact to be found in support of these allegations.

I do not for a moment doubt your wish to serve India, but to effectively perform any work of that kind, facts must be faced and hallucinations dismissed.

This reply, so far as he was concerned, was to be the end of the correspondence. But Dadabhai would not let him have the last word. He said, in another letter, he would pass over subordinate matters and confine himself to the main point of difference between the two.

You say to me: "You announce yourself as a sincere supporter of British rule; you vehemently denounce the conditions and consequences which are inseparable for the maintenance of that rule".

This shows you have not sufficiently known my views. I repeat that I am a sincere supporter of British rule, i.e. of true British rule founded upon honourable, "faithful and conscientious fulfilment" of "solemn pledges." I denounce the present system, which is not British rule but an un-British, despotic and destructive system which, in its declaration of policy, is based upon solemn pledges but which, in its actual practice, is conducted upon the violation of those pledges. The conditions which you lay down as necessary for the maintenance of British rule in India are exactly the conditions which, in their consequences, will destroy, instead of maintaining, British rule in India.

There was no reply to this communication. But Dadabhai saw in the death of Queen Victoria an occasion to revert, in a further letter to Lord George (February 26, 1901), to the great and good Queen's wishes and prayers for India.

Though the beloved Empress has passed away she has left her will—her greatest, her most noble and her most gracious legacy to the Indian people—worthy of herself and of the great British nation over whom she reigned. . . . Her son and our new Emperor thrice declared—before his very first Council, before the world, by his Proclamation issued by yourself, and before Parliament in his very first gracious speech—that he will walk in his good mother's steps. Who now is to be the executor of that gracious and glorious will? She prayed: "And may the God of all power grant to us and to those in authority under us, strength to carry out these our wishes for the good of our people." And who are those who are "in authority tinder us" ? You are the head of those who are under such authority. . . . Will you rise to the height of this great and glorious responsibility and opportunity?

After referring to the two courses open to Lord George, either to fulfil the great and solemn pledges or to persist in their violation and their probable consequences, Dadabhai appealed to his sense of duty, justice, honour and righteousness and concluded with the assurance that his whole desire was that Britain and India might remain together on British lines.

This communication was formally acknowledged, but as regards the question of the obligations of the British Government to India, it was stated that the Secretary of State had nothing to add to what was contained in his Lordship's letter of December 6.

There was, however, yet something to follow for the delectation of Lord George Hamilton. Under the caption, "Facts and Hallucinations," the following paragraph appeared in India of June 7, 1901:

The Hallucination: That the famine in India is the Famine of Food. The Fact: That the famine is a Famine of Money.

"The supply of food," said Lord George Hamilton in the House of Commons, July 26, 1900, "is almost the least of the difficulties with which the Indian Government have to contend.

There is always a sufficiency of food in the great continent of India even in years of drought."

In the same journal, and under the same heading, there was another paragraph, on June 21, maintaining that the belief that the charge of the India Office was borne by the tax-payers of the United Kingdom was a hallucination, whereas the fact was that it was borne entirely by India.

Hopes blighted by the bureaucracy were, however, once more revived by the message given by King Edward VII, which formed the theme of another letter sent by Dadabhai to the Tribune and the Morning Leader (February 22, 1906):

Reading yesterday's proceedings in Parliament (said he) I may venture to say that there is and there has been for a long, long time, a subject of far more serious importance, namely, that under British rule in India millions and millions of human beings are perishing by famine and plague. Would British instincts and sense of duty, conscience and humanity ever lead to deal with the true remedy...? By a divine and blessed inspiration the King himself unconsciously speaks the true and only remedy.

This refers to the hope expressed by King Edward VII that in the South African Colonies as elsewhere throughout his dominions the grant of free institutions would be followed by an increase of prosperity.

6

Golden Words of Dada Bhai

- I am a Liberal in politics, prepared to support the great measures of Social Reform, including a change in the Land Laws affecting dwellers alike in towns and country.
- At one time Home Rule was synonymous with rebellion, but the Irish leaders had managed their affairs in such a way that it was now synonymous with patriotism. The time had come when the greatest statesman of the age held out the hand of fellowship to them, gave them a message of peace, and they thankfully accepted the offer made to them and said now will begin the regeneration of the country.
- When law refuses its duty, when Government denies the right of the people . . . those people are driven back from law and from the ways of civilization to that which is termed the law of nature, and if not the strongest, the law of the vindictive.
- When any question of reform arises, the only remedy that suggests itself to British officials' minds is, "Apply more European leeches, apply more European leeches." Now the Police Commission Report is out, and other Commissions, resolutions, and Reports for "Reforms"

(Heaven save us from those "Reforms") have been coming out, with the same eternal cry, "More European leeches, more European leeches," and add to that hideous drain of £30,000,000 or more, as if India had no people of her own, and, if she had, as if they existed only to be "bled" and "plundered," with all the ghastly consequences of famine and plague—deaths of millions and starvation of scores of millions! When will this curse end?

- What about the people of India? Where do they come in? They had not the slightest voice whatever in the matter; the main object of the European military expenditure in India is to secure from Russian attack British power, British prestige and British exaction of forty to fifty millions a year for British interests.
- This high-handed and narrow-minded project of rousing the estrangement and hatred of the vast Bengal population, by the partition of Bengal, cannot but be productive of mischief to the British rule.

7

Great Life at a Glance

1825, September 4: Dadabhai Naoroji was born in a poor Parsi priest family.

1829: He lost his father, Naoroji Dordi, when he was four years old.

1840: At age 15, he received Clare's scholarship and was considered a scholar. Professor Orlebar called him "Promise of India".

1845: At age 20, he became the first Indian professor (of Mathematics & Philosophy) at Elphinstone Institute.

1849, August 4: He laid the foundation of female education in Bombay.

1851, August 3: At age 26, he started a society Rahnumae Mazdayasnane Sabha in cooperation with educationist Naoroji Furdunji, which still exists and has regular meetings.

1855, June 27: He sailed to London with K.R.Cama and M. H. Cama to join the first Indian business started in England by the Cama family.

1856: He left the Cama family business and became a Professor of Gujarati, in the University college, London, and worked there for 10 years.

1859: He started his campaign of agitation about injustice in the system of recruiting for the Indian Civil Service.

1861: He founded the London Zoroastrian Association and remained its president until 1907.

1886; He was active in the newly founded "East India Association" to promote the welfare and interest of Indians.

1869, July: A public meeting was called by Maharaja Bhagwat Singhji of Gondal and the Sheriff of Bombay, at the Framji Cowasji Institute, to honour Dadabhai and a purse of Rs. 25,000 was presented, most of which he donated to the East India Association Fund.

1875, January 11: After introducing many reforms as Diwan of Baroda, he resigned and left Baroda.

1875, July 26: At age 50, he was elected to the Bombay Municipal Corporation.

1876, August: He resigned from the Corporation and went to England for business.

1883: He was re-elected to the Bombay Municipal Council and worked there until 1886. As an appreciation for his public services a marble statue of Dadabhai adorns the Corporation Hall.

1885: He was the moving spirit and Founder of the Indian National Congress, which had its first meeting in 1885, at the Gokuldas Tejpal Pathshala, at Gowalia Tank.

1886: He went back to England in 1886, where he contested in the election for the British Parliament but was unsuccessful.

1886: At the end of 1886, he was called to attend the second session of the Indian National Congress in Calcutta, where he was elected President.

1906: In 1906, at the age of 80, Dadabhai was invited for a third time to be president of the Indian National Congress in Calcutta. In October, he returned to India, where at his house in Versova, Dr. Maneckbai, his daughter and granddaughter Dr. Mehrbanoo looked after his health.

1916: At age 91, Bombay University bestowed the honorary degree of L.L.D. on him.

1917, June 30: Dadabhai Naoroji passed away and his body was consigned to the Tower of Silence.

Bibliography

Amales Tripathi, and De, Barun: *Freedom Struggle,* National Book Trust, New Delhi, 1982.

Bhagwan, V.: *Indian Freedom Movement and Constitutional Acts,* Atma Ram, 1999.

Bhattacharya, B. K.: *India's Freedom Movement: Legacy of Bipin Chandra Pal,* Deep and Deep, New Delhi, 2007.

C. L. Parekh: *Naoroji, Dadabhai, Essays Speeches and Writings,* Bombay, 1887.

Chakravarty, Shachi: *Quit India Movement: A Study,* New Century Publication, 2002.

Chandra, Bipan: *India's Struggle For Independence,* Penguin Books India (P) Ltd., New Delhi, 1989.

Chandra, Shailesh: *90 Years of India's Struggle for Independence: 1857-1947,* Alfa Pub, 2008.

Ganjoo, S.: *Muslim Freedom Fighters of India,* Anmol Publication, New Delhi, 2002.

Ghosh, Ratna: *Netaji Subhas Chandra Bose and Indian Freedom Struggle (2 Vols-Set),* Deep and Deep, 2006.

Goyal, P. K.: *Battle of India's Freedom Movement,* Vista International, 2005.

Gupta, Shantinath: *Great Freedom Fighters of India,* Anmol, 2006.

Hari Hara Das: *The History of Freedom Movement in India (1857-1947),* National, 1998.

Indu Dave: *Indian Personality in Its Developmental Background,* Himanshu, 1991.

Iyengar, A. S.: *Role of Press and Indian Freedom Struggle: All through the Gandhian Era,* APH, 2001.

Jesudasan, Ignatius: *A Gandhian Theology of Liberation. Gujarat Sahitya Prakash: Ananda India,* Maryknoll, NY: Orbis, 1984.

Kailash Khanna: *History of Indian Freedom Struggle,* Commonwealth Publication, 2004.

Kaushik, A. S.: *Great Freedom Fighters of India,* Indian Publication, 2007.

Khan, Sir Syed Ahmad: *The Complete Collection of Lectures and Speeches, (Urdu, edited by M.I. Gujarati),* Nawal Kishore, Lahore, 1985.

Kumar, Debendra Das: *Great Indian Economists : Their Creative Vision for Socio-Economic Development,* Vol. I: *'Dadabhai Naoroji (1825-1917) : Life Sketch and Contribution to Indian Economy,* Deep and Deep, New Delhi, 2004.

Kumar, Prafulla Pattanaik: *The First Indian War of Independence: Freedom Movement in Orissa, 1804-1825,* APH, 2005.

Kumar, Raj: *Essays on Indian Freedom Movement,* History and Culture Series, Discovery, 2003.

Kumar, Ravindra: *Champaran to Quit India Movement,* Mittal, 2002.

Lion Agrawal, M. G.: *Freedom Fighters of India (4 Vols-Set),* Isha Books, 2008.

Manju Verma: *The Role of Women in the Freedom Movement in Punjab (1919-1947),* Abhijeet, 2003.

Martin, Briton: *New India, 1885; British Official Policy and the Emergence of the Indian National Congress,* University of California Press, Berkeley, 1969.

Masani, R.P.: *Dadabhai Naoroji: The Grand Old Man of India,* George Allen and Unwin Ltd., London, 1939.

Maulana Syed Mohammad Mian: *The Prisoners of Malta (Asira'n-E-Malta): The Heart-Rending Tale of Muslim Freedom Fighters in British Period,* Manak, 2005.

Mazhar Kibriya: *Gandhi and Indian Freedom Struggle*, APH, 1999.

McLane, John R.: *Indian Nationalism and the Early Congress*, Princeton University Press, New Jersey, 1977.

Morris, Morris D.; M. B. McAlpin: *Measuring the Condition of India's Poor: The Physical Quality of Life Index*, Promilla & Co. Delhi, 1982.

Muthaiah, S.: *Women Freedom Fighters*, The Hindu, 2004.

Nanda, S. P.: *Freedom Movement and Constitutional Development in India*, Dominant, 2004.

Nussbaum, M.: *Women and Human Development: The Capabilities Approach*, Cambridge University Press, Cambridge, 1990.

Om Prakash: *Encyclopaedic History of Indian Freedom Movement (12 to 21 Vols)*, Anmol, 2003.

Omesh Saigal: *Shaheed Bhagat Singh: Unique Martyr in Freedom Movement*, Gyan Publication, 2002.

P. D. Hajela: *Economic Thoughts of Dadabhai Naoroji*, Deep & Deep, New Delhi, 2001.

Pash, Nandhra: *Dadabhai Naoroji*, Politico's, 1998

Pasricha, A.: *Poverty and Un-British Rule in India : Dadabhai Naoroji*, B.K.P., 2006.

Pasricha, Ashu: *Encyclopaedia of Eminent Thinkers, Vol XI. The Political Thought of Dadabhai Naoroji*, Concept, 2008.

Pearse, Andrew: *Seeds of Plenty, Seeds of Want: Social and Economic Implications of the Green Revolution*, Clarendon Press, Oxford, 1984.

Rafiya, Nisar: *Shaikh-Ul-Hind Maulana Mahmud Hasan and Indian Freedom Movement*, Manak Pub, 2008.

Ram Sharma, S.: *Education of Women and Freedom Movement*, Discovery, 1996.

Ramanathan, K. V.: *The Satyamurti Letters, Vol. II: The Indian Freedom Struggle Through the Eyes of a Parliamentarian*, Dorling Kindersley for Pearson Longman an Imprint of Pearson Education, 2008.

Ramu, P. S.: *Azad Hind Fauj (I.N.A.) and The Freedom Movement,* Freedom Movement Memorial Comm, 1998.

Ravallion, M.; G. Datt; M. v.d. Walle: *Quantifying Absolute Poverty in the Developing World",* 1991.

Robb, Peter.: *A History of India,* Palgrave, Hampshire, 2002.

Rustom P. Masani, *Dadabhai Naoroji,* 1939.

S. R. Bakshi: *Dadabhai Naoroji: The Grand Old Man,* Anmol Publications, New Delhi, 1991.

Smith, Adam: *Naoroji, Dadabhai, Speeches and Writings,* Madras, 1955.

Smith, Adam: *The Wealth of Nations,* Cannon Edition, New York, 1985.

Swan, S.: *Naoroji, Dadabhai, 1901, Poverty and un-British rule in India,* Swan Schonnenhein & Co. London,

Verinder, Grover: *Dadabhai Naoroji: A Biography of His Vision and Ideas,* Deep & Deep Publishers, New Delhi, 1998.

Zaidi, Moin A.: *Dadabhai Naoroji, Speeches and Writings,* Indian Institute of Applied Political Research, New Delhi, 1985.

Zerbanoo, Gifford: *Dadabhai Naoroji: Britain's First Asian MP;* Mantra Books, 1992.

Index

S

U

W

❑❑❑